FORGIVENESS, MERCY, AND CLEMENCY

DATE DUE

7	5	18	

Forgiveness, Mercy, and Clemency

Edited by

AUSTIN SARAT AND

NASSER HUSSAIN

STANFORD UNIVERSITY PRESS

Stanford, California, 2007

Stanford University Press
Stanford, California
© 2007 by the Board of Trustees of the
Leland Stanford Junior University.
All rights reserved.

Printed in the United States of America on acid-free, archival-quality paper

Library of Congress Cataloging-in-Publication Data
Forgiveness, mercy, and clemency / edited by Austin Sarat and Nasser Hussain.
p.   cm.
Includes bibliographical references and index.
ISBN-13: 9780804753326 (cloth : alk. paper)
         9780804753333 (pbk.: alk. paper)
1. Capital punishment—Moral and ethical aspects.   2. Criminal justice,
Administration of—United States.   3. Clemency.   4. Pardon.   I. Sarat,
Austin.   II. Hussain, Nasser
KFI1765.C2 F67 2006
364.6/3 22   2006012940

Original Printing 2006

Typeset by Newgen in 10/14.5 Minion

Acknowledgments

The work gathered here was first presented at a conference held at Amherst College on March 26–27, 2005. We are grateful to all of the participants in that event, but especially to our colleagues Christopher Dole, Thomas Dumm, Marissa Parham, Andrew Parker, Jill Stauffer, and Paola Zamperini. We also wish to thank Amherst's Dean of the Faculty, Gregory S. Call, for his generous financial support.

Contents

Contributors

MEIR DAN-COHEN is Milo Reese Robbins Professor in Legal Ethics at the University of California at Berkeley.

NASSER HUSSAIN is Assistant Professor of Law, Jurisprudence, and Social Thought at Amherst College.

DANIEL T. KOBIL is Professor of Law at Capital University Law School.

LINDA ROSS MEYER is Professor of Law at Quinnipiac University School of Law.

BRUCE ROBBINS is Professor of English and Comparative Literature at Columbia University.

AUSTIN SARAT is William Nelson Cromwell Professor of Jurisprudence and Political Science and Five College Fortieth Anniversary Professor at Amherst College.

ADAM SITZE is Assistant Professor of Law, Jurisprudence, and Social Thought at Amherst College.

CAROL S. STEIKER is Professor of Law at Harvard Law School.

FORGIVENESS, MERCY,
AND CLEMENCY

Toward New Theoretical Perspectives on Forgiveness, Mercy, and Clemency: An Introduction

NASSER HUSSAIN

AUSTIN SARAT

We begin with the simple proposition that justice exerts, as it should, a powerful pull on the human imagination. And at least part of what constitutes a sense of justice is a world of rules and laws, responsibility, and fair punishment. Yet a world run strictly and solely in accordance with the dictates of the law would be a world in which few would want to live and few could truly thrive. A life lived as if the law were one's only guiding principle would be as much of a tragedy or a farce as a triumph of good over evil. To humanize the world in which we live, to make it possible for people to thrive and survive, the law needs the company of other virtues, such as mercy.

Such an assertion is, of course, hardly a lightning bolt of original insight. Arguments for forgiveness, mercy, and clemency abound; they flourish in organized religion, fiction, philosophy, and law, to say nothing of the conversations of daily life among parents and their children, teachers and their students, criminals and those who judge them, lovers, friends, business associates, and so forth. Yet as common as these arguments are, we are left often with an incomplete understanding of what we mean and do when we speak about forgiveness, mercy, and clemency. Are they different names for a single thing? Do they name attitudes or actions? Are they directed at persons or at the things people do? Can we have one without necessarily bringing the others along? Can we have any of them without committing ourselves to a religious perspective, without invoking some divine or supernatural presence? The purpose of *Forgiveness, Mercy, and Clemency* is to map the terrain on which such questions might be addressed; to examine various registers on which to chart the relations among forgiveness, mercy, and clemency; and to understand their place in our lives and the society in which we live. In this introduction, we offer an accounting of three such registers, what we call the registers of exception, of being, and of history.

We begin with a letter written by Hannah Arendt to W. H. Auden in February 1960 on the subject of forgiveness.[1] The letter was a response to a response: The previous year, Auden had reviewed Arendt's *The Human Condition* and further considered some of her arguments in an essay published later that year. From *The Human Condition* to Auden's essay and Arendt's response, we have a remarkable exchange between two of the great philosophical and poetic minds of the twentieth century on the very subject of this book. In *The Human Condition*, Arendt argues that forgiveness (along with the capacity to make promises) is a political faculty, as it facilitates our living with other human beings, allowing us to let the consequences of ill-conceived actions come to an end: "Without being forgiven, released from the consequences of what we have done, our capacity to act would, as it were, be confined to one single deed from which we could never recover."[2] Indeed, as she notes a little later, the capacity to forgive and be forgiven is what enables humans to dare something new, to initiate novel and necessarily unpredictable actions: "Only through constant mutual release from what they do can remain free agents, only by constant willingness to change their minds and start again can they be trusted with so great a power as that to begin something new."[3]

Auden's response to this argument, as was his response to much of *The Human Condition*, was one of enthusiastic interest and agreement. Nonetheless, he argues that Arendt elided a crucial distinction between forgiveness and clemency. In his essay on "The Prince's Dog," Auden considers whether drama can adequately capture and reveal the Christian command of love and forgiveness. Thus, in *Measure for Measure*, he claims, the only way for Shakespeare to show forgiveness in action is to show it through the decision of the Duke to forgive Angelo. This may suggest that forgiveness and clemency are the same, but they are not: "The law cannot forgive, for the law has not been wronged, only broken; only persons can be wronged. The law can only pardon what it has the power to punish . . . The decision to grant or refuse pardon must be governed by prudent calculation . . . But charity is forbidden to calculate in this way: I am required to forgive my enemy whatever the effect on him may be."[4]

Arendt answers Auden by admitting her failure to properly distinguish forgiveness from pardon. She does not, however, accept his notion of forgiveness, embedded as it is in the Christian commands of love and charity. "Of course I am prejudiced namely against Christian Charity," she writes, "but let me at least make a stand for my prejudices." Charity goes too far in its stance of humility and nonjudgment, or as she puts it, "it forgives uberhaupt."[5] This would remove from forgiveness the quality that Arendt values most in it and what gives it for her a public character—namely, that forgiveness emerges from mutuality and judgment.

A number of questions emerge from this exchange. The first concerns what may be called the many names of pardon and the relationships between them. In the title of this volume, we use the term *clemency* to refer to the political capacity to reduce or remove any lawfully imposed punishment, but this power is also variously referred to as executive clemency, the sovereign prerogative of mercy, the pardon power, and so on. Nor is this merely a semantic issue. Does the more interpersonal term *forgiveness* share anything with the public act of pardoning? Or are they, as some scholars believe, mutually exclusive? Is mercy an act or an attitude? Could it function as the term that joins forgiveness and clemency?

The second part of the exchange between Auden and Arendt highlights the relationship of pardon to politics and history, understood as both the past and the internal specifically theological history of forgiveness itself. Arendt is suspicious of the theological heritage of both forgiveness and clemency. She believes that the tendency of Christian charity to forgive uberhaupt destroys the element of judgment that forgiveness invites and, indeed, even demands. Without such calibration and judgment, forgiveness would lack the mutuality and reciprocity needed for it to become a proper principle of public life. But what does it mean to try to make forgiveness or pardon into a systematic principle? Could one make forgiveness a moral principle but not a legal one? Indeed, do forgiveness, mercy, or clemency have any place in a political and legal system dedicated to the principles of formal equality and respect for rules?

It may seem self-evident that one way to begin to parse the differences in the many forms of forgiveness would be by making a clear distinction between a private interpersonal form of forgiveness and the public institutional form of clemency. And yet even this seemingly clear distinction does not hold up to scrutiny. On the one hand, there are different kinds of public pardons, each with a varying emphasis on the individual and the particular. Thus, Linda Ross Meyer opens her chapter in this volume with a catalogue of the various forms of pardon. While what Meyer calls the "pardon as equity" or the "pardon as compassion" often draws on a "sympathetic connection in a person-to-person exchange," the peace pardon, such as Lincoln's amnesty after the Civil War, is not individually oriented but rather foundational to the restoration of the body politic.

It is somewhat curious that even though all of us have forgiven a friend or lover at some point in our lives, we have such an inexact sense of how to define forgiveness.

In a well-known book on *Forgiveness and Mercy*, philosopher Jeffrie Murphy offers one detailed definition of forgiveness. Murphy takes his cue from Bishop Butler's teaching that forgiveness is the forswearing of resentment: "the resolute overcoming of the anger and hatred that are naturally directed towards a person who has done one an unjustified and non-excused moral injury."[6] But Murphy goes further than Bishop Butler by examining the quality of such resentment and by recasting it in a more positive light.

Resentment, Murphy suggests, is a passion directed at an unwarranted affront to the self and thus actually defends the value of self-respect. In this account, forgiveness without proper reason, too quick and forthcoming, is not the uncontested virtue it is so often taken to be. Murphy notes: "if I am correct in linking resentment to self respect, a too ready tendency to forgive may properly be regarded as a vice because it may be a sign that one lacks respect for oneself."[7] Nor does just any cessation of resentment amount to forgiveness. Forgiveness, Murphy notes, is not the same thing as excuse or justification. Thus, more stringently, he defines forgiveness as the forswearing of resentment for a moral reason. Such reasons can be guessed at from our own daily lives: Repentance and apology are the preeminent reasons, but there are others, such as when we forgive a single transgression in the name of a lifelong loyalty and friendship. Murphy has more to say about each of these "appropriate" grounds for forgiveness, but for our purposes, what is salient in his account is that forgiveness be earned and be granted on stated moral grounds.

Although we find this analysis somewhat convincing, we doubt that forgiveness will always fit with such a reasoned and reasonable account. Indeed, Jacques Derrida, in his work on pardon, articulated a similar skepticism. For Derrida, no reasoned accounting could ever fully anticipate or explain how or when we forgive. As such, the pardon is mad, belonging to a "hyperbolically ethical vision."[8] Contrary to Murphy's balanced accounting of sufficient conditions for earning and granting forgiveness, Derrida asks, "must not one maintain that a pardon worthy of the name, if there ever is one, must pardon the unpardonable and without condition?" For Derrida, the theological tradition from which pardon and forgiveness emerge as well as their current theological forms already hold within them an ambivalence and tension between two contrary positions of the conditional and the unconditional. On the one hand, the Christian conception of forgiveness is akin to an economic exchange, whereby the repentance of the sinner earns God's forgiveness. On the other hand, no amount of repentance can guarantee such forgiveness, which, in the end, is an act of grace given and received without reason or explanation. Pardon, then, relays as if it were between the two poles of the conditional and unconditional, the relation between which Derrida says is "irreconcilable and indissociable."[9] For Derrida, pardon comes as a shock, an ultimately unaccountable disruption. This conception owes much to the work of philosopher Vladimir Jankélévitch, whose 1967 work, Le pardon, only recently translated as Forgiveness, is receiving long delayed and much deserved attention.[10]

It is certainly a testament to the difficulties in defining the term that Jankélévitch spends much of the book discussing what forgiveness is not. Although it may be associated with a "temporal decay," with a forgetting that accompanies the passage of time, forgiveness, he contends, is too conscious and too determined an event to be confused with such an accidental diminution of resentment. Nor is forgiveness the same thing as excuse.

In addition, the reasons for forgiveness should not, he argues, be aligned with some sense of mental or social hygiene, such as the sentiment that I should forgive because holding onto resentment is not good for me or that I should forgive to facilitate the rehabilitation of the offender. Forgiveness, then, is neither a reasoned action nor a process; it is an event. Forgiveness for Jankélévitch: "forgives in one fell swoop and in a single indivisible élan, and it pardons undividedly; in a single radical and incomprehensible movement, forgiveness effaces all, sweeps away all, and forgets all. In one blink of an eye, forgiveness makes a tabula rasa of the past, and this miracle is as simple for it as saying hello and good evening."[11]

In Jankélévitch's account, as in others, we find a consistent effort to distinguish the personal attitude of forgiveness from the public act of clemency. Thus, Kathleen Dean Moore notes that only the aggrieved party can forgive. Although an official may reduce a punishment, to call such an action forgiveness should strike us as a kind of moral usurpation. Somewhat ironically, in Moore's account, what maintains forgiveness as a personal rather than a legal condition is that only the aggrieved party has the right or the standing, as Moore puts it using a legal idiom, to forgive.[12]

Nonetheless, these efforts to distinguish clemency from forgiveness emphasize a common trait in forgiveness and clemency: their exceptional quality. The power to grant forgiveness and clemency is just that, a power, a capacity that is not, in the end, subject to rule and cannot be rendered regular or predictable. If Jankélévitch insists that the philosophical condition of forgiveness shows that the event in the end escapes all reason and rule, such a condition is intrinsic to the definition of the clemency power. In a 1997 decision, the U.S. Court of Appeals for the Sixth Circuit explained the nature of clemency in stark terms: "The very nature of clemency is that it is grounded solely in the will of the dispenser of clemency. He need give no reasons for granting it, or for denying it . . . The governor may agonize over every petition; he may glance at one or all such petitions and toss them away."[13]

Such a magisterial disregard for rules is perhaps the reason the pardon power is so readily associated with monarchical privilege. Thus, in the inaugural texts of modern jurisprudence and the first systemic consideration of the pardon power in the Anglo common law tradition, William Blackstone's *Commentaries on the Laws of England*, Blackstone calls clemency "[o]ne of the great advantages of monarchy in general . . . that there is a magistrate, who has it in his power to extend mercy, whenever he thinks it is deserved: holding a court of equity in his own breast, to soften the rigour of the general law, in such criminal cases as merit an exception from punishment . . . . [T]hese repeated acts of goodness, coming immediately from his own hand, endear the sovereign to his subjects."[14] Like *all* sovereign prerogatives, its essence is discretionary, its efficacy bound up to its very disregard of declared law. Thus, more than half a century before Blackstone, Locke famously defined prerogative as "the power to act according to discretion, for the public good, without the prescription of the Law, and sometimes even against it."[15] It is little wonder, then, that despite his admiration for the monarchical prerogative of pardon, even Blackstone felt that such a power had no place in a democratic system of a rule of law; for "in democracies . . . this power of pardon can never subsist; for there nothing higher is acknowledged than the magistrate who administers the laws."[16]

James Wilson answered Blackstone's concerns by emphasizing that in a democracy the "supreme power" remains with the people who can hold those granting clemency accountable for their actions.[17] Placing the clemency power in an executive who could override the considered judgments of the magistrates did not mean that it would be a lawless power because it could be contained within a framework of law that, on Wilson's account, "is higher" than those who administer it. Yet Wilson conceded some territory to Blackstone by acknowledging that such a power, which allows executives "to insult the laws, to protect crimes, to indemnify, and by indemnifying, to encourage criminals," was indeed "extraordinary" in a democratic political system.[18]

We suggest that clemency is best understood as a form of "legally sanctioned alegality," or as we have elsewhere called it, a "lawful lawlessness." Theorists and judges alike have identified the ambivalence and instability that clemency introduces into the fabric of legality and that neither jurisprudence nor legal theory can fully resolve.

In regard to executive clemency, law recognizes, albeit ambivalently, its own limits and concedes that it cannot regulate adequately what it authorizes. The existence of such a particular—and perhaps in a constitutional democracy, peculiar—form of sovereign prerogative serves as a powerful reminder of the still relevant distinction between lawfulness and the rule of law. Indeed, for us, absent such a reminder of the occasional gap between law and predictive rules, it is impossible to understand some of the anxieties that attend the exercise of sovereign prerogative in a modern constitutional democracy.

Some of those anxieties are surveyed by Carol S. Steiker in this volume. Steiker's chapter, "Tempering or Tampering? Mercy and the Administration of Criminal Justice," examines the paradox of mercy in the daily administration of criminal justice. As if to reaffirm Martha Nussbaum's well-known insistence on the role of stories in the production of judgment, Steiker begins by turning to two different stories by O. Henry: one that illustrates the redemptive potential in mercy and another that reveals its inherently unfair and uneven application. For Steiker, these two conditions correspond to two of the more salient features of the contemporary administration of criminal justice: the excessively harsh mandatory lengths of punishment and the strong racial disparity in prison populations. In such a system, there is a particular need for justice to be tempered with mercy, but the relation between the two terms is a difficult one. What is the place of mercy in a system dedicated to formal equality? And even if one demonstrates the need for mercy in a system of a rule of law, what sort of institutional design would best accommodate it?

Steiker goes through a few specific approaches to the relation, or lack thereof, between mercy and justice, each endorsed by a particular set of theorists. The first, which Steiker labels "the skeptical view," insists that mercy should have no place in the system of law and justice. This approach, most readily associated with retributivism, insists that offenders be given their just deserts, no more and no less. Moreover, to the claim that mercy brings a calibration and individuation necessary for justice to be done, those skeptical of the claims of mercy, such as Jeffrie Murphy, assert that this is an incorrect understanding of mercy and justice. To carefully calibrate, to consider individual and singular circumstances, is, in his view, not to exercise mercy but rather to do justice in the first place.

This may be a persuasive answer, but it does not address one of the more consistent critiques of retributivism—that is, how is one to know with such surety what a given offender's "just deserts" are? Punishment is a mixture of social norms, political pressures, and cultural assumptions, and there is no correct and ultimate answer waiting to be accessed.

Steiker considers other approaches to the disjunction between mercy and justice, such as that of the so-called "social welfare school," for whom mercy and justice are two distinct possibilities in the larger goal of promoting social welfare and deterring crime. In this view, Steiker contends, there is no conflict between justice and mercy because each is "subsumed on equal footing into the larger calculus of social welfare." But for Steiker, the problem with such an approach is the same as that which afflicts another approach—that of restorative justice—namely, each fails to account for any intrinsic moral good to punishment at all.

If Steiker shows us that the conceptual relationship between justice and mercy is a difficult one, Daniel T. Kobil opens his chapter by noting that such a relation is almost entirely absent in the daily practices of law and politics. While instances of executive clemency are on the decline everywhere, even in the rare cases when a pardon is granted, it is on the grounds of a miscarriage of justice and almost never by an appeal to mercy. For the retributivists, as we have seen, this is as it should be: a system in which pardons are only used to calibrate justice, adjusting a punishment that might not otherwise be just. But if we dispense with the idea of mercy as a public institution altogether, Kobil sensibly urges us to do so with at least some reflection. "What, if anything," Kobil asks, "are we giving up when we allow our leaders to set aside mercy as a basis for their actions?"

Kobil distinguishes between what he calls merciful acts and his desired objective of "mercy-based clemency." The latter would for Kobil be the result of reflection and judgment and would be taken "in order to achieve for society the benefits of benevolence and compassion." Thus, Kobil categorically dismisses the well-known and oft-cited pardon of Darrell Mease by Missouri Governor Mel Carnahan in 1999. Mease, guilty of a triple murder, was scheduled to be executed the same day that the pope was to visit St. Louis. When the pontiff faced the governor and asked him to spare Mease's life, Carnahan agreed. For Kobil, this was neither the result of deep reflection on the particulars of the case nor a way of showing society the benefits of compassion.

Kobil's insistence on the distinction between merciful acts and mercy-based clemency, although important, does not move us away from the problem of lawful lawlessness that we identified earlier. One may recommend deep reflection and considered judgment to the executive in dispensing pardons, but there is no way to monitor such a recommendation without tampering with precisely the condition that gives clemency its power.

Having drawn out the distinction between merciful acts and mercy-based clemency, Kobil asks what it would take to convince politicians and a public increasingly hostile to acts of public mercy. He speculates about some "instrumental benefits," pointing to studies that have shown a link between the practice of forgiveness and better mental and physical well-being. But a surer case would need to rely on so called "expressive claims," ones that enact certain norms and moral behaviors for a society at large. Thus, Kobil argues that if the death penalty demonstrates, as its supporters contend, the strength of the law and the robust power of the state, the occasional grant of mercy would not reduce this power but rather would amplify it. Kobil quotes former Ohio Governor Celeste that mercy shows there is "strength as a community." Or as Justice Anthony Kennedy puts it, mercy shows "confidence."

Kobil's argument returns us to some of the concerns we mentioned at the opening of this introduction. It is extremely difficult to get away from theological and, indeed, distinctively Christian conceptions of mercy, conceptions that like all conceptions of mercy tie it deeply to the exercise of power. This is because the exercise of mercy is constitutively hierarchical: I can only show mercy to someone who is at my mercy. Moreover, Christian conceptions of mercy are implicated even in modern understandings of sovereign power. God's grace, it seems, is the ultimate sovereign prerogative. It is no wonder, then, that Blackstone believed the pardon most suited a monarch. In democratic cultures, however, this particular theological heritage of mercy is more troublesome. As Derrida astutely notes, "what renders the 'I forgive you' sometimes unsupportable or odious . . . is the affirmation of sovereignty."

Are we then to conclude that the legal question of clemency will not only remain part of an aporia in the law, a legally sanctioned power above the rules and procedures that make up modern law, but also will remain incommensurable to an understanding of forgiveness? If we are only to consider the role of clemency in theories of punishment, in arguments with retributivists, this would perhaps be an inescapable conclusion. But there are at least two other possible approaches to the question of mercy and to the possible relations between forgiveness and clemency. The first emphasizes mercy as not just an act, a decision, or an exception but as a cultivated attitude among rulers and ruled. The second would consider the role of forgiveness and pardon in addressing the past.

For Linda Ross Meyer, arguments of various retributivists, while they could be answered in detail, rely on a foundational assumption that is, in the end, Kantian. Instead of offering us a point-by-point critique of the Kantian position, Meyer considers what happens if "we begin in a different place." To articulate this new point of departure, she turns to Heidegger and to his foregrounding not of reason but of a being-with others. Such a mode of existence is finite, practical, and based on complex and continuous interaction. Moreover, this is distinct from notions of empirical sympathy and so on. Rather, being-with is the first condition that motivates all thinking and feeling and, indeed, is prior to any emotional experience. Such an embeddedness has some distinct consequences for a theory of pardon. Meyer argues that it removes the objection that pardon must be discarded on the basis of a formal equality. Rather, the grounds for arguing for or against a theory of pardon shifts to our daily practices of living with one another. Thus, for example, Meyer suggests that only a being-with perspective rather than strict retributivism can account for the role of remorse and mercy.

This is clear in instances of what Meyer calls the "allegiance pardon." In the military, for example, a transgression may be forgiven by a superior officer, thereby creating a personal bond. A further transgression would then be not just a violation of the law but more saliently a personal breach of trust.

Meyer anticipates that we might object to all of this as too hierarchical, too personal, but one of the more compelling arguments that Meyer offers is that the role of discretion and mercy, power and forgiveness, is not subject to an abstract argument for or against, for discretion and mercy already exist in the legal system. The prosecutor who declines to file charges because it would ruin the life of a young first-time defendant or the jury who declines the ultimate penalty in response to the remorse of a defendant are already practicing the many forms of mercy that some theorists argue for or against in the abstract. "Moral luck pervades the system," Meyer argues, and we need to base our critiques of clemency on such an acknowledgment.

It is not that this leaves us with no basis for offering a criticism of clemency, but it does force us to draw on different norms that emerge from a foundation of being-with: norms such as respect. Thus, Meyer argues that what strikes us as repugnant in Justice O'Connor's infamous example of tossing a coin to decide to whom to grant a clemency decision is that such a mode of deciding someone's fate shows no respect or consideration. Such a moral and political if not legal judgment is, for Meyer, the kind of organic, contextual, and richer conclusion that can only emerge from a being-with-others perspective.

The other condition that characterizes both forgiveness and pardon is their ability to undo the past, to cancel out the continuing consequences of a previous action. Recall that for Arendt this was the most valuable quality of both forgiveness and pardon (she uses the terms interchangeably perhaps because they both contain what was for her this desirable ability to perform a revision of the past). Thus, from the everyday proverbial counsel of forgiving and forgetting to the etymological link between amnesty and amnesia, there is, it seems, a deep connection between forgiveness–clemency and remembering and forgetting.

Indeed, in his chapter in this volume, Meir Dan-Cohen takes this link one step further by grouping even repentance with forgiveness and pardon as a distinct set of activities that he terms *revisionary practices*. These practices are for Dan-Cohen united by the common ability of bringing the negative response to a past transgression to an end. One may, of course, object that repentance does not bring anything to an end, as it merely facilitates the possibility of forgiveness that alone ends the past. But for Dan-Cohen, each of these activities is related in their activity, and the only real difference is the subject of each activity: In forgiveness, it is the victim; in clemency, it is the official; and in repentance, it is the wrongdoer.

Dan-Cohen, like Arendt, emphasizes the ability of both private forgiveness and public pardon to revise the past. But Dan-Cohen wonders *how* such a revision of the past is achieved and what it entails. The conventional wisdom on the topic would suggest that it is repentance that facilitates forgiveness and a new beginning by excising the offensive action, by making the wrongdoer anew.

Dan-Cohen asks if this could really be the case. If, in fact, repentance has made the wrongdoer into a "new person" (putting aside the question of if this is ever possible), who or what is one forgiving? "If we allow," he notes, "that as a result of the change in identity there is no one to resent or attach stigma to anymore, we must also recognize that for the very same reason there is no one to forgive or pardon either." What is required, then, is a theoretical model that can explain both continuity and change brought about by repentance and forgiveness in the wrongdoer's identity.

Dan-Cohen illustrates the temporal quality of forgiveness and identity by turning to a spatial hypothetical. His imaginary town of Arcadia contains within its borders a source of pollution. It might then be reasonable for us to assume that Arcadia is responsible for the pollution. But if by treaty there is a redrawing of borders so that the source of the pollution is no longer in Arcadia's territory, we would feel it inappropriate to continue blaming Arcadia. What is key to the extension of this hypothetical to a wrong committed in a person's life, to the redrawing of the border's of the self, is the notions of responsibility or inappropriate responses, both of which Dan-Cohen insists are normative and not just psychological positions. Thus, in the give-and-take of repentance and forgiveness even between two private individuals, forgiveness redraws the boundaries of the wrongdoer's self by making it normatively inappropriate to demonstrate a negative response. Similar to the drawing of spatial borders, forgiveness for Dan-Cohen is a normative stand on the nonrelevance of a prior act. This does not actually excise the wrong from the wrongdoer's past, but it does oblige others to act as if that wrong had never happened.

Dan-Cohen's analysis of revisionary practices is useful in emphasizing forgiveness as a normative process and not just a more inchoate psychological one. The normative dimensions of remembering and forgetting become, in our time, a more urgent question. As Derrida notes, we live in an age of forgiveness. Every year, it seems, we are witness to an apology by a head of state for a past atrocity committed on a population more than a half-century ago. (Most of these reparations and apologies stem from the events of World War II though certainly not all of them; others include apologies for apartheid and colonialism and so on.) But just as compelling are the various idioms these apologies can adopt, the negotiations that can decide or derail an apology. And then there are those apologies that seem to be demanded but consistently refused, such as the United States' refusal to acknowledge a wrong, much less apologize for it, with the dropping of atomic bombs on Japan. Derrida thus notes, "we see not only some individuals but entire communities, professional corporations, church representatives and hierarchs, sovereigns and chiefs of state asking for 'pardon.' They do this in an 'abrahaminque' language which is not (in the case of Japan or Korea, for example) that of the dominant religion of their society, but which has already become the universal idiom of law, of politics." The theological idiom of repentance and the legal idiom of pardon merge in a global language of coming to terms with the past.

But this raises new questions. As Bruce Robbins asks in his chapter in this volume: Can countries forgive? Can entire collectivities be forgiven? Of course, a necessary prelude to these questions of national repentance and forgiveness is the question of how to assign national blame. Answering this question requires a complicated calculus that Robbins terms "comparative national blaming." How and when do collectivities recall the atrocities they have endured? When do they indulge in what may be called strategic forgetting? Bruce Robbins explores these urgent questions through a reading of W. G. Sebald's *On the Natural History of Destruction*.

Sebald's work is animated by a single question: Why, after World War II, was there so little remembrance of the Allied firebombing of German cities? One possibility that Sebald entertains but ultimately dismisses is that the flames that instantly consumed Dresden, for example, went beyond what humans can grasp. In Sebald's account, what emerges as a more compelling rationale for the postwar silence is national shame. That is, German suffering of the fire-bombing could not compare to the horrors the country had been responsible for in the Holocaust. What Robbins wants Sebald and us to move toward, however, is a more sophisticated cosmopolitanism that understands national shame and pride in conjunction to reach a more nuanced reckoning with the past.

The final chapter brings together the numerous theoretical approaches we have been considering. Adam Sitze's "Keeping the Peace" not only addresses the role of mercy in the construction of a sovereignty but also its part in the role of memory and the possibility of a more participatory politics.

His chapter contains an intriguing illustration of the link between amnesty and amnesia, a general pardon and a forced forgetting. Sitze explores the shape and consequences of what he calls an "indiscernibility" between amnesty and the right of grace by first turning to Kant and then to Plato, and he considers the Athenian amnesty of 403 B.C. The rupture that this amnesty sought to heal was not so easily categorized in the extant terminology of *polemos* or external war, and it was more horrible because of fratricidal stasis or civil war. Moreover, drawing on the work of Nicole Loraux, Sitze shows how this restoration that the amnesty of 403 B.C. capped did not only involve Athenian citizens but was due in large part to the "democratic faction" of slaves and women. The amnesty thus involved a specific prohibition against recall: an oath taken by all that they would not raise past grievances. And although this is surely illustrative of Arendt's approval of the power of pardon—namely, its ability to unchain us from the past—Sitze shows us a less sanguine version of this power. The amnesty of 403 B.C. was in effect the mechanism by which democracy was defeated and silenced at the very moment of its victory. Political differences were put away, and all future legal recourse was closed once the amnesty was completed. In this way, the amnesty certainly did found the body politic, but it did so by curiously evacuating the political.

But if one part of Sitze's work shows the political limitations of pardon as a means of addressing the past, the other strand in his chapter speaks to our understanding of pardon as a form of decision and judgment. Sitze shows how a rupture in the organizational schema of the polity, introduced in Plato's *Laws* by the death of the intestate man, requires a particular use of *sungnômon*. This is a concept that designates a sense of flexible or nonruled-based judgment. It is a concept Martha Nussbaum uses to show how the later Roman clementia in Seneca accords with a sense of humanitarian sympathy. Sitze finds these accounts of *sungnômon* doubtful. Instead, he points to how the concept is used in the laws as a "constitutively divided judgment." That is, when the lawgiver must encourage a breaking of the laws to restore the mathematical harmony that is disrupted by the intestate man, *sungnômon* is required not only by the lawgiver in giving the laws but by the citizens in receiving them. Sitze thus begins to point us toward as conception of judgment and mercy that would not be solely an affirmation of a sovereign and his decision.

Taken together, the chapters in *Forgiveness, Mercy, and Clemency* map some of the crucial domains of inquiry into their complex relations, domains that link those concepts to judgment and exception, being and acting, history and forgetting. They point toward an enriched understanding of the links and disjunctures among forgiveness, mercy, and clemency and of the registers of individual psychology, religious belief, social practice, and political power that circulate in and around those who forgive, grant mercy, or pose clemency power. Finally, they collect and build on existing theories. They suggest that in many ways necessary theoretical work on the questions of forgiveness and pardon, on the connection between mercy and justice, are only just beginning. They invite scholars to renew and revitalize that work.

Notes

1. Arendt to Auden (February 14, 1960, no. 004864 and 004865) in *General Correspondence, 1938–1976* (Hannah Arendt Papers, Manuscript Division, Library of Congress, Washington, DC). A digitized version of this letter can be found at http://memory.loc.gov/ammem/index.html.

2. Hannah Arendt, *The Human Condition* (Chicago and London: University of Chicago Press, 1958), 237.

3. Ibid., 240.

4. W. H. Auden, "The Prince's Dog," in *The Dyer's Hand and Other Essays* (New York: Random House, 1962), 201.

5. Arendt to Auden, (February 14, 1960), 1.

6. Jeffrie Murphy and Jean Hampton, *Forgiveness and Mercy* (Cambridge: Cambridge University Press, 1988), 15.

7. Ibid., 17.

8. Jacques Derrida, "The Century and the Pardon," *Le Monde des Debats* 9 (December 1999). Found at http://fixion.sytes.net/pardonEng.htm. Last visited January 17, 2006. Hereafter, all citations refer to this translated version.

9. Ibid., 6.

10. Vladimir Jankélévitch, *Forgiveness*, Andrew Kelley, trans. (Chicago and London: University of Chicago Press, 2005).

11. Ibid., 153.

12. Kathleen Dean Moore, *Pardons: Justice, Mercy, and the Public Interest* (New York and Oxford: Oxford University Press, 1989), 184.

13. *In re Sapp*, 118 F. 3d 460, 465 (6th Cir. 1997).

14. William Blackstone, *Commentaries on the Laws of England: A Facsimile of the First Edition of 1765–1769* (Chicago: University of Chicago Press, 1979), 390–391.

15. John Locke, *Second Treatise on Civil Government*, C. B. Macpherson, ed. (Indianapolis, IN: Hackett, 1980), §§ 159–160.

16. 4 Blackstone, *Commentaries*, 390.

17. James Wilson, "Executive Department," *Lectures on Law* in *The Works of James Wilson*, vol. 2, Robert McCloskey, ed. (Cambridge, MA: Harvard University Press, 1967), 442–444.

18. Ibid.

Tempering or Tampering? Mercy and the Administration of Criminal Justice

CAROL S. STEIKER

Mercy has long been a topic addressed by many disparate written traditions—religious, literary, philosophical, and legal, to name only the most prominent. Although writers among and within these traditions have given the topic of mercy widely differing treatment, a common thread emerges connecting many otherwise radically dissimilar approaches. Writers who vary hugely on the very meaning of mercy, on its relationship to justice, and on its relative status as a virtue (or a vice) find common ground in their resort to stories. From biblical parables, to the plays of Shakespeare, to the driest philosophical and legal disquisitions, treatments of mercy typically invoke the particularities of human experience to an unusual degree.

In accordance with this helpful convention, I begin my own remarks with reference to two stories written in the early years of the twentieth century by a former prison inmate who dealt, not surprisingly, with issues of crime, punishment, and redemption. A long-time resident of Texas in an era of rough-and-ready justice, William Sidney Porter eventually served three years of a five-year prison term for bank embezzlement. While in prison, he adopted his future pen name from one of the prison guards, whose given name was Orrin Henry.[1] Writing under the pseudonym O. Henry, Porter became famous for his turns of phrase, his unexpected twists of plot, and his sharp eye for the contradictions of the human situation. It is his appreciation of ambiguity and irony in connection with his fondness for themes of crime and punishment that recommend O. Henry here. The two stories I have chosen, though they were written nearly a century ago, reflect two quite different faces of mercy and capture what I believe is the central paradox of mercy as it relates to criminal justice today.

The first story, "A Retrieved Reformation,"[2] begins with the corrupt pardon and release from prison of Jimmy Valentine, a brazen but extremely well-connected bank robber. Jimmy, unrepentant and outfitted with "the finest set of burglar's tools in the East," soon becomes a one-man crime wave, breaking into bank safes in small towns separated by long distances. On his trail is Ben Price, the lawman who put Jimmy away before his untimely release. But upon alighting in Elmore, Arkansas, Jimmy falls in love at first sight with Annabel Adams, the local bank president's daughter. A year later, Jimmy has completely abandoned his old identity and his life of crime. Under the new name of Ralph Spencer, he is now well established in Elmore, running a legitimate shoe business and engaged to be married to Annabel. He writes to a former compatriot, explaining that he has gone straight and arranging a meeting to hand off his no longer needed burglar's tools. Unbeknownst to Jimmy, however, Ben Price is closing in and has arrived in Elmore looking for him. On the very day that Jimmy is planning to abandon his tools, his fiancée's two nieces are playing in their grandfather's bank, and the nine-year-old accidentally locks the five-year-old in the time-locked vault in such a way that the safe cannot be opened before the little girl will perish from suffocation. Knowing that his actions will uncover his former identity, Jimmy nonetheless uses his tools to crack open the safe and rescue the child. Believing that his new life is over, Jimmy Valentine spots Ben Price, the lawman, at the entrance to the bank, greets him by name, and offers himself into custody. But the lawman only replies, "Guess you're mistaken, Mr. Spencer. Don't believe I recognize you."

This story presents the attractive face of mercy as both the agent of and the reward for human redemption. It was Jimmy Valentine's initial pardon, however corrupt, that gave him the second chance to make a life outside of crime. And it was Ben Price's decision to let Jimmy remain at large that paid appropriate tribute to that new life. O. Henry's words say it best: The lawman did not "recognize" Jimmy Valentine; he was truly another person. We, the readers, cheer when the law, in the form of Ben Price, takes less than it could in the face of a powerful story of love, redemption, and sacrifice. There is also the suggestion that Ben Price himself, the mercy giver, may be transformed by his experience. The very last line of the story is about Ben, not Jimmy: The reader's eye follows Ben as "he turned and strolled down the street." The cynical and vigilant lawman himself changes—"turns"—and walks with a lighter hearted "stroll" rather than the stalk of the professional detective.

The second story, "Law and Order," [3] shows an altogether different face of the merciful lawman. The tale takes place in Texas, a story within a story told by a former deputy sheriff reminiscing to the narrator about the good old days of law and order when "cases was decided in the chambers of a six-shooter instead of a supreme court." The deputy tells the tale of his friend, a former cattle rancher, who married a beautiful woman and fathered a much-loved son. When the boy was two, the rancher learned of his wife's dalliance with another man and promptly bribed a local judge to give him an order of divorce granting him sole custody of his child. But before he could present the order to his wife, she disappeared, taking the boy with her, and the rancher never found them. Well, the years went by and the rancher became the local sheriff, with our storyteller as his deputy. A group of rich tenderfeet from New York City arrive in town, with a teen-aged boy proud of his new cowboy finery and pearl-handled pistol. The deputy witnesses a local man named Pedro Johnson laugh at the teenager and physically assault him, and the deputy sees the boy shoot Pedro in response. The boy and his group quickly return to New York City, but the sheriff, enraged, follows them with his deputy to bring the boy back to Texas justice. Just as he bribed a Texas judge for the divorce decree many years previously, he bribes a New York City judge to give him an extradition order for the boy and prepares to take him back to Texas. But the deputy notices an unusual scar on the boy's face and recognizes him as the sheriff's long-lost son. Upon learning of the boy's identity, the sheriff is overjoyed and pulls out his dog-eared order of paternal custody, planning to teach the willing boy all he knows about ranching. His deputy, however, notes that law and order require taking the boy into criminal custody for the shooting of Pedro Johnson, "a respectable and well-known citizen." "Oh, hell," responds the sheriff, in the last words of the story. "That don't amount to anything. That fellow was half Mexican, anyhow."

In this story, the sheriff's decision to grant his son special dispensation from punishment overrides the deputy sheriff's sardonic appeal to "law and order" in a way that places mercy and justice squarely at odds. The possibility of bias and therefore error in the exercise of merciful forbearance is shown in both of its possible guises. The sheriff is biased in favor of his son by the strong attachment of paternity, just as we are all more likely to be moved by the plight of those close to us not only by virtue of blood relation but also by other ties and similarities that make it easier for us to engage sympathetically in another's pain. And the sheriff is biased against the victim, Pedro Johnson, whose "half-Mexican" status makes it easier for the sheriff to devalue his suffering and, indeed, to err gravely in assessing Johnson's very status as a person and a citizen. Although there are many competing voices in the story—among them the voice of the narrator who is being told the story and the deputy sheriff who is telling it—the sheriff's blithe about-face on the need for justice for Pedro Johnson gets the last word, literally, silencing the two other competing voices in their joint reminiscences about law and order in Texas.

These two stories capture both the attractiveness and the danger of the power of mercy within any system of criminal justice. At this particular point in time in the development of our particular institutions of criminal justice, however, the paradox of mercy is especially compelling because the two faces of mercy sketched by O. Henry mirror the two most serious critiques of the American criminal justice system at the turn of the twenty-first century. On the one hand, our punishment practices, especially when compared to those of many Western European countries, appear exceedingly and often excessively harsh. Along virtually every dimension, our system of criminal justice has become significantly more punitive over the course of the past three decades. Criminal sentences have become substantially longer, prison populations significantly larger, and the use of capital punishment has increased nationwide to a point not seen in more than fifty years.[4] Initiatives like "three strikes, you're out" laws and the "war on drugs" have resulted in the incarceration of greater numbers of nonviolent offenders for much longer periods of time. Moreover, juvenile offenders are increasingly treated as adults and sent to adult prisons, where rehabilitation has been abandoned, often formally, as a goal of incarceration.[5] Partially as a consequence of overcrowding, but also partially as a reflection of the punitive moment, prison conditions are frequently degrading, dehumanizing, and dangerously violent.[6] In such times, the creation of institutional possibilities for the exercise of mercy within the criminal justice system is extremely attractive as a way of mitigating the draconian harshness of our current penological regime.

On the other hand, however, the second critique of our criminal justice system addresses its extreme racial disparate impact. At every level, from on-the-street policing, to bail policies, to the provision of defense resources, to sentences and the use of capital punishment, it appears that we have not one criminal justice system but two—one for the white and relatively privileged and another for indigent minorities.[7] Viewed through the lens of this issue, the exercise of mercy has a different face and a far more problematic one, for it is likely that the institutional opportunities for the exercise of mercy in the criminal justice system are also sources of a substantial part of the system's disparate impact along the lines of race, ethnicity, and class.

Addressing the possible role of mercy in our current institutions of criminal justice is thus a matter of urgent importance. One central question for our legal system is whether there is a coherent and normatively attractive conception of mercy that is also consistent with the ideal of the rule of the law—the fundamental commitment to treating like cases alike. A second crucial question, this one more institutional than normative, follows from the first: What would such a conception mean for the reform of our current institutions of criminal justice and for the self-conception of the institutional actors within them?

The first and openly normative question immediately implicates a host of related inquiries. What is the relationship between mercy and justice? Does justice require the imposition of deserved punishment? Is mercy related or opposed or indifferent to the moral desert of an offender? Does mercy describe merely an act, or does it describe something about the state of mind of the mercy giver? Or something about the relationship between the mercy giver and receiver? What is the relationship between mercy and the constellation of emotions or attitudes we call pity, empathy, compassion, and forgiveness? Is mercy opposed to reason? Can the exercise of mercy be evaluated? How, if at all, can whatever view of mercy we choose to embrace guide us to its proper application? In short, is mercy a good normative lens, among others, through which to judge the exercise of discretion within our criminal justice system?

The second, more institutional question comes with its own host of corollaries. Is mercy appropriate for the public sphere at all? If so, is it possible to realize institutionally? Which institutional actors would be best suited to promote any particular vision of mercy? Should prosecutors think of themselves as open to appeals for mercy in the exercise of their charging discretion? What about juries? Should their power to render acquittals that are unreviewable be recognized as a proper locus for the power of mercy? Should sentencing judges consider appeals for mercy, or are such appeals more properly directed toward those with the powers of executive clemency and pardon? Can legislatures be merciful? Or is mercy necessarily individual, perhaps the province only of discrete victims of crime? Under this last view, should the legal system have any role in fostering conditions for reconciliation between victims and offenders? By attempting to carve out and protect a power of mercy within our criminal justice system, do we inevitably increase the problems of arbitrariness and bias beyond what we would endure without such a commitment?

The urgency of these questions may be new, but not the questions themselves. The normative question about the relationship of mercy to justice was famously posed in the theological realm by St. Anselm of Canterbury in the eleventh century, who noted two paradoxes of God's mercy. St. Anselm's first paradox asks how judgment and salvation can emanate from the same source. If God is perfectly just, how can he also show compassion and grant mercy to the wicked? In St. Anselm's words: "What justice is it that gives him who merits eternal death everlasting life? How, then, gracious Lord, good to the wicked, can you save the wicked if this is not just, and you do nothing that is not just?"[8] St. Anselm's second paradox is concerned with equal treatment, asking how we can understand God's choice to show mercy only to some. In St. Anselm's words: "But if it can be comprehended in any way why you can will to save the wicked, yet by no consideration can we comprehend why, of those who are alike wicked, you save some rather than others, through supreme goodness, and why you condemn the latter, rather than the former, through supreme justice."[9] St. Anselm's two paradoxes of God's mercy are startling in their relevance to contemporary treatments of human mercy (though his resolution of the paradoxes is wholly theological and without human analog). Indeed, St. Anselm's paradoxes are often the starting point for modern moral philosophers struggling with the conundrums of individual and institutional mercy. They figured prominently in Jeffrie Murphy's chapter on "Mercy and Legal Justice," in his 1988 book with Jean Hampton, *Forgiveness and Mercy*, which itself can be credited with a substantial role in promoting moral philosophical and legal interest in the topic since 1988.[10]

Questions of institutional design, perhaps because they lack the same theological provenance, have not been the subject of as much interest and attention. While particular features of legal institutions of mercy have engaged thinkers for centuries—think, for example, of Montesquieu's disquisition on the relative roles of the pardoning power in a monarchy and a republic[11]—it is hard to find comprehensive treatments of what mercy might mean for our varied institutions of criminal justice.[12] The legal scholars who have become interested in the topic of mercy have generally been drawn in through some particular feature of the current criminal justice system—many of them by capital sentencing,[13] some by the issue of discretionary sentencing more generally,[14] others by the powers of pardon and clemency,[15] and still others by the potential for legislative leniency.[16] What lawyers have added and can continue to add to the work of moral philosophers—and theologians, classicists, historians, playwrights, and poets—is an understanding of what our normative presumptions commit us to institutionally and whether these commitments are feasible within the general outlines of the structures of legal justice that we have already established.

So how best to begin to tackle the large and multifaceted normative and institutional issues raised by the relationship of mercy to criminal justice? There are many tasks of "first principle" involved here, from defining mercy, to defining justice, to considering the essential functions of particular institutions within the legal system that might mediate between the two. The most helpful route through this difficult terrain is by charting a map of possible destinations and considering the attractions and deficiencies of each. In what follows, I briefly sketch several possible approaches to the relationship of mercy to criminal justice (each of which is actually endorsed by one or more theorists) and attempt to understand their advantages and disadvantages from the perspectives both of normative theory and institutional consequences. Of course, there are many more positions on the matter that it is possible to take and that, indeed, have been taken. But the ones that I have chosen give a sense both of the sweep of the landscape and the shape of my larger project, and it is my hope that this bird's-eye perspective will provide enough of a view to provoke further discussion and thought.

The first and perhaps most provocative position, taken by Jeffrie Murphy and Ross Harrison, among others, is that there is simply no place for mercy in our public institutions of criminal justice. Although mercy can be a virtue in private law— appropriately exercised, for example, when an individual rightfully owed a debt forgives a suffering debtor—it has no place in the public institutions of criminal law because institutional actors have a duty to pursue justice.[17] Mercy, under this view, is either a part of justice or opposed to it. When what we might commonly call mercy—such as individualized consideration during sentencing that leads to leniency—is actually the same as doing justice, there is no independent need for the concept of mercy. And when mercy would call on the criminal justice system to depart from doing justice, then the concept is, in Murphy's words, "a product of morally dangerous sentimentality."[18] In his most provocative passage, Murphy concludes, "There thus simply is no room for mercy as an autonomous virtue with which the[] justice [of judges, prosecutors, and parole boards] should be tempered. Let them keep their sentimentality to themselves for use in their private lives with their families and pets."[19]

It is important to realize that under this skeptical view of mercy, justice embraces a piece, perhaps a very large one, of what in common parlance goes by the name of mercy. Murphy makes clear that many examples sometimes offered of appropriate exercises of mercy—such as using discretion to take into account individuating details to modify a punishment that would otherwise be too harsh under the strict application of legal rules—is really the pursuit of moral justice within the retributivist tradition, which demands that offenders be punished according to their moral desert. Ross Harrison agrees, arguing that it is the gap between rules and moral justice, not between justice and mercy, to which we need to attend in apportioning punishment. In Harrison's view:

> It is important to distinguish . . . between the mechanical operation of rules and the question of justice in the particular case. Obviously a simple or mechanically operated rule may not take appropriate account of the complexity or individuality of a particular case, and, if applied, justice would not be done. This is because the case is importantly different from others which are, by contrast, appropriately covered by that rule. So the rule should not be applied in this particular case. But this, it seems to me, is quite different from saying that law should be suspended, or that a mechanism is needed outside the law which can suspend it. . . . Difficult cases should not be taken outside the law and handed over to political amateurs, in the name of justice. Rather, if justice is to be done, the decision made should be taken for reasons and be rationally defensible.[20]

Under Harrison's approach (and Murphy's), what one needs in order to decide when to mitigate or forego punishment is a full-blown theory of just punishment, not recourse to some idea outside the realm of justice, such as compassion, forgiveness, or love.

Thus, one virtue of the skeptical view is that it embraces as justice many of the most powerful examples of lenient treatment that might also be claimed to be the product of mercy. For example, Murphy addresses an example that is very similar to the story of our Jimmy Valentine in which an offender "has so reformed that he is, in a very real sense, a 'new person.'"[21] Although he deems himself "suspicious of 'new person' talk," Murphy nonetheless concludes that "if there really are cases where we should take it literally, then it is obviously a matter of justice that one does not punish one person for the crimes of another. Why talk of mercy here?"[22] Another attraction of the skeptical view is that it has the potential to curb arbitrariness and bias in the granting of leniency by its emphasis on reasons that are of general application. Under the skeptical view, institutional actors within the criminal justice system should not think of whatever discretion they hold as an empty vessel to be filled as they choose or are emotionally moved to fill it. Instead, they must be forced to think of and articulate reasons for their discretionary actions rather than merely to identify motives. And they must be able, in Kantian terms, to will those reasons as universal law for their reasons to count as reasons of justice.

Despite these advantages, the skeptical view runs into a number of problems. First, as the foregoing makes clear, for justice to embrace some of the most compelling examples of leniency, we need a theory of just punishment, and needless to say, this gets us into arduous territory—arduous not only because there is serious contention about theories of just punishment even within the retributivist tradition but also because it is difficult to know when the demands of any such theory are being met in an individual case. It is all very well to say that offenders ought to be punished in accordance with their moral desert, but of what does moral desert consist? Choice? Character? Harm? In what proportion? Even if we could answer those questions, how can whatever retributive theory we choose provide the kind of metric that we need to decide individual cases: How can we ever know what precisely the just punishment is for a particular individual, who made a particular choice, with a particular character, and inflicted a particular harm? Is it really possible for a theory of just punishment to take us all the way to particular punishments, or do we always need something else? If we do, why isn't some conception of mercy appropriately part of that "something else"?

A second, related problem is that many theories of just punishment in the retributive tradition would leave out of justice some of the situations in which mercy is most attractive. Murphy's suspicion of what he calls "'new person' talk" is connected, I think, to his commitment to retributivism. It simply isn't clear how remorse, repentance, and redemption fit into retributive theories of punishment if they do at all. The story of Jimmy Valentine, for all of its emotional and moral force, quite possibly lies outside of what Murphy or other retributivists would embrace as justice. This possibility—that something important will be lost by the abandonment of any independent content for the concept of mercy in the criminal justice system—defies the instinct, so well-expressed by Milton, that justice is appropriately "tempered" by mercy.[23] Can it really be that justice never needs tempering, especially justice in punishment, which is usually the paradigm first pictured when justice is summoned to mind?[24] A resonant literary tradition joins common intuition in questioning this assertion.

A final problem for the skeptics is the role conception their view promotes for institutional actors within the criminal justice system. Thomas Jefferson, who shared the skeptics' repudiation of discretionary mercy, articulated an extreme view of the proper mind-set of a judge or other wielder of discretionary authority as follows: "Let mercy be the character of the law-giver, but let the judge be *a mere machine*. The mercies of the law will be dispensed equally and impartially to every description of men; those of the judge, or of the executive power, will be the eccentric impulses of whimsical, capricious designing man."[25] Murphy and company might fairly reply that it is not discretion that they object to but rather discretion unmoored from an anchoring concept of justice. However, their anchoring concept, with its emphasis on moral desert subject to rational divination, does suggest that judges should use reason as opposed to emotion and exercise judgment as opposed to compassion. Do we want prosecutors, judges, juries, governors, and presidents to consider compassion beyond their purview? What kind of presentations and considerations—in charging decisions, trials, sentencings, and clemency proceedings—would this conception render irrelevant? Discretionary decision makers under the skeptical view might not necessarily be Jefferson's "mere machines," but they could not draw fully on all of their human capacities.

Last, but certainly not least, let us consider the victim as institutional actor. It is, after all, a victim's suffering that puts the criminal process in motion in most cases and in all of the most serious ones. Victims thus play the role of complainant, and frequently that of witness as well, in both trials and sentencing hearings. Under the skeptical view, mercy has no place in criminal justice because justice is served only when offenders are punished in accordance with their desert. But this view does not attend to the possibilities of forgiveness by victims or their reconciliation with offenders; it puts such possibilities outside of the domain of appropriate criminal justice. This is one of the most compelling and now most frequently voiced critiques of retributivism as a theory of just punishment. Because it is retributivism that leads the skeptics to reject mercy as an aspect of criminal justice, it is also a powerful critique of the skeptical view.

What alternatives are there to the skeptical view? I sketch a handful without going into as much detail as I gave the skeptical view, partly because of constraints of time and space and partly because the pros and cons of the skeptical view already lay a good deal of the groundwork for the alternatives. The alternatives to mercy skepticism fall into three main groups. The first group directly contradicts the skeptical thesis and asserts both that the concept of mercy has content independent from justice and that it is reconcilable with the demands of justice. The second group depicts justice and mercy as separate and incommensurable goods that must be traded off against each other. Finally, the third group rejects the retributive justice of skeptics altogether, offering a variety of competing theories of criminal justice with a variety of conceptions of and roles for mercy within them.

One powerful way to reconcile mercy with justice is to build on Murphy's concession that justice permits, indeed requires, individuation. This alternative to Murphy's skepticism takes the process of individuation and fashions it into a conception of mercy that is often called "equity" after both the ancient concept of equity[26] extolled by Aristotle and Seneca among others in the classical world and the more recent Anglo-American legal tradition of equity.[27] Martha Nussbaum translates the ancient concept of equity as dually "the ability to judge in such a way as to respond with sensitivity to all the particulars of a person and situation, and the 'inclination of the mind' toward leniency in punishing."[28]

The first and most obvious challenge for this version of mercy is to distinguish itself from mere individuation, which the skeptics are happy to claim as part of justice.[29] Nussbaum maintains that equity requires more than mere individuation or, rather, that true individuation both requires and leads to an internal attitude distinct from the feelings of retributive anger that retributivist mercy skeptics tend to endorse on behalf of victims and other institutional actors within the criminal justice system. She also insists that equity demands consideration of emotional appeals for compassion more characteristic of novels than of judicial proceedings as we now know them (Nussbaum would like O. Henry's treatment of Jimmy Valentine). The skeptics might reply that mature and discerning moral judgment requires exactly the kind of mind-set endorsed by Nussbaum but that nothing about such a mind-set necessarily mitigates appropriate retributive anger; rather, it only gives us a more nuanced appreciation of when such anger is truly justified.[30] As to the structural implications of the equity view, skeptics might reply that the unfettered emotionalism of the narrative approach endorsed by Nussbaum undermines the public reason we must demand of our institutions of criminal justice.[31] Whatever the proper resolution of such disputes, it is clear that the distinction, if there is one, between retributivist mercy skeptics and the promoters of equity derives from differences about what individuation entails internally in the character and attitude of institutional actors and procedurally in the presentations properly addressed to those actors.

Even if one were convinced that mercy as equity is truly distinct from and not merely a part of retributive justice, the equity alternative runs into a further difficulty. The concept of mercy as commonly understood, as instituted historically in criminal justice practices, and even as translated into institutional structures by such equity promoters as Nussbaum,[32] is irreducibly supererogatory. And yet if individuation is a requirement of justice, is it not problematic to conceive of mercy as something for which one "pleads" or "begs," as we commonly say? Murphy articulates it best: "One could introduce a sense of 'mercy' that means 'seeking to tailor our response to morally relevant individual difference.' But this would be . . . dangerous because it might lead us to suppose that individuation is not owed to persons as a right and is thus somehow optional as a free gift or act of grace."[33]

A different attempt, within the first general type of responses to mercy skeptics, to assert the independence of mercy and yet reconcile it with justice relies on scaling back the requirements of justice by taking a weaker or softer view of what retributivism requires. The mercy skeptics start from the presumption that justice ordinarily requires that we punish offenders according to their moral desert. The soft retributivists make room for mercy by loosening this demand of justice, asserting, for example, that retributivism permits but does not require the imposition of deserved punishment[34] or, for another example, that retributivism requires the imposition of deserved punishment but it cannot specify a particular punishment. Rather, there is always a range of deserved punishments among which mercy can help us choose.[35] These proposals definitely do dissolve the conflict between justice and mercy, but they do so at the expense of providing criteria for just punishment. The idea of retributivism as an outer limit on punishment fails to tell us how to choose punishments up to that limit, and the idea of retributivism as setting a range of punishments likewise fails to guide us in choosing among them. We still need a theory of what weight compassion and the mercy that it might call forth should have in the balance of all the permissible reasons to choose a punishment up to the retributive limit or within the retributive range.

The second general type of response to the mercy skeptics does not attempt to reconcile justice with mercy. Rather, this type of response acknowledges that justice and mercy are necessarily incompatible but insists that they are both indispensable goods. This incommensurable view of mercy embraces retributive justice and accepts that it generally requires rather than merely permits punishment. However, it also treats mercy as an independent virtue that necessarily conflicts with justice whenever it is exercised. This is the position Jean Hampton takes in her pas de deux with Murphy in their book written in chapters alternating between their two voices. We have a moral obligation to punish offenders, agrees Hampton, but that duty can conflict with "other obligations, in particular, to the wrongdoer as a human being."[36] This acknowledgment of irreconcilable conflict is refreshing in its honest recognition of the complexity of the human condition; as another theorist notes, agreeing with Hampton, "we should resist the temptation to suppose that life cannot confront us (cannot be allowed to confront us) with such irresoluble conflicts between incommensurable values."[37] But neither Hampton nor any other proponent of incommensurability offers us much guidance on who within the criminal justice system should weigh the competing demands of justice and mercy or how they should do so. The challenge for such a view is to offer us some way of working out substantive positions and institutional arrangements that mediate between justice and mercy rather than merely to leave us with the sense that the best we can hope for is to muddle through somehow.

The third and last general type of response to the mercy skeptics rejects wholesale rather than modifies or limits the retributive premises from which the skeptics begin. However, what anti-retributivists put in the place of retributivism varies greatly, and consequently, their conceptions of and roles for mercy vary greatly as well. I consider two diametrically opposed examples of antiretributive thought, perhaps the two most significant challenges to retributivism in theory and practice at the present time.

On the one hand, social welfare theorists from the school of "law and economics" seek to replace retributivism—and indeed, any and all deontological theories of justice—with a theory of social welfare, which holds, in essence, that normative questions of justice, including criminal justice, should be determined solely by considering how legal rules affect individuals' welfare in the aggregate.[38] In the criminal domain, this theory sometimes goes by the name of deterrence theory because deterring crime is obviously one of the main ways that criminal law affects social welfare. But it need not be so narrow: The expressive function of criminal law is also a significant way that criminal law can affect social welfare, as the "new Chicago school" elaborates.[39] Even punishing people according to their desert may itself promote social welfare.[40] Similarly, showing mercy may contribute to social welfare under certain conditions.[41]

Under this view, there is no conflict between justice and mercy because each is subsumed on equal footing into the larger calculus of social welfare. Justice is pursued if and only to the extent to which it contributes to social welfare; the same is true for mercy. Individuals' preferences for justice—that is, their desires to see offenders punished according to their moral desert—are taken into account in the calculus, as are individuals' preferences for a criminal justice system that allows compassion to produce leniency. But these preferences are given no more weight than any other preferences individuals might have for anything they value. There are no distinctively *moral* values that take precedence over others, nor are any outcomes that the calculus of social welfare produces ruled out a priori. Although this view neatly eliminates St. Anselm's paradoxes of justice and mercy, the ease with which it does so should give us pause. Social welfare theory solves the conundrum of mercy's relationship to justice because it denies that either justice or mercy is an independent good; indeed, it denies the possibility of moral theory altogether, except perhaps as a useful proxy or shorthand for the workings of the calculus of social welfare. Clearly, this theory, in its exclusive form, faces a daunting challenge from our deep-seated moral intuitions and thousands of years of human history, not to mention institutional challenges in the feasibility of performing a plausible calculus of social welfare within the structures of the criminal justice system.

A very different rejection of retributivism comes from a group of theorists who call their view "restorative" as opposed to "retributive" justice. Under this view, we have no obligation to punish offenders according to their moral desert; indeed, we have no obligation to "punish" at all. Rather, as one of the leading proponents of restorative justice describes it, "Restorative justice is a process by which all the parties with a stake in a particular offense come together to resolve collectively how to deal with the aftermath of the offense and its implications for the future."[42] Under such a view, mercy is not opposed to justice because justice does not entail the imposition of deserved punishment. But if that is the case, for mercy to have a role in a system of restorative justice, it must mean something different from declining to inflict deserved punishment out of compassionate concern for the offender. In such a system, mercy must implicate not the outcome of the restorative process but rather the attitude with which participants, particularly those who have been wronged by the offense, approach the restorative process. Many theorists in many different theoretical camps want to maintain that mercy entails something about the internal state of mind of the mercy giver.[43] In the theory of restorative justice, this entailment of mercy achieves full flower because the internal attitude of the victim and others in the community harmed by the offense is crucial in creating the possibility of something other than revenge or retribution. Indeed, one of the goals of the restorative justice movement is to move beyond the cycles of violence that communities and whole nations face; it is striking and not accidental that the language of the restorative justice movement is echoed by one of the proponents of mercy within our more traditional criminal justice system: "this virtue brings into the world those sorts of actions that break the cycle of revenge and retribution into which actors and even whole communities can so easily fall. It promotes harmony in the community, reconciliation, and flourishing. It encourages the resolution of problems and does all of these things through a thorough examination of the cause of discord."[44] Moreover, within a restorative justice system, the idea that mercy is a good for the mercy giver also has more force because the mercy giver is not merely an institutional actor playing an institutional role but one personally harmed by the offense. In such circumstances, there is a stronger case that, as one scholar put it, mercy "enriches the soul" of the mercy giver,[45] or as Shakespeare put it, "It is twice blessed; / It blesseth him that gives and him that takes."[46]

A critic might say that restorative justice makes room for mercy only by abandoning justice. Restorative justice theory thus faces some of the same challenges that social welfare theory does in that it rejects wholesale a venerable conception and tradition of punishment as a moral good. Moreover, it faces a different set of challenges as well. Whereas social welfare theory takes better account than either retributive justice or restorative justice of commonly held beliefs that the first job of a criminal justice system is to protect society by deterring or incapacitating criminals, restorative justice must explain how it can take account of those concerns as well if it rejects the imposition of punishment as we know it.

That concludes my whirlwind tour of the most substantial approaches to the conundrums of justice and mercy. It is fair to ask at this point, "Well, which one is right?" As you no doubt have guessed, I have my own take on the question of mercy, and I plant my flag in the anti-skeptic, pro-mercy camp. My own account, which I only sketch here, as it is the subject of the next chapter of my larger project, is simultaneously both more modest and more ambitious than the others I have canvassed. My account is more modest in that it is a prudential account rooted in the predictable failures of other accounts rather than on some new normative terrain. But my account is more ambitious in that it argues for a place for the virtue of mercy in institutions of criminal justice regardless of which normative theory or theories the criminal justice system seeks to promote or instantiate.

In brief, I argue that both retributivism and social welfare theory, at least as they play out within our current institutions of criminal justice, have predictable biases toward too much punishment. In other words, the several-decade-long trend toward increased harshness in punishment in our country is not, or not only, the product of an inevitable pendulum swing in criminal justice policy. Rather, it is the likely if not inevitable result of the way the two reigning theories of punishment operate within our institutions. Retributivism is limited and skewed by its inability to make nuanced judgments about freedom of action and choice in a world of great inequality; this limitation is reflected in the on-off switch of culpability that characterizes much of substantive criminal law. Once such determinations of culpability are made by law, they reinforce social and systemic tendencies toward attitudes of smugness and even satisfaction in punishing "evil" that are always latent in a society with deeply rooted religious attitudes toward personal responsibility for sin. In a different vein, social welfare theory is limited by its unwillingness to posit any a priori limits on the quantity or quality of punishment. Social welfare theory's thin conception of "personhood" prevents it from giving any purchase to a strong commitment to "human dignity" that can place limits on extreme punishments that aggregation of preferences might permit or require, especially when such punishments are likely and predictably to be imposed on minority groups within the larger population. Moreover, the tendencies of both theories toward harsh punishment are exacerbated by current and longstanding institutional arrangements that create legislative and prosecutorial incentives to maintain or increase extreme criminal penalties. The growth of plea bargaining as the prime mechanism of disposition in a context of recognized, protected, and celebrated prosecutorial discretion has given legislatures incentives to raise potential criminal penalties so as to make the prosecution of crime cheaper for prosecutors. In addition, prosecutors have their own individual incentives to seek high penalties, in a context of intense local accountability, largely through electoral politics, for local crime rates coupled with minimal local responsibility for bearing the costs of high penalties.

Given the predictability of an ever-upward tending ratchet of punishment for both of the two reigning paradigms of punishment within our current institutional arrangements, we need some counterratchet, some way of checking this tendency and working against it. I contend that the ideal of mercy—taken quite self-consciously from the very religious tradition that contributes to retributivism's ratchet—is that necessary counterbalance. Mercy can offer a normative vocabulary to evaluate the many exercises of discretion that occur throughout the criminal justice system and that are thought to be either beyond evaluation (because discretionary) or subject to evaluation only along other dimensions (promoting the values of accuracy or efficiency, for example). Moreover, mercy is virtue that can be cultivated not only by the actors who exercise discretion within the criminal justice system but also by the general public through changes in the nature of public discourse about crime and punishment. But the cultivation of the virtue of mercy is not without cost. Discretion, which is necessary for the virtue of mercy to be cultivated, has dark sides, to which I have alluded in my reservations about some of the pro-mercy theories explored earlier. Thus, while I join the pro-mercy camp and bring new arguments as reinforcements of that position, I do so with some fear and trepidation. These fears need to be fully confronted and explored, and potential mitigation of them considered, before the case for the cultivation of mercy within our current institutions can prevail.

In this vein, I close with yet another story by O. Henry—a quick one and probably his most famous—that both captures and validates my own ambivalence. In "The Gift of the Magi,"[47] O. Henry tells the simple story of a young couple with very little money, each of whom wants to buy the other a special gift for Christmas. The couple have two prized possessions in their household: his gold watch and her long chestnut hair. She impulsively cuts off her hair and sells it to buy him a beautiful watch chain, and he pawns his watch to buy her magnificent combs for her hair. O. Henry portrays the young couple as both "foolish children" who made a "most unwise[] sacrifice[]" and as "the wisest" on a par with "the wonderfully wise" Magi who brought gifts to the Babe in the manger. O. Henry's piercing eye for the paradoxes of humanity aptly captures the paradox of mercy: Depending crucially on our point of view, the granting of mercy can be an act of foolish profligacy or one of wise loving kindness. The view is ours to choose.

Notes

1. *The Best Short Stories of O. Henry* (Modern Library Edition, 1994), x.

2. "A Retrieved Reformation" was published in O. Henry's 1909 collection of stories, *Roads of Destiny*. See *The Complete Works of O. Henry*, vol. 1 (Doubleday, 1953). It is one of his best-known stories and was made into a smash dramatic hit entitled *Alias Jimmy Valentine*. See *The Best Short Stories of O. Henry*, supra note 1, x.

3. "Law and Order" was published posthumously in O. Henry's 1911 collection of stories, *Sixes and Sevens*. See *The Complete Works of O. Henry*, vol. 2 (Doubleday, 1953). O. Henry died in 1910.

4. See Michael Tonry and Richard S. Frase, eds., *Sentencing and Sanctions in Western Countries* (New York: Oxford University Press, 2001); Franklin E. Zimring and Gordon J. Hawkins, *Capital Punishment and the American Agenda* (New York: Cambridge University Press, 1986).

5. See Barry C. Feld, *Bad Kids: Race and the Transformation of the Juvenile Court* (New York: Oxford University Press, 1999); Simon I. Singer, *Recriminalizing Delinquency: Violent Juvenile Crime and Juvenile Justice Reform* (New York: Cambridge University Press, 1996).

6. See Scott Christianson, *With Liberty for Some: 500 Years of Imprisonment in America* (Boston: Northeastern University Press, 1998); David Garland, *The Culture of Control: Crime and Social Order in Contemporary Society* (New York: Oxford University Press, 2001).

7. See David Cole, *No Equal Justice: Race and Class in the American Criminal Justice System* (New York: New Press, 1999); Jerome G. Miller, *Search and Destroy: African-American Males in the Criminal Justice System* (New York: Cambridge University Press, 1996); Jeffrey Reiman, *The Rich Get Richer and the Poor Get Prison: Ideology, Class, and Criminal Justice* (Boston: Allyn & Bacon, 2001); Michael Tonry, *Malign Neglect: Race, Crime, and Punishment in America* (New York: Oxford University Press, 1995).

8. *Proslogium* IX, in Brian Davies and Gillian Evans, eds., *Anselm of Canterbury: The Major Works* (New York: Oxford University Press, 1998).

9. *Proslogium* XI, in Davies and Evans, eds., *Anselm of Canterbury*.

10. There had been a smattering of interest among moral philosophers on the question of mercy from the late 1960s to the late 1980s. See, e.g., Claudia Card, "On Mercy," *Philosophy Review* 81 (1972), 182; H. Scott Hestevold, "Disjunctive Desert," *American Philosophical Quarterly* 20 (1983), 357; H. Scott Hestevold, "Justice to Mercy," *Philosophy and Phenomenological Research* 46 (1985), 281; John Kleinig, "Mercy and Justice," *Philosophy* 44 (1969), 341; Lyla H. O'Driscoll, "The Quality of Mercy," *Southern Journal of Philosophy* 21 (1983), 229; H. R. T. Roberts, "Mercy," *Philosophy* 46 (1971), 352; Alwynne Smart, "Mercy," *Philosophy* 43 (1968), 345; James Sterba, "Can a Person Deserve Mercy?" *Journal of Social Philosophy* 10 (1979), 11; Steven Sverdlik, "Justice and Mercy," *Journal of Social Philosophy* 16 (1985), 36; P. Twambley, "Mercy and Forgiveness," *Analysis* 36 (1976), 84. The publication of Jeffrie G. Murphy and Jean Hampton's book, *Forgiveness and Mercy* (New York: Cambridge University Press, 1988), however, gave new life to the topic; it both generated a rich moral philosophical response and has been cited in the very recent flare of interest in the topic of mercy among legal scholars. For moral philosophical responses to Murphy and Hampton, see, e.g., Andrew Brien, "Saving Grace," *Criminal Justice Ethics*, Winter–Spring (1990), 52; Andrew Brien, "Mercy Within Legal Justice," *Social Theory & Practice* 24 (1998), 83; R. A. Duff, "Justice, Mercy and Forgiveness," *Criminal Justice Ethics*, Summer–Fall (1990), 51; Ross Harrison, "The Equality of Mercy," in *Jurisprudence: Cambridge Essays 107*, ed. Hyman Gross and Ross Harrison (Oxford: Clarendon Press; New York: Oxford University Press, 1992); Carla Ann Hage Johnson, "Entitled to Clemency: Mercy in the Criminal Law," *Law & Philosophy* 10 (1991), 109; Herbert Morris, "Murphy on Forgiveness," *Criminal Justice Ethics*, Summer–Fall (1988), 20; George W. Rainbolt, "Mercy: An Independent, Imperfect Virtue," *American Philosophical Quarterly* 27 (1990), 169; Nigel Walker, "The Quiddity of Mercy," *Philosophy* 70 (1995), 27. For legal scholars on mercy and criminal justice, see those cited in notes 13 to 16 infra.

11. See Charles de Montesquieu, *The Spirit of Laws* (1748) (Legal Classics Library, 1984), explaining that while executive pardons can have "admirable effects," they have no place in a republic where they would usurp the will of the people.

12. Perhaps the closest thing to a comprehensive institutional assessment is Kent Greenawalt's discussion of "Institutions of Amelioration," in his book *Conflicts of Law and Morality* (New York: Oxford University Press, 1987), Part IV.

13. See, e.g., Anthony V. Alfieri, "Mitigation, Mercy, and Delay: The Moral Politics of Death Penalty Abolitionists," *Harvard Civil Rights–Civil Liberties Law Review* 31 (1996), 325; Paul W. Cobb Jr., Note, "Reviving Mercy in the Structure of Capital Punishment," *Yale Law Journal* 99 (1989), 389; Stephen P. Garvey, "'As the Gentle Rain from Heaven': Mercy in Capital Sentencing," *Cornell Law Review* 81 (1996), 989; Malla Pollack, "The Under Funded Death Penalty: Mercy as Discrimination in a Rights-Based System of Justice," *University of Missouri Kansas City Law Review* 66 (1998), 513.

14. See, e.g., Frank O. Bowman III, "The Quality of Mercy Must Be Restrained, and Other Lessons in Learning to Love the Federal Sentencing Guidelines," *Wisconsin Law*

Review (1996), 679; Richard G. Fox, "When Justice Sheds a Tear: The Place of Mercy in Sentencing," *Monash University Law Review* 25 (1999), 1; Eric L. Muller, "The Virtue of Mercy in Criminal Sentencing," *Seton Hall Law Review* 24 (1993), 288.

15. See, e.g., Clifford Dorne and Kenneth Gewerth, "Mercy in a Climate of Retributive Justice: Interpretations from a National Survey of Executive Clemency Procedures," *Criminal & Civil Confinement* 25 (Summer 1999), 413; Daniel T. Kobil, "The Quality of Mercy Strained: Wresting the Pardoning Power from the King," *Texas Law Review* 69 (1991), 569; Joan H. Krause, "Of Merciful Justice and Justified Mercy: Commuting the Sentences of Battered Women Who Kill," *Florida Law Review* 46 (1994), 699; Kathleen Dean Moore, *Pardons: Justice, Mercy, and the Public Interest* (New York: Oxford University Press, 1989).

16. See, e.g., Robert L. Misner, "A Strategy for Mercy," *William & Mary Law Review* 41 (2000), 1303.

17. After much agonizing, Murphy would allow one exception when everyone in a community unanimously agrees upon a departure from justice and authorizes it, say, through a vote. Though this is an exception, in theory, from the "no mercy in criminal justice" position taken by Murphy, in practice, it would be no exception at all.

18. Murphy and Hampton, *Forgiveness and Mercy*, 167.

19. Ibid., 174.

20. Harrison, "The Equality of Mercy," 121.

21. Murphy and Hampton, *Forgiveness and Mercy*, 173.

22. Ibid. Nigel Walker also treats the case of leniency to an offender whose offense is "stale" and out of character as a form of justice rather than mercy (though he distinguishes leniency based on unrelated good acts and leniency based on remorse as examples of true mercy). See Walker, "The Quiddity of Mercy," 33–34.

23. John Milton, *Paradise Lost*, Book 10, in *The Works of John Milton*, ed. F. Patterson (New York: Columbia University Press, 1931), 307.

24. Isn't this why, when justice is personified, she carries a sword? (Or think of "the hammer of justice" from the folk song "If I Had a Hammer.")

25. Thomas Jefferson, "Letter to Edmund Pendleton, 26 Aug. 1776," in *Papers of Thomas Jefferson*, ed. Julian P. Boyd (Princeton, NJ: Princeton University Press, 1950), 505 (emphasis added).

26. See Martha C. Nussbaum, "Equity and Mercy," *Philosophy & Public Affairs* 22 (1993), 83, 85–86, discussing the Greek term *epieikeia*, which is translated as both "equity" and "mercy."

27. See Johnson, "Entitled to Clemency: Mercy in Criminal Law," 111.

28. Nussbaum, "Equity and Mercy," 85–86.

29. See A. T. Nuyen, "Straining the Quality of Mercy," *Philosophical Papers* 23 (1994), 61, criticizing Nussbaum's argument for equity as failing to distinguish it from justice.

30. See, e.g., Murphy and Hampton, *Forgiveness and Mercy*, 171.

31. See, e.g., Mary Sigler, "The Story of Justice: Retribution, Mercy, and the Role of Emotions in the Capital Sentencing Process," *Law & Philosophy* 19 (2000), 339.

32. See Dan M. Kahan and Martha C. Nussbaum, "Two Conceptions of Emotion in Criminal Law," *Columbia Law Review* 96 (1996), 269, 366–372, urging a two-step process in which pleas for mercy are heard only after fault is established.

33. Murphy and Hampton, *Forgiveness and Mercy*, 171–172.

34. See O'Brien, *Saving Grace*, 57.

35. See Hestevold, "Disjunctive Desert," 360–362.

36. Murphy and Hampton, *Forgiveness and Mercy*, 159.

37. Duff, "Justice, Mercy and Forgiveness," 63.

38. See Louis Kaplow and Steven Shavell, "Fairness Versus Welfare," *Harvard Law Review* 114 (2001), 961.

39. See, e.g., Dan M. Kahan, "Social Meaning and the Economic Analysis of Crime," *Journal of Legal Studies* 27 (1998), 609.

40. See Paul H. Robinson and John M. Darley, "The Utility of Desert," *Northwestern University Law Review* 91 (1997), 453.

41. See Meir Dan-Cohen, "Decision Rules and Conduct Rules: On Acoustic Separation in Criminal Law," *Harvard Law Review* 97 (1984), 625, arguing that "acoustic separation" in the structure of the defenses of necessity and duress, which exempt some offenders from punishment, works to achieve both a higher degree of compliance with the law and greater leniency toward offenders than could otherwise be obtained.

42. John Braithwaite, "Restorative Justice: Assessing Optimistic and Pessimistic Accounts," *Crime & Justice* 25 (1999), 1, 5, quoting Tony Marshall.

43. See, e.g., Brien, "Mercy Within Legal Justice," 104, arguing that the virtue of mercy is the stance of those with discretionary powers to "be sensitive to the vulnerability of others and focused upon the individuality of cases"; Muller, "The Virtue of Mercy in Criminal Sentencing," 329, arguing that in the sentencing process, "mercy is a frame of mind induced by the imaginative effort to see both the impact of the possible sentences and the nature of the criminal conduct from the defendant's perspective"; Nussbaum, "Equity and Mercy," 103, suggesting that a merciful attitude "requires, and rests upon, a new attitude toward the self"—an attitude of "identification" with and "sympathetic understanding" of offenders; O'Driscoll, "The Quality of Mercy," 232, contending that "[t]he term 'mercy' encompasses an attitude and the modes of treatment which are natural or conventional ways of expressing it."

44. Brien, "Mercy Within Legal Justice," 106.

45. Stephen J. Morse, "Justice, Mercy, and Craziness," *Stanford Law Review* 36 (1984), 1485, 1495.

46. William Shakespeare, *The Merchant of Venice*, act 4, sc. 1.

47. "The Gift of the Magi" was published in O. Henry's 1906 collection of stories, *The Four Million*. See *The Complete Works of O. Henry*, vol. 1, supra note 2, x.

Should Mercy Have a Place in Clemency Decisions?

DANIEL T. KOBIL

I have always found that mercy bears richer fruits than strict justice.[1]
—Abraham Lincoln, discussing pardons granted to soldiers who had deserted

Mercy is completely dead.[2]
—Mark Stevens, capital defense attorney describing the Texas clemency process

The word *mercy*, as a matter of common usage, is often employed as a synonym for *clemency*. But at least in the official sphere, it seems today that the two terms are completely distinct and that mercy is the thinnest of reeds on which to base a request for executive clemency. As most clemency attorneys would attest, claims for executive clemency are best supported with arguments about justice and fairness ("this punishment is not deserved") rather than mercy ("this punishment, while deserved, should not be imposed"). Perhaps this should not surprise us. After all, the most eloquent and oft-quoted plea for mercy in the English language—that of Portia in *The Merchant of Venice*—fails utterly. Shylock rejects Portia's moving words seeking remission of the forfeiture of a pound of Antonio's flesh, responding that he "crave[s] the law, the penalty, and the forfeit of my bond."[3] Indeed, it is not a desire to grant mercy but the fear of harsh justice that ultimately persuades Shylock to relinquish the forfeiture: He realizes that he will be severely punished if he violates the letter of the bond by taking a drop of Antonio's blood along with the flesh.

Like Shylock, when those in a position to remit punishment actually do so, they almost always are persuaded, if we are to take them at their word, by arguments about justice rather than mercy. Illinois Governor George Ryan's sweeping 2003 grant of clemency to all prisoners on death row, as I have noted elsewhere,[4] was justified not by mercy but because the Illinois system of capital punishment was so unreliable that there was no way to determine whether any death sentences were justly deserved. The rhetoric he employed to explain his actions placed these commutations, in the words of Austin Sarat, "well within the anti-mercy conceptions of clemency" embraced by most modern political leaders.[5] Likewise, in the forty-eight cases where clemency was granted to individuals sentenced to death between 1976 and 2003, only four were based on what could arguably be characterized as merciful reasons.[6] Nor is mercy any more popular in noncapital cases where it is rarely cited as a reason for remitting punishment. Almost always when clemency is granted, the reason cited is to rectify some sort of disparity in the punishment that is justly deserved: The offender is innocent, or arguably innocent, or did not receive a fair trial, so we do not know what is deserved, or the offender received a disproportionately severe punishment relative to other participants in the crime.

The removal of mercy from clemency and the prevailing focus on justice-based rationales have also coincided with an overall decline in clemency in most jurisdictions. Federal grants of clemency have dropped steeply since the middle of the twentieth century, with commutations evaporating almost completely and pardons becoming infrequent, even for offenders who have long completed their sentences.[7] Though comprehensive figures are difficult to come by, it also appears that in most states the rate at which clemency is granted has fallen off. For example, in Florida between 1924 and 1966, there were 59 commutations and 196 executions in capital cases,[8] but between 1983 and 2000, the clemency requests of all 161 Florida prisoners on death row were denied.[9] Reports show a similar decline in capital clemency in states such as Texas and California, a decrease that at least in part has been associated with an unwillingness by governors to treat mercy as a permissible reason for acting.[10] In noncapital cases, there has likewise been a reluctance to use the clemency power to remit punishment. A survey of all commutations granted from 1995 to 2003 revealed that most states averaged fewer than one hundred commutations per state, with thirty-four states, including California, Texas, Ohio, and Pennsylvania, having dispensed twenty or fewer during the eight-year study period.[11]

Although it is impossible to establish whether the divergence of mercy and clemency is responsible for, or a symptom of, the overall decline in clemency, this separation of the two concepts is of relatively recent vintage, and many believe it represents the loss of something valuable. Elizabeth Rapaport and other commentators[12] have forcefully argued that the absence of mercy from the clemency process is based on a reductionist approach to criminal justice that exalts the goals of retribution and deterrence at the expense of important competing values such as rehabilitation and reconciliation. The dearth of mercy in the clemency process even prompted Supreme Court Justice Anthony Kennedy to call for more merciful clemency practices in a speech to the American Bar Association in 2003. In the speech, he remarked on the infrequency of clemency and observed that "the pardon process, of late, seems to have been drained of its moral force."[13]

However, as Justice Kennedy suggested in the remainder of his talk, "a people confident in its laws and institutions should not be ashamed of mercy."[14] It is by no means certain that we benefit as a society from the unstinting harshness of our punishments, nor is it inevitable that mercy should be an unpersuasive ground for remitting punishment. Despite the tendency of our political leaders to exclude mercy from clemency, few would deny that as a people, Americans consider mercy an important, indeed a noble, human virtue. The Bible frequently admonishes us to be merciful[15]; Thomas Aquinas counted mercy among the greatest of virtues.[16] Our most revered president, Abraham Lincoln, was noted for his forgiving nature and frequent merciful use of the clemency power. Mercy, insofar as it moves individuals to forgive transgressions committed against us, is widely acknowledged to quell resentment and contribute to a peaceful spirit.

In the legal context, pardons and commutations have long been described by our jurists as based on principles of mercy. It is a commonplace for courts to refer to executive clemency as a manifestation of the "sovereign's prerogative of mercy"[17] or to state that the inherent nature of clemency is "grace."[18] As Justice Kennedy wrote in *Dretke v. Haley*, clemency "holds out the promise that mercy is not foreign to our system."[19] The framers of the U.S. Constitution likewise were explicit in connecting clemency with mercy. Alexander Hamilton wrote that the unfettered power to dispense "the mercy of government" had been placed in the hands of the president for reasons of "humanity" so that justice did not appear too "sanguinary and cruel."[20] At the North Carolina convention to ratify the Constitution, James Iredell argued that the power to pardon is necessary because a man may violate "the letter of the law, yet peculiar circumstances in his case may entitle him to mercy."[21]

Of course, our understanding of clemency may have fundamentally changed in recent years. Perhaps we no longer see a need to preserve in any regularized fashion a value as difficult to pin down and defend as mercy. Maybe clemency, as a device lodged in the political sector, should be exercised only for reasons about which there is pervasive societal agreement, which today seems to mean ensuring that punishments are fair in a retributive sense. According to this approach, clemency should only be used in what I have described as a "justice-enhancing" manner,[22] to calibrate punishments more finely than the courts are capable of doing, for example, by ensuring that perpetrators of similar crimes receive similar punishments or that those who are less culpable receive lesser punishments. But mercy would be left entirely to philosophers and theologians or higher spheres. Some commentators are comfortable with this narrow conception of clemency and defend it as necessary to ensure that clemency is not used in an arbitrary manner.[23] After all, one person's "mercy" is another's "favoritism" or worse.

However, in light of the forceful arguments raised by proponents of mercy, its historic connection with clemency, and the significance of mercy as a societal value, any decision to discard it as a justification for pardons and commutations should be made in a considered manner. What, if anything, are we giving up when we allow our leaders to set aside mercy as a basis for their actions? In the remainder of this chapter, I consider whether a compelling case can be made to retain mercy in any "official" sense as a basis for clemency in our legal systems. To address this question, it is first necessary to explain in more detail what I mean by mercy-based clemency and how it differs from exercises of the power that are sometimes described as merciful.

Mercy-Based Exercise of the Clemency Power

There is substantial scholarship devoted to the meaning of "mercy,"[24] and a detailed exploration of the complex issues associated with this concept (and related terms such as forgiveness, reconciliation, and redemption) is beyond the scope of this chapter. For purposes of this discussion, I propose a definition of mercy denoting "an act of benevolence or compassion that reduces what is owed." Such a definition embraces the sort of mercy Portia seeks from Shylock and also most of the other actions that we typically describe as merciful (God reducing the punishment we deserve to have imposed on us for our sins; creditors acting mercifully by forgiving monetary debts; people reducing the amount of stigma that is exacted from others as the result of a social transgression, etc.). It also excludes the enhancement of justice as a rationale for action: Since mercy reduces what is "owed," it is not present in those instances where punishment is remitted because there is doubt about whether the sanction is deserved. Thus, I agree with Garvey that we should not include within our definition of mercy instances of what he calls "mercy as equity"—that is, the remission of punishment designed to "produce the result the rules should have produced in the first place" if the system had operated correctly.[25]

In addition, when mercy is used as a basis for clemency, the representative nature of the action has to be taken into account. Because clemency is something performed by public officials on behalf of those they represent, all acts of clemency, mercy-based or otherwise, in order to be legitimate should be the product of considered judgment and done for the good of society. Thus, when I speak of mercy-based clemency, I mean "an act of judgment by one in a position of authority that reduces what is owed to achieve for society the benefits of benevolence or compassion." By this definition, I seek to exclude from the discussion arbitrary or idiosyncratic acts by one who happens to possess the power to remit punishment. Justice O'Connor's oft-cited hypothetical example of a grant of clemency based on a coin toss would not constitute a mercy-based grant of clemency—though some might casually refer to it as a "merciful" act.[26] Such a remission of punishment would not be based on any sort of considered judgment, and it obviously does not manifest any qualities of benevolence or compassion toward the offender or society. Indeed, there is an element of cruelty inherent in its arbitrariness.[27]

Nor would I characterize the commutation of Darrell J. Mease, which Missouri Governor Mel Carnahan granted in 1999 because of a personal appeal by Pope John Paul II, as an act of mercy by the governor.[28] Mease had confessed to a brutal triple murder for which he had been tried and sentenced to death. Though Mease had become a born-again Christian in prison, he publicly expressed little remorse for the killings (beyond regret at having killed a paraplegic boy who had witnessed two of the murders), and his case had not attracted a great deal of public support. But in an embarrassing accident of timing for the state of Missouri, Mease was scheduled to be executed on January 27, 1999, the precise date of the pope's visit to St. Louis. When the scheduling faux pas came to light, Mease's execution date was abruptly postponed. The rearrangement of the execution did not escape the notice of Pope John Paul, and on the last day of his visit, he personally approached Governor Carnahan at a prayer service and asked if he would "please have mercy on Mr. Mease."[29] The governor, a Baptist and a staunch supporter of the death penalty, commuted Mease's sentence to life imprisonment without the possibility of parole.

Though Governor Carnahan and others described the grant of clemency as an act of mercy, this seems a misnomer. His decision had surprisingly little to do with Mease or the facts of his case: When considering the pope's request, he told his legal counsel he did not "want to know everything about the case" because in a capital case the facts were unlikely to be "good."[30] He explained that the commutation was the product of "one of those moments that one would never expect to happen in one's life" and had been granted "out of respect for the pope."[31] There was little pretense that Darrell Mease should be given special compassion or benevolence or that society would somehow be better because of this act. Indeed, Mease's own attorney seemed surprised by the commutation and conceded that Mease had "one of the weaker clemency cases."[32] Carnahan's action ultimately was more arbitrary and confusing than it was merciful, a point suggested by an editorial of the *St. Louis Post-Dispatch*:

> Paradoxically, the governor's generosity in this single instance underscores the case against the death penalty. Unlike the governor's commutations in other cases, this one was divorced from any details or legal issues connected to Mease's case. The clemency was granted, apparently, because the pope asked. . . . While merciful, it is also arbitrary and capricious.[33]

The newspaper, which was on record as opposing capital punishment, approved of the commutation but could not ignore its arbitrary nature.

Governor Carnahan's grant of clemency to Darrell Mease did not signal a change in his approach to imposition of the death penalty generally and indeed appeared to ensure that others who sought clemency thereafter would not be given serious consideration. After the Mease commutation in 1999, Governor Carnahan presided over nine executions in one year—the "most prolific stretch of executions" in Missouri history.[34] Among those executed was Roy Roberts, who had a compelling claim for clemency based on innocence. Many believe that Governor Carnahan ignored Roberts's claim because of the criticism he had encountered for commuting Mease.[35] In the end, Governor Carnahan's action in commuting Mease's death sentence resembled the coin flip envisioned by Justice O'Connor more than it did an act of compassion: The pope happened to be in town for the first time in history and asked a favor that the governor felt he could not refuse. Although the pope's request could certainly be described as based on mercy, the decision of Governor Carnahan to honor the request would not satisfy the definition of mercy that I am advocating in this chapter.

Finally, I wish to exclude from the discussion of mercy-based exercises of the clemency power remissions of punishment that are granted to benefit the state. For example, when the governor of South Dakota recently issued commutations to a large number of prisoners in exchange for their performing work for the government, this was not an example of mercy, at least in the sense that I am urging. The primary purpose of the commutations was obviously to benefit sparsely populated South Dakota, not to act out of compassion or benevolence. In the view of many, the state, which lacked ready workers to perform onerous or hazardous tasks, took advantage of the prisoners' desire for freedom, their inability to obtain it in other ways, and their fear of additional punishment if they refused to perform community service work.[36] In the same category would fall recent commutations in Kentucky and Oklahoma that were granted to nonviolent offenders to create savings for the public fisc because the state could not afford to imprison them.[37] These commutations fit comfortably in a long line of utilitarian pardoning practices such as those of the British crown, which historically used conditional pardons to provide cheap labor for the American colonies and to supply recruits for the royal navy.[38] Certainly, such grants of clemency may be useful or desirable as a matter of public policy. There is even historical precedent for using the term *mercy* to describe remissions of punishment that benefit the state, as when a pardon was issued in exchange for the defendant paying a fine to the crown.[39] However, in this chapter, I seek to exclude such acts that overtly advantage the state or the decision maker and focus on a narrower conception of mercy that emphasizes compassion and benevolence and the benefits that might derive from such acts.

What, then, would mercy-based clemency look like? The most widely discussed case for mercy in recent years provides a good example: Karla Faye Tucker's unsuccessful request for a commutation in Texas in 1998. The troubled life of Ms. Tucker, marked by drug addiction, prostitution, and violence, culminated in her being sentenced to death for two grisly murders she and an accomplice committed in 1983 with a pickax. Several months after she entered prison and gave up drugs, Tucker experienced a religious conversion to Christianity, the sincerity of which does not seem to have been doubted by those who met her.[40] Following her conversion, she evidently became an entirely different person who expressed great remorse for her crime, sought to make amends to the families of her victims, and married a prison ministry worker. Her spiritual transformation and repentant demeanor prompted persons all over the world, including representatives of the United Nations, Pope John Paul II, and death penalty proponents such as television evangelist Pat Robertson and William F. Buckley, to support her request for clemency.[41] Plainly, remission of Tucker's punishment could be defended only on merciful grounds because there was no doubt that she was guilty of a heinous crime and there were no compelling arguments that she did not otherwise deserve her sentence. Thus, it was her rehabilitation and apparent spiritual transmutation that caused many to support her plea for mercy. The comments of Pat Robertson echoed those of many Tucker supporters:

> [M]y feeling was—and I think the feeling of thousands of others in America was—that the woman who had been convicted thirteen years before was not there any longer. This was a different person and to execute her was an act of barbarity that was totally unnecessary.[42]

In Robertson's view, Tucker's profound personal transformation made her a worthy object of compassion. Though some contended Tucker deserved to be executed in light of the heinous nature of her crimes, the overwhelming tenor of the public debate favored mercy for Tucker. Ultimately, however, Governor Bush relied on a justice-based conception of clemency and denied Tucker's request for a temporary reprieve because "the role of the state is to enforce our laws and to make sure all individuals are treated fairly before the laws."[43]

Although I contend that Governor Bush missed an opportunity to exercise the clemency power mercifully, there were some complicating factors in Karla Faye Tucker's case that highlight the difficulties that attend acting on such grounds. For one thing, Ms. Tucker, like Governor Bush and many of those urging him to act mercifully, was a white, evangelical Christian. Because Governor Bush and the Texas Board of Pardons had summarily denied every other prior request for clemency in a capital case, a deviation from his longstanding policy in Tucker's case might have suggested political favoritism or paternalism rather than mercy. Moreover, as some of the opponents of clemency pointed out, one of the reasons that Tucker evoked such widespread support for leniency was that she was an attractive young woman with a winning smile.[44] Texans, like Americans generally, have historically been reluctant to execute women: Prior to Tucker, the last execution of a female in Texas occurred in 1863.[45] Far from promoting the benefits of compassion or benevolence for society, a commutation for Tucker may have merely reinforced a sense that the legal system is unfair or fraught with gender bias, illustrating why grants of mercy can be so problematical.

A lesser known example of clemency being sought on grounds of mercy was the 1990 commutation granted to William Neal Moore by the Georgia Board of Pardons and Paroles. Moore received a death sentence for murdering an elderly man during a robbery in 1974. He confessed to the murder and pleaded guilty without a jury trial.[46] Immediately after his arrest, Moore expressed remorse for the killing to the family of the victim. While on death row, he underwent a religious conversion

and reached out to others through his prison ministry, becoming a "prime example of the redemptive possibility of condemned prisoners."[47] As Moore's execution approached, his petition for commutation drew support from a broad array
of persons including the Reverend Jesse Jackson, Mother Teresa, a Georgia state
representative, and even members of the victim's family—a fact that especially
impressed the Georgia Board of Pardons and Paroles. A day before he was scheduled to die, the board commuted his sentence to life imprisonment. There was
no doubt that Moore was guilty of the crime for which he was sentenced to death
and that the only basis for commutation was compassion for the man that he had
become.[48] The merciful nature of the board's decision was widely acknowledged
by the press. As the *Atlanta Journal-Constitution* put it:

> The state Board of Pardon and Paroles did a wonderful thing Tuesday by commut-
> ing the death sentence of murderer William Moore. The unanimous vote for clemency
> saved the people of Georgia from killing a good man, and for that we should be grate-
> ful. . . . Moore has demonstrated that his crime represented a momentary, if very serious,
> mistake by a man of otherwise strong and redeeming character. He embraced Christian-
> ity, as do many inmates seeking to impress the authorities, but Moore, by his attitude
> and behavior, convinced even jailhouse cynics that his repentance and faith were real.[49]

Moreover, Moore's commutation was not fraught with problems of possible
favoritism that plagued Karla Faye Tucker's appeal for clemency. As a black male
in a state where black offenders have received a disproportionately high number
of death sentences,[50] there was little chance that Moore's commutation would be
perceived as the product of influence peddling by a member of a politically connected group. Also, since Moore is a man, there was no argument that he was
granted mercy because of his gender. Finally, members of the Georgia Board of
Pardons and Paroles are jointly appointed by the Senate and governor,[51] largely
insulating them from direct political influence and charges that their decision was
designed to curry favor with voters. Based as it evidently was on compassion for a
transformed person, Billy Moore's commutation presents a compelling instance of
mercy-based clemency uncluttered by allegations of bias or paternalism.

Although both the Moore and Tucker cases for mercy-based clemency are
predicated on compassion for offenders who effectively became different persons
through rehabilitation, there could also be other objects of mercy. A governor
might grant merciful clemency to an unrehabilitated offender because meting
out the deserved punishment would indirectly impose great hardship on others.

Consider a father convicted of theft and sentenced to prison for a lengthy period. If he were the sole provider for several minor children and his imprisonment would force his children to become wards of the state, a commutation might be warranted on merciful grounds. In such a case, the object of the mercy would be the children rather than the offender, but the purpose of the clemency would be to obtain the benefits of compassion on behalf of society.[52]

Possible Approaches to Mercy-Based Clemency

What, then, is the best case that can be made in favor of merciful commutations? If an offender commits a crime that we agree deserves a particular punishment, some would contend that mercy never constitutes a proper ground for refusing to impose the appropriate sanction. According to this view, justice demands that every criminal should receive no less and no more punishment than he or she deserves. Unless every similarly situated offender also receives mercy (in which case, it is not really mercy but a tacit overturning of the sentencing laws via the clemency power), no principled basis exists for distinguishing Billy Moore from other death row inmates who also were "good" people in prison, such as Karla Faye Tucker. To grant clemency to some based on mercy, while letting others be executed, would erode the principle of equal punishment and undermine confidence in our legal system. Indeed, the incompatibility of mercy with equality prompted Kant to observe that a pardon given to one who has committed a crime "constitutes the greatest injustice" toward society.[53] In another well-known passage, Jeffrie Murphy has argued that there is no room for mercy in our legal systems and that public officials should keep what amounts to sentimentality "to themselves for use in their private lives with their families and pets."[54] Another legal commentator contends that any mercy-based deviation from imposing full punishment, whether undertaken by police, prosecutors, juries, judges, or executives, "is a source of especial shame" for our nation because of its unfairness.[55]

There is substantial force to this argument from equity, particularly given the high premium we place on fairness in our legal system. Indeed, it is not difficult to imagine that the remission of punishment based on mercy could give rise to constitutional challenges under equal protection or due process principles.[56] And by retaining the flexibility needed to dispense mercy, we undoubtedly leave clemency open to abuse by decision makers. For example, in South Carolina, Governor

Coleman Blease had this to say about the pardon of a murderer named William H. Mills, whom Blease pardoned in 1912 to fulfill a promise made to a rowdy crowd on the campaign trail: "I took the position that I was the servant of the people[,] . . . and when a community where a crime had been committed, with the best people, the white people, signing the petition, said that the criminal had been punished enough, I turned him out without regard to criticism."[57] Invidious discrimination in the use of clemency was also evident in Kentucky during the state constitutional convention of 1890, where a Mr. Ramsey observed that the governor had granted 845 pardons during a period of less than sixteen months. In 390 of those cases, pardons were granted to "persons convicted of kukluxing in Laurence County upon the request of the judge of that district."[58]

Thus, if we urge our leaders to ignore the dictates of equal punishment and utilize their broad discretion to grant merciful clemency, we must articulate good reasons for such action. There are two types of justifications commonly advanced in favor of mercy-based clemency, neither of which seems to me entirely persuasive. The first might be termed the "expediency rationale": It generally focuses on the dispenser of mercy and contends that granting mercy will benefit the decision maker in some discernible way. The second group of arguments rejects, at one level or another, the retributive underpinnings of prevailing definitions of justice and suggests that justice should achieve other goals beyond strictly exacting what is owed from offenders. I refer to this as the "false dichotomy" rationale because it asserts that justice, understood broadly enough to embrace goals such as redemption, really is not at odds with mercy and in fact needs mercy to achieve its goals.

The expediency rationale was one of the earliest arguments made in favor of mercy-based clemency. Seneca famously advanced this argument to the Roman Emperor Nero in his essay "On Clemency":

> [G]entleness enhances the security of kings, because while frequent punishment does crush the hatred of a few, it provokes the hatred of all. . . . Clemency therefore assures not only higher honor but higher safety; it is at once sovereignty's ornament and surest preservation.[59]

Portia echoes this rationale (admittedly, in rather vague terms) to Shylock when she asserts that mercy "blesses him that giveth."[60] Blackstone similarly contends that acts of merciful pardoning benefit the king:

> To him therefore the people look up as the fountain of nothing but bounty and grace; and these repeated acts of goodness, coming immediately from his own hand, endear the

sovereign to his subjects, and contribute more than any thing to root in their hearts that filial affection, and personal loyalty, which are the sure establishment of a prince.

Lord Coke agrees that clemency strengthens the king's throne.[61]

Although the expediency argument may have been persuasive when a monarch wielded the clemency power, it rings hollow in the context of a representative democracy where we expect our leaders to exercise delegated power on behalf of their constituents, not to consolidate their political power or vindicate their personal beliefs. Even Alexander Hamilton, notoriously one of the framers most tolerant of monarchy, did not seek to justify vesting the clemency power in the president because it would benefit the executive per se.[62] Rather, according to Hamilton, "humanity and *good public policy*" dictate that the power to dispense mercy of the government be vested in the president.[63] Today, we would no more tolerate our leaders wielding the clemency power to improve their personal or political standing than we would accept the common monarchical practice of selling pardons for the financial benefit of the executive.[64] Much of the outrage that followed President Clinton's eleventh-hour grants of clemency in 2001, particularly his pardon of financier Marc Rich, arose from the perception that he was using the clemency power in a politically expedient fashion to benefit his cronies.[65] The last governor who openly admitted using the clemency power to gratify his personal sense of morality, Tony Anaya of New Mexico, was roundly criticized when he commuted everyone on death row because "my personal beliefs do not allow me to permit the execution of an individual in the name of the state."[66] Moreover, even if Americans tolerated the openly expedient exercise of governmental power by our leaders, it is doubtful that self-interest would prompt merciful grants of clemency. Given the "tough on crime" sentiment that continues to dominate public debate,[67] the expediency rationale would most likely push our leaders to reject mercy rather than to dispense it in the hope that their compassion would "endear" them to their constituents.

The "false dichotomy" argument, by contrast, has much to commend it as a justification for mercy-based clemency. Proponents of this view seek to broaden our understanding of criminal justice to include redemptive or restorative goals in addition to the prevailing retributive goal of rendering punishment that is due. For example, Elizabeth Rapaport argues that clemency should be granted for merciful reasons based on the offender's positive transformation. She contends that hope and rehabilitation are proper goals of justice, and thus, mercy-based clemency actually furthers the ends of justice.[68] On this view, the tension between mercy and justice disappears because justice includes goals that are conducive to mercy. Rapaport asserts that the redemptive perspective draws on "the common store-house of Judeo-Christian norms and expectations" and that merciful clemency can best be defended by recalling that it is "an extraordinary measure, a failsafe to redress system failure and extraordinary cases."[69]

Stephen Garvey advances a narrower argument but, like Rapaport, attempts to make a place for mercy-based clemency by modifying our understanding of justice. He contends that instead of presuming that the primary purpose of our justice system is retribution, we should think about it as a process designed to achieve atonement between victim and criminal in which punishment plays an integral role.[70] Atonement allows violators of the law to make amends for their transgression, ideally achieving reconciliation with the victims of their crime and also with the larger community.[71] Under Garvey's theory, mercy could be defended morally in every case where the punishment is death (and for different reasons in some nondeath cases) because otherwise the possibility of atonement and reconciliation expires with the death of the offender.

I am sympathetic to the false dichotomy rationale, for I believe that the prevailing retributive account of justice is incomplete. It ignores other, more humane goals of punishment to which I believe many of us aspire and mistakenly treats the offender as one who is completely outside our society rather than still a part of it. As long as the entire focus of our justice system is on ensuring that criminals pay the entirety of their debt to society, we will perpetually be in the business, like Shylock, of collecting more and more, regardless of the toll in human and economic resources.[72]

Nevertheless, if we are to attempt to make an argument for mercy-based clemency, these reasons must be persuasive in the society that we have, not the society we wish we had. As Garvey himself admits, a theory of atonement-based remission of punishment is "of course, an ideal theory" because atonement seldom happens in the real world.[73] Rapaport likewise concedes that the redemptive perspective, with its emphasis on community, may in many ways "so little resemble . . . a vast heterogeneous country like the contemporary United States, as to appear irrelevant" (though she also argues that the benefits that would attend a shift to the redemptive perspective make it a plausible criminal justice goal).[74] Unfortunately, when it comes to our current approach to justice, it appears that we solidly subscribe to the retributive creed, with goals such as rehabilitation, redemption, or atonement playing secondary roles at best. Although the debate that these and other scholars have initiated about the proper approach to justice is certainly an important one to have as a society, it is not one that is likely to be resolved in favor of mercy in the immediate future. Certainly, a day will come when our faith in the benefits of unmitigated retributive punishment will waver, but I find myself persuaded by the concluding observations of James Whitman in his influential book, *Harsh Justice*:

> [American] traditions of authority—really our traditions of opposition to au-
> thority—have given us a criminal justice system long on degradation and short on
> mercy. This may be the way we want it. If it is not, there is certainly nothing to stop us
> from trying to overcome the traditions that have brought us to this point—though it is
> hard to be confident that we can really transcend them. . . . For the moment, in any case,
> real change does not loom; and real change would mean change, not just in punishment
> practices but in much grander American cultural traditions. It would be foolish to think
> that such change is coming soon.[75]

Although there have been a few exceptions, when it comes to clemency practices, most leaders seem to view themselves as implementers rather than arbiters of societal values.[76] Until we decide as a society that retributive notions of justice are too limited, it seems unlikely (outside a handful of isolated cases) that we will be able to persuade public officials to expand their conception of justice to include mercy.

The Benefits of Mercy-Based Clemency

In light of the pervasiveness of retributive justifications for punishment and the force of equity-based objections to mercy, it is quite frankly much easier to come up with reasons not to use mercy than to marshal compelling arguments in its favor. Yet if we are to make a case for mercy to those who are skeptical of its value, as our public officials certainly are,[77] we must identify distinct, practical benefits that justify making exceptions to our usual practice of inexorably meting out retributive justice. These benefits should accrue not to the representatives who grant clemency on our behalf but to society, which vests in leaders the broad discretion that allows for merciful acts.

Mercy-based clemency, like other political acts, can potentially bring both instrumental and expressive benefits. Murray Edelman describes instrumental aspects of political actions as those that get society certain tangible benefits from government, whereas expressive effects pertain to what the act means to the public and whether they are placated or aroused by it.[78] In terms of making a case for mercy, society does not obtain obvious instrumental benefits from specific merciful acts. Certainly, a commutation or pardon results in instrumental effects that benefit the offender, his or her family, and friends. These effects no doubt are of great importance to those directly involved and, in the aggregate, may arguably be of significance to society in general. However, most of these benefits (release from incarceration; removal of collateral consequences of conviction; freeing up of economic resources otherwise used to punish) would attend any remission of punishment and are not specific to clemency granted for merciful reasons.

To justify mercy on instrumental grounds, it would be helpful to identify distinctive benefits that flow from the merciful aspect of punishment remission. Although this may seem a quixotic task, at least two possible benefits come to mind that deserve discussion. First, there is intriguing research being done suggesting that forgiveness and reconciliation offer distinctive emotional and physical health benefits for individuals. Recent medical and psychological studies indicate that people who are unwilling to exercise mercy and forgive have higher levels of stress-produced hormones and report greater anger, sadness, and stress.[79] Those who practiced forgiveness had lower blood pressure and heart rates and also felt calmer. Obviously, it cannot be said with certainty that what is good for individuals would translate into a societal benefit if done by political leaders on our behalf. However, in light of the fact that we regularly enact laws for symbolic reasons, it is plausible to suppose that the observation of representative acts of mercy would prove influential to others in the community, thereby contributing to the broader societal good.[80] To return to the example of Karla Faye Tucker, if Governor Bush had stepped in and granted a mercy-based reprieve of her execution, would that not have been a dramatic exemplar of forgiveness for many who admired him and his policies? Perhaps such a striking act of mercy would have legitimated the act of forgiving by those who were otherwise disposed to debilitating emotions of hatred and vengefulness, like the protesters at Tucker's execution who chanted songs to celebrate her death and mocked her execution with signs such as "Axe and ye shall receive."[81] Though admittedly difficult to quantify, the fostering of forgiving attitudes in society through example could be a significant positive effect of acts of merciful clemency.[82]

Another potential instrumental benefit of mercy is that it could lead to lower recidivism rates by recipients of mercy-based clemency. Although I am aware of no recidivism studies specifically directed at mercy, the annual report of Canada's

National Parole Board suggests that those who receive postpunishment pardons have a very low risk of reoffense. The board compiled statistics on 306,985 pardons issued in Canada before 2004. These numbers indicate that only about 3% of all persons receiving pardons have them revoked as a consequence of their committing a subsequent criminal offense.[83] This demonstrates, according to the board, "that most people remain crime free after receipt of a pardon." By contrast, the total recidivism rate for Canadian offenders who were granted full parole or subject to statutory release has ranged between 7.9% and 13.8% over the past three years for which statistics are available.[84] This is not an entirely satisfactory comparison because unlike the parolees, those who received pardons had already proved themselves successful in society by being crime-free for a period of at least five years. Also, making similar recidivism comparisons using pardon statistics in the United States would be difficult, at least at the federal level, because the number of presidential pardons issued is infinitesimal. For example, in the three-year period from 1998 to 2000, the Canadian National Parole Board granted and issued 25,532 federal pardons, while President Clinton granted only 125, less than 0.5% of the Canadian total.[85] Still, the Canadian experience suggests that further study of a potential correlation between mercy and diminished rates of reoffense is warranted.

Ultimately, though, given the difficulty of establishing obvious, measurable benefits of merciful acts, the case for mercy must rest primarily on its expressive aspects. Shakespeare dramatizes the expressive quality of clemency in *The Merchant of Venice* in a scene that is overshadowed by Portia's famous plea. As Shylock faces death for having contrived to murder Antonio, the Duke grants him merciful clemency and does so to communicate an important message about the Venetian community: *"that thou shalt see the difference of our spirit,* I pardon thee thy life before thou ask it."[86] The Duke's action illustrates the superiority of generous Venetian society over Shylock's inhumane, "justice-at-any cost" world.

Moving from literature to politics, former Ohio Governor Richard Celeste, who granted eight death penalty commutations in 1991 and pioneered the systematic use of clemency for battered women who had committed crimes because of their abuse, has also attempted to identify the expressive benefits of merciful clemency:

> Writing after my clemency decisions on behalf of the battered women, Judge Lawrence Grey pointed out that "clemency is granted more for the benefit of society than it is for the prisoner." In the words of *Sterling v. Drake* more than 125 years ago, the clemency power "is entrusted to the governor for merciful and beneficent purposes." In the end,

I believed that we must live in a society that reflects our best instincts, a society that nurtures our higher nature. I believed then and I believe now, that to show mercy is a sign of our strength as a community, not a sign of our weakness. It is also, in a way, a reminder of our shared pain. For whatever punishment we impose, we can never replace the victims.[87]

Governor Celeste's comments confirm that the principal benefits of merciful acts of clemency arise from their communicative effect, raising questions about what, exactly, acts of mercy might signify. In a similar vein, Austin Sarat argues that acts of mercy-based clemency, while fraught with difficulties, serve as an invitation for us "to join an ongoing conversation about memory and aspiration, a conversation about sovereign prerogative and associated risks."[88]

As these examples suggest, merciful acts of clemency can express something important about our society. I would like to conclude this chapter by outlining several of the messages that merciful clemency conveys that warrant its use today. First, granting mercy to one deserving of punishment, particularly the ultimate punishment of death, makes an eloquent statement that our society is a strong and confident one. Second, acts of merciful clemency say to the world that while we are strong, we are also a community that is humble rather than arrogant; reflective rather than dogmatic. Finally, by treating with compassion even those who have transgressed our fundamental laws, we express a profound commitment to one another, demonstrating that we are a cohesive group who share a system of justice mediated by mercy.

With regard to how mercy demonstrates our strength, some argue that the imposition of harsh punishment provides a tangible demonstration of the power of the government. "Don't do the crime if you can't do the time," the macho boast of the television detective, captures some of this sentiment.[89] One commentator makes the point graphically with regard to capital punishment: "Executed bodies perform their political mission well when their utter impotence, their absolute lack of vitality, testifies to the robust agency of the state."[90] But if punishing demonstrates strength, how much stronger does our society appear if we couple with our demonstrated power to imprison or kill wrongdoers the confidence to treat them occasionally with mercy? George Rainbolt puts it this way:

> One who is in a position to show mercy is in a position of power—the power to treat another harshly. Having power and not using it can reflect a confidence in one's abilities. If another has unjustifiably harmed you and you therefore have a right to treat that person harshly, and if you do not do so, your action sends the message that this harm was not that important, that it was a punch you can take. In this way, mercy reveals a strength.[91]

This is the expressive message of clemency that Governor Celeste argues for when he says that mercy reveals our "strength as a community." It also seems to capture Justice Kennedy's meaning when he told the ABA that a people "confident" in their laws and institutions need not be afraid of mercy. By showing mercy, we demonstrate society's magnanimity, literally its "greatness of soul."

But mercy does not just reveal strength; it also shows humility. Merciful clemency expresses that we acknowledge our own imperfection and the fallibility of our laws. This is the humbling message of Hamlet to Polonius when he reminds him that if we "[u]se every man after his desert, . . . who should 'scape whipping?"[92] In one respect or another, we are all guilty and all in need of mercy. Shylock, in his arrogance, cannot grasp this message of humility. Thus, he can hardly expect the mercy that is extended to him when the tables are turned and his former supplicants have power over him. Alexander Hamilton in *The Federalist* (No. 74) recognizes the fallibility of all systems of criminal law because they "partake[] of such necessary severity," making ready access to merciful exceptions necessary.[93] Such honesty about both our laws and the human condition keeps us tethered to reality and helps ensure that we do not delude ourselves into thinking that our institutions are never wrong or unfair. By keeping us from responding inexorably to every injustice, merciful clemency also helps temper our retributive spirit and prevents us from becoming the very sort of "raging ungentle people" against whom we react when we punish.[94]

Finally, extending mercy to those who have violated our laws says that no one ever completely forfeits their humanity—that we are all, to one extent or another, still members of the same society and can at least make a request for mercy that will be considered. As Rapaport puts it, when our political leaders argue for the inexorable application of retributive justice, they typically offer a vision of a bifurcated community, divided by a great moral chasm into depraved, hopeless transgressors and law-abiding, worthwhile citizens.[95] The option of mercy as a potential response to an offender's actions reinforces instead the cohesion of our community and leaves open the possibility that considerations other than justice "ground the relationships between individuals."[96]

This could well be a message of great significance in a society increasingly riven by racial, ethnic, religious, and political differences. Recent studies of the role of forgiveness in resolving international conflicts find that the atmosphere of conflict existing in fragmented societies often "eliminate[s] the vocabulary of civil relations—the ability to say 'we' pretty much vanishes."[97] Examining the process of rebuilding societies in various countries shattered by powerful conflicts, these researchers assert that merciful responses to violations of the law are crucial in repairing these communities.[98] To shrink these observations down to an individual level, mercy's positive effect on community can be seen in the life of Billy Moore, who was eventually released in 1991 following his commutation from death row by the Georgia Board of Pardons and Paroles. Since that time, Moore has apparently led a productive life, becoming a minister and also a friend of the family of the man he murdered many years ago.[99] But for the board's willingness to use mercy as a ground for clemency, these bonds of community would have been severed with Moore's execution and never reconstituted.

Of course, the difficulty with predicating a case for merciful clemency on these expressive benefits is that there is nothing inevitable about the meaning we take from such acts. People can and will disagree with the assertions that mercy demonstrates strength tempered by humility and that it fosters social cohesion. Acts of clemency are often criticized as showing weakness ("clemency shows we lack the moral strength to punish wrongdoing") or as a manifestation of arrogance rather than humility ("the governor is high-handedly second-guessing the decision of the judge and jury"). And social cohesion is not the message that everyone will take away from acts of mercy: Some will inevitably seek to maintain the "us-them" division and contend that public officials are making the world unsafe for the law-abiding by siding with the criminals.

We should not conclude, however, that we must despair of making the case for mercy or abandon our efforts to advocate its use. Rather, we can continue to seek to demonstrate its benefits to society. Advocates of mercy should also forcefully and openly defend the benign account of mercy as more accurately reflecting human experience and our aspirations as a society. Unfortunately, that is not how acts of clemency have always been discussed by our leaders. Often, like President Clinton's eleventh-hour pardons and commutations issued on his last days in office in 2001, acts of clemency occur at the last minute with inadequate justification. Governor Celeste candidly confessed to similar shortcomings when he granted numerous pardons and death penalty commutations in Ohio at the end of his final term in office:

> Unlike my decision on the battered women, these death penalty commutations stirred up a firestorm of protest. Part of this had to do with the widespread support for the death penalty. But part of it had to do with the nature and timing of my decision. In

this instance, I did not have a well-developed process nor did I have a strong constituency for the issue. Rather, coming in the final hours of my second term and without the engagement of the Corrections Department or the Adult Parole Authority, this action seemed hasty and ill considered.[100]

Executives often seem embarrassed by mercy and, if they use it at all, do so clumsily without mounting any real defense of their actions. This allows critics to claim the rhetorical field, characterizing merciful acts as weakness, arrogance, or worse.

Officials who use clemency in a merciful way should clearly explain the reasons for their actions and unapologetically defend the value of mercy to the community. This would require executives to abandon the common practice of waiting until the end of their term in office to consider most clemency requests and instead to grant clemency with regularity, as part of a considered, deliberative process.[101] This would also allow an opportunity, as Governor Celeste suggests, for building a strong constituency for acts of mercy. Although the possibility of marshaling political support for mercy might seem somewhat farfetched given the predominance of retributive values in today's society, in particular cases, executives could elicit support for mercy among religious and other moral leaders, just as many supported mercy for Karla Faye Tucker.[102]

In the end, the case for mercy is a difficult one to make but not impossible. As examples of the unyielding harshness of our justice system come to light, there seems to be some softening in the cries for justice at any cost. Moreover, despite the dearth of mercy in our public institutions, we continue to espouse mercy as an important American value in literature, in religion, and in our descriptions of ourselves as a people, suggesting that we are not so committed to unmitigated justice as our leaders seem to believe.

I would like to conclude this chapter by quoting a passage from Marilynne Robinson's beautiful novel, *Gilead*, that illustrates why mercy is indeed a value that is worth fostering, despite its indeterminacy. John Ames, the narrator, is a minister looking back on his life as death nears. In reviewing one of his old sermons connecting the parable of the Prodigal Son with the Old Testament practice of forgiving slavery and all debts in certain years, Ames describes the transforming nature of forgiveness that lies at the core of mercy:

> I believe [the sermon] concludes quite effectively. It says Jesus puts His hearer in the role of the father, of the one who forgives. Because if we are, so to speak, the debtor (and of course we are that, too), that suggests no graciousness in us. And grace is the great gift.

So to be forgiven is only half the gift. The other half is that *we* also can forgive, restore, and liberate, and therefore we can feel the will of God enacted through us, which is the great restoration of ourselves to ourselves.[103]

Viewed in this light, it plainly would be a shame if we conclude that our commitment to justice demands that we abandon mercy and with it the chance to forgive and be forgiven.

Notes

1. Francis Browne, *The Everyday Life of Abraham Lincoln* (New York and St. Louis: N. D. Thompson Publishing, 1886), 627.

2. Mike Tolson, "State Shows Condemned Little Mercy; Panel Is Reluctant to Stop Executions," *Houston Chronicle* (May 20, 2001), A1.

3. William Shakespeare, *The Merchant of Venice*, act 4, sc. 1.

4. Daniel Kobil, "How to Grant Clemency in Unforgiving Times," *Capital University Law Review* 31 (2003), 227–228.

5. Austin Sarat, *Mercy on Trial* (Princeton, NJ, and Oxford: Princeton University Press, 2005), 139.

6. These "mercy-based" grants of clemency were made to David Cameron Keith (Montana, 1988), who reportedly received a commutation because of Keith's partial paralysis and blindness, remorse, religious conversion, and the possibility that he may have shot the victim as a reflex action; William Moore (Georgia, 1990), whose death sentence was commuted by the Board of Pardons and Paroles because of his exemplary prison record, remorse, religious conversion, and the pleas for clemency from the victim's family; William Saunders (Virginia, 1997), whose sentence was commuted because of his rehabilitation and because the prosecutor and judge from the trial recommended clemency; and Darrell Mease (Missouri, 1999), whose sentence was commuted by Governor Carnahan at the personal request for mercy of Pope John Paul II during a visit to Missouri. Death Penalty Information Center Web site at http://www.deathpenaltyinfo.org/article.php?did=126&scid=13.

7. Daniel Kobil, "The Quality of Mercy Strained: Wresting the Pardoning Power from the King," *Texas Law Review* 69 (1991), 601–604; and Appendix of presidential clemency statistics, The Jurist Web site, "Presidential Pardons: Clemency Statistics" at http://jurist.law.pitt.edu/pardons5a.htm.

8. Margaret Vandiver, "The Quality of Mercy: Race and Clemency in Florida Death Penalty Cases, 1924–1966," *University of Richmond Law Review* 27 (1993), 315, 322.

9. Randolph Pendleton, "Clemency Rarely Given in Florida," *Florida Times-Union* (Jun. 24, 2000), A1.

10. Tolson, "State Shows Condemned Little Mercy," A1; Bob Egelko, "California Governor Sets High Bar for Clemency," *San Francisco Chronicle* (Jan. 21, 2005), B3.

11. Stu Whitney, "Prison-Time Cuts Lead U.S.," *Sioux Falls-Argus Leader* (Jun. 29, 2003). According to Whitney's study, only six states (South Dakota, Oklahoma, Kentucky, Arkansas, Illinois, and Arizona) granted more than one hundred commutations during the eight-year period, with the most states issuing fewer than ten.

12. Elizabeth Rapaport, "Retribution and Redemption in the Operation of Executive Clemency," *Chicago-Kent Law Review* 74 (2000), 1501–1535; Austin Sarat, "Governor Perry, Governor Ryan, and the Disappearance of Executive Clemency in Capital Cases: What Has Happened to Mercy in America?" Findlaw's Legal Commentary, at http://writ.news .findlaw.com/commentary/20041229_sarat.html (Dec. 29, 2004).

13. Anthony M. Kennedy, "Speech at the American Bar Association Annual Meeting" (Aug. 9, 2003), http://www.supremecourtus.gov/publicinfo/speeches/sp_08-09-03.html.

14. Ibid.

15. E.g., Luke 6: 36 ("Be ye therefore merciful, as your Father also is merciful."); Psalms 123: 4 ("Have mercy on us for we have had more than enough of contempt"); Psalms 103: 8–10 ("The Lord is merciful and gracious, slow to anger, and plenteous in mercy. He will not always chide; nor will he keep his anger forever. He hath not dealt with us after our sins, nor rewarded us according to our iniquities."). Perhaps the most famous call for human mercy is in the Sermon on the Mount, which uses divine mercy as the exemplar: "Blessed are the merciful: for they shall obtain mercy." Matthew 5: 7 (King James).

16. Thomas Aquinas, *Summa Theologica*, "Whether Mercy Is the Greatest of Virtues."

17. *Commissioner v. Sutley*, 378 A.2d 780, 789 (Pa. 1977).

18. *United States v. Wilson*, 32 U.S. 150, 160 (1833); *Bacon v. Lee*, 549 S.E.2d 840, 852 (N.C. 2001).

19. *Dretke v. Haley*, 541 U.S. 386, 399 (2004).

20. Alexander A. Hamilton, *The Federalist* (No. 74) (New York: Mentor Publishing, 1961), 447–448.

21. James Iredell, "North Carolina Ratifying Convention, July 28, 1788," in *The Founders Constitution*, vol. 4, eds. Philip B. Kurland and Ralph Lerner (Chicago: University of Chicago Press, 1987), 17.

22. Kobil, "Quality of Mercy." In this article, which represented my first academic foray into the subject of clemency, I noted the ongoing atrophy of the clemency power and argued that justice-enhancing reasons for granting clemency, broadly defined, were entirely consistent with prevailing retributive theories of justice and should be utilized more frequently. Mercy, it seemed to me, was sufficiently controversial and so little employed in practice that it offered an unlikely foundation on which to ground the revival of the clemency power that I advocated. Thus, I was essentially agnostic as to whether any "justice-neutral" grounds for granting clemency, including mercy, were defensible, leaving this question for future discussions such as this one.

23. Kathleen Dean Moore, *Pardons: Justice, Mercy, and the Public Interest* (Oxford: Oxford University Press, 1989); Dan Markel, "Against Mercy," *Minnesota Law Review*, 88 (2004), 1421. Indeed, Markel has gone so far as to assert that mercy is a source of shame for our nation. "Against Mercy," 1481.

24. E.g., Moore, *Pardons*; Jeffrey Murphy and Jean Hampton, *Forgiveness and Mercy* (Cambridge: Cambridge University Press, 1988); Alwynne Smart, "Mercy," *Philosophy* 43 (1968), 345; Peter Digeser, *Political Forgiveness* (Ithaca, NY: Cornell University Press, 2001).

25. Stephen P. Garvey, "Is It Wrong to Commute Death Row? Retribution, Atonement, and Mercy," *North Carolina Law Review* 82 (2004), 1328–1329: "Retribution's first theory of mercy is therefore a theory of justice in disguise."

26. *Woodard v. Ohio Adult Parole Authority*, 523 U.S. 272, 289 (1998): "Judicial intervention might, for example, be warranted in the face of a scheme whereby a state official flipped a coin to determine whether to grant clemency."

27. In this regard, I disagree with Garvey's contention that a grant of clemency for capricious reasons, such as political expediency, can be properly described as merciful. Garvey, "Is It Wrong to Commute Death Row?" 1331.

28. Michael Cuneo, *Almost Midnight* (New York: Broadway, 2004). This book offers a detailed and engrossing account of the Darrell Mease murder case, as well as the commutation by Governor Carnahan, though it sometimes lacks corroborating citations.

29. Ibid., 292.

30. Ibid., 289.

31. Terry Ganey, "Carnahan Spares Murderer's Life: Brief Meeting with Pope Led Governor to Cancel Execution," *St. Louis Post-Dispatch* (Jan. 29, 1999).

32. Pam Belluck, "Clemency for Killer Surprises Many Who Followed Case," *New York Times* (Jan. 31, 1999).

33. Editorial, "The Quality of Mercy," *St. Louis Post-Dispatch* (Jan. 29, 1999).

34. Cuneo, *Almost Midnight*, 309.

35. Kit Wagar, "Carnahan Rejects Appeal for Reprieve," *Kansas City Star* (Mar. 10, 1999): "Roberts would have had a stronger case for clemency if Carnahan had not taken so much criticism in the Mease case"; Editorial, "Killing an Innocent Man?" *St. Louis Post-Dispatch* (Mar. 8, 1999): "For political reasons, Gov. Carnahan undoubtedly doesn't want to stop any more executions, given the criticism he faced for saving triple murderer Darrell Mease at the pope's request."

36. Stu Whitney, "Sentence Reform Led to Cuts in Time," *Sioux Falls-Argus Leader* (Jun. 30, 2003), recounting the death of inmate Neil Ambrose who was electrocuted while battling fire on a private farm.

37. Stu Whitney, "Prison-Time Cuts Lead U.S.," *Sioux Falls-Argus Leader* (Jun. 29, 2003).

38. Leslie Sebba, "Clemency in Perspective," in *Criminology in Perspective: Essays in Honor of Israel Drapkin*, eds. S. Landau and L. Sebba. (Lexington, MA: Lexington Books, 1977), 224; W. Holdsworth, *History of English Law* 6 (1938), 573.

39. At English common law, the punishment for some crimes could be reduced at the discretion of the court to a financial penalty. In such circumstances, the defendant was said to be "in mercy," from which derives the word *amercement*. *Webster's New Twentieth Century Dictionary Unabridged* (New York: Simon & Schuster, 1983).

40. Bruce Nolan, "Minister Who Baptized Tucker Calls Her Poster Child for Grace," *New Orleans Times Picayune* (Feb. 4, 1998): "I never met a guard, or volunteer or anyone who ever met her who questioned her sincerity after they got to know her. She was, and is, a very kind human being."

41. "Woman Executed in Texas; Governor, High Court Reject Final Appeals of Killer Karla Faye Tucker," *Akron Beacon Journal* (Feb. 4, 1998).

42. Pat Robertson, "The Importance of an Escape Valve for Mercy," *Capital University Law Review* 29 (2000), 580–581.

43. "Texas Governor Refuses to Intervene," *New York Times* (Feb. 4, 1998). It should be noted that under Texas law, Governor Bush could only grant a temporary reprieve but lacked the authority to set aside Tucker's death sentence permanently absent a favorable recommendation from the Texas Board of Pardons. However, it is widely assumed that had he wanted to grant clemency, it was likely that he could have influenced the Board of Pardons to make a recommendation that would have allowed Tucker's life to be spared.

44. Scott Baldauf, "Death Row Has Its Own Gender Gap," *Christian Science Monitor* (Jan. 23, 1998).

45. Sam Howe Verhovek, "Her Final Appeals Exhausted, Tucker Is Put to Death in Texas," *New York Times* (Feb. 4, 1998): "The last execution of a woman in Texas was in 1863, when Chipita Rodriguez was hung from a mesquite tree for the ax murder of a horse trader."

46. Holly Morris, "Board Spares Murderer; Term Commuted to Life in Prison," *Atlanta Journal-Constitution* (Aug. 22, 1990).

47. Ronald Smothers, "Day Short of Death, Convict in Georgia Is Given Clemency," *New York Times* (Aug. 22, 1990).

48. "Former Death Row Inmate Billy Moore: 'I was considered the worst of the worst,'" *The New Abolitionist* (Jun. 2004, Issue 32), reproduced at www.nodeathpenalty.org/ newab032/14_BillyMoore.html. As Moore states in *The New Abolitionist* interview, "I've never said that I wasn't guilty. If we're going to get people to oppose capital punishment, they have to deal with me—a person who's guilty."

49. Editorial, "Parole Board Saved a Worthy Man's Life," *Atlanta Journal-Constitution* (Aug. 23, 1990).

50. *McCleskey v. Kemp*, 481 U.S. 279 (1987), upholding Georgia system of capital punishment despite disproportionately high numbers of blacks executed in cases where victims were white.

51. *Georgia Code Annotated*, § 42-9-2 (2005).

52. On December 12, 2005, California Governor Arnold Schwarzenegger denied clemency to convicted murderer and antigang activist Stanley Tookie Williams who sought

clemency primarily on grounds of mercy. Schwarzenegger argued that Williams was not deserving of mercy because he had not admitted his guilt or sought to atone for his crimes, casting doubt on the claim that he presented a compelling case of redemption. Stacy Finz, Peter Fimrite, and Bob Egelko, "Schwarzenegger, Supreme Court Won't Halt Execution; Governor Denies Clemency While High Court Rejects Request for a Stay," *San Francisco Chronicle* (Dec. 12, 2005). Perhaps a more compelling argument for mercy, suggested by the foregoing discussion, would have been that a commutation would have proved merciful toward others in California—the young men who could have been saved from a life of gang-related crime through Williams's efforts.

53. Immanuel Kant, *The Metaphysical Elements of Justice* (Indianapolis, IN: Hackett, 1999), 100.

54. Murphy and Hampton, *Mercy and Forgiveness*, 174.

55. Markel, "Against Mercy," 1480.

56. *Connecticut Board of Pardons v. Dumschat*, 452 U.S. 458 (1981), rejecting a procedural due process challenge alleging that prisoners had acquired a protected liberty interest because of the frequency with which the Board of Pardons granted clemency.

57. James D. Barnett, "The Grounds of Pardon," *Journal of Criminal Law, Criminology and Police Science* 17 (1927), 507, quoting *Governor's Conference Proceedings* 53 (1912).

58. Christen Jensen, *The Pardoning Power in the American States* (Chicago: University of Chicago Press, 1922), 62.

59. *The Stoic Philosophy of Seneca*, trans. Moses Hadas (New York and London: W. W. Norton, 1958), 151.

60. *The Merchant of Venice*, act 4, sc. 1.

61. E. Coke, *The Third Part of the Institutes of the Laws of England*, 4th ed. (London, 1669), 223.

62. Thus, to the extent that Sarat suggests that the framers vested the pardoning power in the president because it "would ennoble those who wielded it," I find his account unpersuasive. Austin Sarat, *Mercy on Trial*, 145. In *The Federalist* (No. 74), Hamilton expresses little concern about the status of the president or his personal ennoblement but instead argues that placing the pardoning power in the executive alone will advance the public good by improving the quality of justice.

63. Alexander A. Hamilton, *The Federalist* (No. 74), 448.

64. *The Attorney General's Survey of Release Procedures*, vol. 3 (Washington, DC: U.S. Department of Justice, 1939), 150–153, describing the impeachment of Oklahoma Governor J. C. Walton for selling pardons.

65. Hamilton Jordan, "The First Grifters," *Wall Street Journal* (Feb. 20, 2001); James Zirin, "Pardon Me, but It Reeks," *London Times* (Mar. 13, 2001).

66. Robert Reinhold, "Outgoing Governor in New Mexico Bars the Execution of 5," *New York Times* (Nov. 27, 1986), stating that while Anaya was praised by opponents of the death penalty, "general reaction in New Mexico was not so positive, and Mr. Anaya today was surrounded by an unusually heavy cordon of bodyguards."

67. Although the conventional view has been that governors have little to fear politically for refusing to grant clemency but face political repercussions if they reduce punishment, this perception may no longer be accurate. A study of recent death penalty commutations and governor approval ratings done by the Criminal Justice Section of the American Bar Association showed that most governors who commuted death sentences did not suffer "any measurable political consequences for granting clemency." "Clemency and Consequences" (Jul. 2002), reproduced at http://www.abanet.org/crimjust/juvjus/jdpclemeffect02.pdf. See also Daniel Kobil, "Solid Rationale for Clemency in Williams Case," *Indianapolis Star* (Jun. 27, 2004).

68. Rapaport, "Retribution and Redemption in the Operation of Executive Clemency," 1530.

69. Ibid., 1531.

70. Garvey, "Is It Wrong to Commute Death Row?" 1336.

71. For a detailed discussion of Garvey's theory of atonement, see Stephen P. Garvey, "Punishment as Atonement," *UCLA Law Review* 46 (1999), 1801.

72. James Whitman, *Harsh Justice* (Oxford: Oxford University Press, 2003), 3–4.

73. Garvey, "Is It Wrong to Commute Death Row?" 1337.

74. Rapaport, "Retribution and Redemption in the Operation of Executive Clemency," 1530.

75. Whitman, *Harsh Justice*, 207.

76. As Austin Sarat has observed, governors who discuss their reasons for granting clemency usually take great pains to defend their decisions as "grounded in values and beliefs" shared with the citizenry. Sarat, *Mercy on Trial*, 154; see generally Edmund (Pat) Brown and Dick Adler, *Public Justice; Private Mercy* (New York: Weidenfeld & Nicolson, 1989).

77. E.g., Amanda Crawford and Ryan Konig, "Clemency Voice Goes Unheeded," *Arizona Republic* (May 22, 2005), A1.

78. Murray Edelman, *The Symbolic Uses of Politics* (Urbana and Chicago: University of Illinois Press, 1985), 10–12.

79. Roxanne Roberts, "To Forgive, Divine," *Washington Post* (Mar. 31, 2002); Elizabeth Large, "Forgiveness Is Hot: Researchers Cite Health, Personal Benefits," *Baltimore Sun* (Jan. 12, 2005).

80. We frequently pass laws or sanction political acts because of their symbolic effect, with no empirical showing that they will achieve the results claimed for them. Certainly, it cannot be demonstrated that laws forbidding homosexuals from marrying or adopting children will promote heterosexual marriage or preserve the traditional nuclear family. Yet our leaders frequently act on such suppositions when enacting laws or amending constitutions.

81. Sam Howe Verhovek, "Her Final Appeals Exhausted, Tucker Is Put to Death in Texas," *New York Times* (Feb. 4, 1998).

82. First Amendment scholar Lee Bollinger makes an analogous argument with respect to the vigorous protection of harmful extremist speech, positing that the act of allowing that

which we disagree with fosters greater tolerance among members of society. Lee Bollinger, *The Tolerant Society* (Oxford: Oxford University Press, 1988).

83. DPR 2003-04 National Parole Board, reproduced at http://www.tbs-sct.gc.ca/rma/dpr/03-04/NPB-CNLC/NPB-CNLCd3401_e.asp#sec4.3. Persons eligible for pardons by the Canadian National Parole Board must have satisfied the sentence imposed and have shown themselves free of a criminal conviction for a period of five years.

84. Ibid.

85. Cf. Ibid. with "Presidential Clemency Actions by Administration: 1945–2001," prepared by the Department of Justice Office of the Pardon Attorney and reproduced at http://www.usdoj.gov/pardon/actions_administration.htm.

86. William Shakespeare, *The Merchant of Venice*, act 4, sc. 1.

87. Richard F. Celeste, "Executive Clemency: One Executive's Real Life Decisions," *Capital University Law Review* 31 (2003), 141–142 (emphasis added; footnotes omitted). It should be noted that though Governor Celeste now seems to characterize his grants of clemency as acts of mercy, he has previously explained some of them in what I would call justice-enhancing terms, arguing that they were necessary to correct defects in retributive justice. Daniel Kobil, "Do the Paperwork or Die: Clemency, Ohio Style?" *Ohio State Law Review* 52 (1991), 655–704.

88. Sarat, *Mercy on Trial*, 162.

89. This was the catch phrase of the television detective series *Baretta*, 1975–1978, starring actor Robert Blake.

90. Timothy V. Kaufman-Osborn, "Reviving the Late Liberal State: On Capital Punishment in an Age of Gender Confusion," *Signs: Journal of Women, Culture and Society* 24 (1999), 1121.

91. George Rainbolt, "Mercy: In Defense of Caprice," *Noûs* 31 (1997), 238.

92. William Shakespeare, *Hamlet*, act 2, sc. 2.

93. Hamilton, *The Federalist* (No. 74), 447.

94. Martha Nussbaum, "Equity and Mercy," *Philosophy and Public Affairs* 22 (1993), 101.

95. Rapaport, "Retribution and Redemption," 1529.

96. Andrew Brien, "Mercy Within Legal Justice," *Social Theory and Practice*, 24 (1998), 83.

97. William Bole, Drew Christiansen, and Robert Hennemeyer, *Forgiveness in International Politics* (Washington DC: U.S. Conference of Catholic Bishops, 2004), 26.

98. Ibid, 99–103.

99. "Former Death Row Inmate Billy Moore: 'I was considered the worst of the worst,'" *The New Abolitionist* (Jun. 2004, Issue 32), reproduced at http://www.nodeathpenalty.org/newab032/14_BillyMoore.html. Moore recounts the effect of forgiveness on his relationship with the family of the victim:

I got a copy of my transcript and court records, and in those records were the addresses and names of some of the members of the victim's family. When I saw that, I knew in my heart that I had to write to these people to apologize. I did, and they wrote me back and said they were Christian people and forgave me. It was like a breath of life. They were giving me a breath of life. Here are the people who should want me to die—who had every reason to want me to die—saying that they didn't want me to die and that they forgave me. We continue to write, even to this present day, and talk on the phone. I even go visit them at times.

100. Celeste, "Executive Clemency," 142.

101. Margaret Love has discussed this and other improvements in the clemency process that might allow for more merciful decisions to be made. Margaret Love, "Of Pardons, Politics, and Collar Buttons: Reflections on the President's Duty to Be Merciful," *Fordham Urban Law Journal* 27 (2000), 1483–1513.

102. Whitman, though he is not optimistic that mercy will make a comeback anytime soon, suggests that the Christian tradition is the most likely quarter from which reform in America will eventually proceed. Whitman, *Harsh Justice*, 207.

103. Marilynne Robinson, *Gilead* (New York: Farrar, Straus, and Giroux, 2004), 161.

The Merciful State

LINDA ROSS MEYER

The power of the executive to pardon[1] has shown many faces through its long history. It was a sign and derivative prerogative of the absolute power of despots; it was a delegation of divine authority to earthly rulers; it was an implication of personal bonds of fealty between lord and vassal;[2] it was a propaganda tool;[3] it was a tool for quelling political division; it was a tool for enriching the public coffers and filling the navy;[4] it was an equitable ameliorative for harsh, unjust, or superannuated laws; and it was a place for pure, unjustified mercy.

Traditionally, the executive's pardon power is ungoverned by rule or law. It is completely discretionary, to be used for any reason or for none. Hence, the pardon power often seems like sheer, irrational whim, antithetical to enlightened democratic rule, antithetical to reason, to ethics, and to law. Philosophical commentators rarely praise it, more often attempting to tame it to rules or abolish it entirely. Pardon, they argue, must either be transformed into a better law and governed by reason and principle, or it is not appropriate to a modern state. The state must be lawful, not merciful.

This chapter takes the opposite view, defending the position that pardons are not wrong because they are irrational, treat like cases unlike, or stem from a personal judgment rather than a democratic process. As I point out, all these objections to the pardon power are based on a flawed foundation. When we make such objections, we assume that Kantian reason is the ground of ethics, equality, and community and that pardon, by repelling universalizable principles, undoes all three. But I argue that we have gotten the foundation wrong: Reason is not the ground of community or government but comes only after we recognize something more foundational still—that is, our mutual connection with each other and the world as aware, perceiving, engaged beings (as *Dasein*, to use Heidegger's terminology), an immersion and "tuned-in-ness" that founds even reason itself. I argue, then, that far from undoing the grounding principles of government, pardons are grounded precisely in the connectedness, embeddedness, and finitude that undergird community and government and that come before reason and serve as the basis and touchstone for judgments about justice that are abstracted in law.

The problem is, of course, that this same place where law begins and ends also generates the possibility of lawless violence and chaos that makes us ill at ease with pardoning always. The "hole in the law" at the basis of being-with each other is both a place for justice and for destruction, for compassion and for chaos. But I maintain that the hard and murky choices in pardoning are nonetheless ethical choices, even though ungroundable in law (general principles). I argue that the place of openness that is ungoverned by law should not be understood as law's antithesis of unconstrained force or violence for the simple reason that we humans are not gods of unrestricted absolute power. Instead, this openness may be understood as a finite being's half-blind groping response to what cannot be articulated or bound in law but remains as the bone-felt guide of judgment in the always only partially illuminated and finite moment of decision. The justice and compassion that elude the rules of law are what we (lawyers, politicians, philosophers, advocates) are always seeking to adumbrate, what we are always partially formulating, but what are by definition not amenable to complete articulation. Kant calls this elusive guide of decision "reflective judgment,"[5] Derrida, "forgiveness without sovereignty,"[6] Llewellyn, "instinct,"[7] and Nietzsche, most expressively of all, "love with seeing eyes."[8]

If there is such a ruleless way to grope after justice, it must be case by case; hence, an ethical inquiry must wrestle with the concrete and complex. The strategy I suggest we can adopt here for a normative interrogation of pardoning is that of the common law—look for a "clear" case and then turn to the more complex and murky ones, reasoning by analogy, categorizing only provisionally and tentatively, subject to rearticulation and overruling as another case alters our understanding.

Hence, I begin this chapter with a provisional taxonomy of pardons, trying to identify some "central cases" where our intuitions about the appropriate use of the pardon are clearer, and then moving to harder cases. The second section undertakes to respond to the philosophical claims that pardon is unjust and undemocratic and tries to provide a new philosophical foundation for pardon, focusing especially on pardons granted to remorseful or sympathetic defendants. This new foundation helps justify the "personal" in pardons, even pardons by state actors, and clarifies the relation between pardoning and justice and between pardoning and "moral luck." Finally, the third section brings together the first two—a first cut at an ethical analysis of pardoning not tied to rules, as I try to apply the foundational insights in the second section to the kinds of pardons described in the first.

A Pardon Bestiary

Here I give examples of various pardons that I group into several provisional categories. My aim is to break out the pardons that commentators have found more controversial from those that seem less controversial and so to provide some context for the ensuing abstract discussion. The categories are far from original: Digeser, Kobil, Rapaport, Sarat, and many others have divided pardons into similar kinds. The first four categories reflect considerations internal to the case: equity, peacemaking, allegiance/remorse, and compassion. The fifth category consists of pardons that reflect considerations external to the case, for in my view, these pardons represent cases in which an executive is faced with a role conflict: the demands of the adjudicative role in pardoning conflict with the role as enforcer of policy or head of state. Finally, I end with an example of a "hard case" of pardon.

I do not limit my examples to pardons by the chief executive (governor or president) but include "pardons" by anyone who waives or mitigates lawful or deserved punishment, including prosecutors, juries, judges, police, and victims, for the normative concerns at play in many cases are not unique to chief executives.

Pardons as Equity

In October 2004, Peter J. Rose was exonerated by DNA evidence of the rape of a thirteen-year-old girl. At his sentencing in 1996, he had sobbed, "this crime is sick, it's not me!" Through the Innocence Project and the efforts of Golden Gate law students, clothing worn by the victim was tracked down and retested twice. Both tests proved that Rose couldn't have been the rapist. He had served ten years of a twenty-seven-year sentence. Rose was the 157th convicted defendant in the United States exonerated by DNA evidence.[9]

Kevin Byrd was convicted of rape in 1985 and served twelve years before he was exonerated by DNA evidence in 1997 and pardoned by then-Governor George Bush. The evidence used to exonerate him was slated for destruction in 1994 but, owing to recordkeeping snafus, had been preserved. Just after his exoneration, DNA evidence preserved in other cases was destroyed.

These cases are central, easy cases for pardon[10]—better justice for old cases that may be procedurally barred by courts.[11] These equity pardons involve individual cases of innocence, where new evidence of innocence is available.

But innocence is not always obvious. Consider Aleck Carpitcher, convicted of child molestation through the testimony of an eleven-year-old girl. Shortly after his trial, she recanted her testimony, saying she had made the allegation because she didn't like his living with her mother and wanted to get him out of the house. The Virginia courts would not hear her recantation because of a rule that barred new evidence twenty-one days after the conviction. But then, the Virginia legislature changed the rule, allowing new evidence ninety days after conviction. With Carpitcher's case now pending before the state appellate court, new hearsay evidence turns up that the victim may have recanted her recantation, and evidence not introduced at Carpitcher's original trial suggests that he may have been involved in molesting young girls in the past.[12] And it is always possible that this "new" evidence could be called into doubt by "newer" evidence. As every good lawyer (and every good mystery writer) knows, at one point in time the question of guilt or innocence seems absolutely clear, but that certainty may not be determinate for all time because the possibility of new evidence placing old evidence in a new light is always lurking. Human justice is ineluctably temporal.

Beyond the individual case of innocence, equity may also account for pardons of classes of cases in which legal rules or procedures have lagged behind our sense of justice.[13] Governor Celeste pardoned battered women who could not make out self-defense claims under traditional rules,[14] and pardons have been extended in compassionate euthanasia cases[15] where the law required verdicts of premeditated murder. Governor Ryan justified his blanket pardon of death row inmates in Illinois in part by the claim that the death penalty was not administered fairly or reliably and that the legislature had repeatedly failed to act to make the law more just.[16]

Still more controversial are equity pardons based on postconviction "reform." The death penalty case of "Tookie" Williams in California is a prime example of a case in which an offender had reformed his life since his crime—a gang leader who became a leader in the fight against gangs. Calls for Governor Schwarzenegger to pardon him emphasized that he was no longer the cold-blooded killer who had murdered the four victims, and his commutation would recognize his good works. But reciting the gruesome details of the murders, the strong evidence of Williams's guilt, and Williams's refusal to acknowledge guilt, Schwarzenegger declined to pardon him despite his "good works," and he was executed.[17]

Finally, pardons may commute sentences where service of the original sentence becomes more onerous than "average" because of old age, illness, susceptibility to rape, loss of custody of minor children, or other circumstances. Kathleen Dean Moore considers this pardon a kind of after-trial equity that equalizes the "pain" of the sentence so that one does the same pain, if not the same time, for the same crime.[18] Dan Markel and P. E. Digeser argue, on the other hand, that this sort of pardon is based on compassion, not equity. If justice required postconviction re-adjustment, they argue, then the only sentencing option is the indeterminate sentence and the concomitant and dangerous problem of giving disparate sentences for disparate "sensibilities."[19] For my purposes, these sorts of pardons could be placed into either category—equity or compassion—as I argue that pardons in neither category should be ethically excluded.

Pardons as Peace

> Whereas it is now desired by some persons heretofore engaged in said rebellion to re-sume their allegiance to the United States, and to reinaugurate loyal State governments within and for their respective States; therefore, I, Abraham Lincoln, President of the United States, do proclaim, declare, and make known to all persons who have, directly or by implication, participated in the existing rebellion, except as hereinafter excepted, that a full pardon is hereby granted to them and each of them, with restoration of all rights of property, except as to slaves, and in property cases where rights of third parties shall have intervened, and upon the condition that every such person shall take and subscribe an oath, and thenceforward keep and maintain said oath inviolate.[20]

Lincoln's and Johnson's post–Civil War pardons were classic examples of executive pardons as peace. Nor were they unique. Washington, Adams, and Jefferson all used the pardon power to settle instances of rebellion and to re-form the national community.[21] In our own time, the South African Truth and Reconciliation Commission provided a new example of pardon as peace, looking into the future to establish and renew community after racial violence.[22]

The peace pardon is usually general, not personal, and extended to all those "at war" with the pardoning community (usually extending to acts that would have been criminal had they not had their genesis in war or political disagreements or to criminal acts that proceeded under color of later-discredited law or illegitimate authority). Lincoln was faced repeatedly with the difficulties of the distinction between war and crime: In 1862, he commuted the death sentences of hundreds of Native Americans involved in hostilities in Minnesota, allowing the execution of only those who "proved guilty of violating females" [two] and those "who were proven to have participated in massacres [forty], as distinguished from participation in battles." His hope, repeated in the Civil War amnesties, was "to not act with so much clemency as to encourage another outbreak on the one hand, nor with so much severity as to be real cruelty on the other."[23]

Margaret Love, Kobil, and Digeser[24] have all emphasized the importance of this aspect of the pardon power. Digeser would separate peacemaking from reconciliation, however, and would place the latter roughly where I put allegiance pardons.

Pardons as Allegiance

To Edwin M. Stanton
February 5, 1864
  Submitted to the Sec. Of War. On principle I dislike an oath which requires a man to swear he has not done wrong. It rejects the Christian principle of forgiveness on terms of repentance. I think it is enough if the man does no wrong hereafter.[25]

In 2004, an American soldier in Iraq refused to obey a direct order to "chamber a round" in his weapon before leaving the base perimeter. The commander could have convened a court martial. But he did not. He knew this soldier well; he was a good soldier and had served well for nearly his entire tour of duty. But the soldier had had enough of killing. The commander decided to avoid a court martial by assigning this soldier to duties within the perimeter for the short remainder of his tour. The commander acknowledged that he could not have done this at the beginning of the soldier's service; other members of the company would have taken it as favoritism, weakness, and it would have destroyed discipline. However, after having served together for some time, many of the company were sympathetic with this soldier, and all understood the commander's act of mercy, for no one wanted someone who had served so well to end his service by court martial. They understood that the soldier had been responsible to the commander, and now the commander was being responsible for the soldier.[26]

Another officer at a military training camp confronted a young soldier who had gone AWOL to visit his girlfriend to try to convince her not to break up with him. The soldier acknowledged fault and expressed remorse. The officer knew him as a good soldier and did not want to ruin his career—the military was this soldier's best chance to rise above a tough childhood. So the commander gave him a minor punishment that would not be reflected in his future personnel records and did not kick him out of the training program. The soldier was extremely grateful because he knew that the officer was putting his own reputation on the line. The soldier felt responsible to the officer; the officer was at future risk himself from the soldier's future bad conduct.

Victim-offender mediation also emphasizes what I call here pardon as allegiance, but here the allegiance is forged between victims and offenders. Mark Umbreit tells the story of David and Maria Sanchez, owners of a local grocery store that was vandalized by Frederico Angeles and his friends. The store owners remember Angeles as a frequent customer; Angeles has often been a patron. Angeles acknowledges the connection: "Everybody knows the 'J.' We get snacks there and meet people there. . . . The parking lot behind the store is a good place to mess around with girls. Usually you don't get hassled there."[27] In their discussion, the Sanchezes express anger but also connection: "You look like a young man who wants to have fun, but you don't look like a bad man. It was important for me to see you. Now I remember you from before. You have been in our store many times. Why don't you help us?"[28] Angeles's cocky grin dissolves when he sees Mrs. Sanchez in tears over the wreckage of her store (and her future). After understanding the extent of the damage he helped cause, and its effect on the people before him, Angeles responds with remorse and agrees to work in the Sanchez store to help repair the damage instead of going to jail.

Personal connection, presence, and remorse play a central role here: "It was important for me to see you" is the theme that echoes through many of these mediation stories—both for the victims and for the offenders. The victims needed to see the offenders out of the context of the crime, to counteract their own fear, express their anger, and to try to understand why the crime occurred. The offenders needed to see the victims face to face to see for themselves the effects of their actions and to have the opportunity to apologize.

The pardon out of allegiance stems from an authority (or victim as authority) who can personally forgive and resettle a preexisting relationship for the future (even if the preexisting relationship is one created only by the crime itself). Executive pardons used to be conceived, at least in part, as "most personal"[29] in this way. Blackstone states: "[I]n monarchies the king acts in a superior sphere . . . Whenever the nation sees him personally engaged, it is only in works of legislature, magnificence, or compassion . . . [T]hese repeated acts of goodness, coming immediately from his own hand, endear the sovereign to his subjects, and contribute more than any thing to root in their hearts that filial affection, and personal loyalty, which are the sure establishment of a prince."[30] Likewise, Justice Marshall in *United States v. Wilson*[31] said: "A pardon is an act of grace, proceeding from the power entrusted with the execution of the laws, which exempts the individual, on whom it is bestowed, from the punishment the law inflicts for a crime he has committed. It is the *private*, though official act of the executive magistrate" (emphasis added).

However, by 1926, Justice Holmes in *Biddle v. Perovich* would deny the "personal" nature of executive pardons, saying, "A pardon in our days is not a private act of grace from an individual happening to possess power. It is a part of the Constitutional scheme. When granted it is the determination of the ultimate authority that the public welfare will be better served by inflicting less than what the judgment fixed."[32]

I argue later that we need not be so afraid of the "personal" pardon, but it is clear that a personal understanding of the pardon power is disfavored in modern times. We have no allegiance to a particular king (a person), but to a "state."[33] Putting the personal power under a "legal" restraint and public purpose seems more democratic: a government of laws and not men.

Pardon as Compassion

To Edwin M. Stanton, Hon. Sec. Of War—
March 1, 1864

A poor widow, by the name of Baird, has a son in the Army, that for some offence has been sentenced to serve a long time without pay, or at most, with very little pay. I do not like this punishment of withholding pay—it falls so very hard upon poor families. After he has been serving in this way for several months, at the tearful appeal of the poor Mother, I made a direction that he be allowed to enlist for a new term, on the same conditions as others. She now comes, and says she can not get it acted upon. Please do it.

Yours truly, A Lincoln.[34]

To George G. Meade
Aug. 21, 1863

At this moment I am appealed to in behalf of William Thompson of Co.K.3rd. Maryland Volunteers, in 12th Army Corps said to be at Kelly's Ford, under sentence to be shot to-day as a deserter. He is represented to me to be very young, with symptoms of insanity. Please postpone the execution till further order.[35]

*

To George G. Meade

October 8 & 12, 1863

    I am appealed to in behalf of John Murphy, to be shot to-morrow. His Mother says he is but seventeen . . . I therefore, on account of his tender age, have concluded to pardon him, and to leave it to yourself whether to discharge him, or continue in the service.

To Stephen A. Hurlbut

December 17, 1863

    I understand you have, under sentence of death, a tall old man, by the name of Henry F. Luckett. I personally knew him, and did not think him a bad man. Please do not let him be executed, unless upon further order from me, and, in the mean time, send me a transcript of the record.[36]

To George G. Meade

August 27, 1863

    Walter, Rainese, Faline, Lae & Kuhne appeal to me for mercy without giving any ground for it whatever. I understand these are very flagrant cases, and that you deem their punishment as being indispensable to the service. If I am not mistaken in this, please let them know at once that their appeal is denied.[37]

These samples of compassion, and lack of compassion, all come from President Lincoln's letters, but clemency for the old, the young, the sick, those with extraordinary family burdens, those subject to child abuse or domestic violence, war veterans, the disabled, and other sympathetic cases is apparent in earlier presidencies[38] and is also reflected currently in the sentencing "downward departure" cases under the Federal Sentencing Guidelines and in clemency actions in the military context.[39] The pardons from compassion often come after an emotional plea by a parent, a respected authority, or the offender himself. Like remorse pardons, they are often founded on a sympathetic connection in a person-to-person exchange. The commonest grounds for compassion are those that most of us would find make either the crime more tempting, the punishment more onerous, or are a response to other hardships the person has endured in life.[40] Compassion may also arise spontaneously based on a sense of common ground that cannot be articulated in these categories, and here it is most controversial. Compassion pardons may be unconnected with remorse or retributive justice.

    Jacques Derrida points out that it is here that pardon or forgiveness is seen in its truth. Only the unforgivable can really be forgiven, he argues, for it is only when there is no reason to forgive, where one does not deserve to be forgiven, that true forgiveness, completely divorced from law and desert, is possible.[41] Forgiveness of the unforgivable, compassion without a ground, is the kind of forgiveness that gives forgiveness its very meaning as "undeserved," according to Derrida, and is therefore forgiveness at its purest. The farther from rational grounds of forgiveness we get, of course, the more controversial the forgiveness becomes, and many authors have argued for a category of "unforgivable crimes."[42]

Extrinsic-Good Pardons

Inside the quiet Governor's Mansion late that November night, I became in a very real sense a scale of justice. The case against Lindsey was loaded with horrible details of the savage brutality that can lie hidden inside a human being until something makes it erupt. It was the kind of crime which seemed to cry out for vengeance, for ritual punishment as swift and terrible as the act itself.

Weighed against this were the doubts raised by his mother's letter about Lindsey's mental history, an issue that I felt had never really been carefully explored during his trial. Then, too, if the death penalty was designed to be a deterrent against future crimes, I couldn't for the life of me see how killing Lindsey would keep another madman from attacking another little girl somewhere down the road.

I had been governor for almost three years, and in spite of some setbacks I had managed to get a lot done. I was fighting a conservative legislature to spend more money on a growing state, to improve its schools and its mental health facilities and its working conditions. Should I risk, did I even have the *right* to risk, destroying any of that because of one demented criminal?

Rose Marie Riddle was dead, and nothing I could do would bring her back. By letting Richard Lindsey go to the gas chamber, I was giving her parents and people like them a chance at a living wage. The scales tipped. I picked up my pen and on the first page of the clemency file wrote these words: "I will take no action." I dated it November 10, 1961, and signed my name. Four days later, Lindsey was dead. That same week, the farm labor bill passed through committee and a few months later was signed into law.

Why then, has the Lindsey case troubled me all these years[?][43]

California Governor Ed Brown refused to pardon Lindsey not because of factors intrinsic to Lindsey's case (the crime, his circumstances and character, his community standing, the harm done, the need to repair the relationships breached, etc.) but because of concerns that had nothing to do with the case or its merits. On the merits, Brown would have pardoned Lindsey because of his long-term mental state that suggested organic brain damage and insanity. Even were one to accept the possibility that pardons can be based on nonretributive justice factors like repentance or compassion or peacemaking, Brown's nonpardon falls into another category of utilitarian or, perhaps more accurately, extrinsic-good pardons. Other examples of extrinsic-good pardons include the pardons used to pacify the public into acquiescing in harsh laws, nonpardons in an election year to convince the public one is tough on crime, pardons to those who will agree to pioneer in new communities or serve in the armed forces, pretrial clemency to a soldier because the commanding officer cannot spare personnel to serve on the court martial,[44] pardons to those supported by others who will reciprocate in political or personal favors, pardons (or immunity) to secure testimony against others,[45] and straightforward pardons for purchase.

Some of these are clear abuses of the pardon power (like bribery), but other cases are not so clear. Is it wrong not to pardon, for example, to gain support for legislation that will help many others? To be reelected (or to put it more kindly, because one's constituency would not approve)? To convince a legislature to pass a moratorium on the death penalty? To avoid insurrection, riot, or mutiny (think of *Billy Budd* or the riots in Los Angeles after acquittals of abusive police officers)? Is it wrong to pardon to gain volunteers for dangerous missions? To avoid tying up key personnel for a trial who are needed in combat? To save administrative resources for other cases?[46]

Unlike courts, which have the obligation to decide cases on their merits, executive officials have multiple roles, and the adjudicative role is only one of them. As they balance these roles and their priorities, pardon decisions may become instrumental to duties and considerations required by the executive's other roles. The ethical problems expand: When considering a pardon application, should the executive's adjudicative role always trump the executive's other roles?

The Hard Case of Darrell Mease

In January 1999, Governor Carnahan pardoned triple murderer Darrell Mease. Mease is a Missouri hillbilly who grew up in the Pentecostal church and was drafted into Vietnam after high school, just after his seventeen-year-old wife bore his first child. He left the United States a good old boy who didn't drink or swear and who wanted to be a preacher someday but returned addicted to alcohol and suffering nightmares. After two failed marriages and a long run of job instability, Ozark drug lord Lloyd Lawrence recruited Darrell for his methamphetamine manufacturing operation. One night, after Lloyd got Darrell to try some crystal meth, Darrell's drug-induced paranoia (and Lloyd's reputation as a rapist) made him believe Lloyd was going to try to molest his girlfriend, Mary, to whom he was devoted. Darrell decided to leave right away, stashing the drugs they had made where Lloyd wouldn't be able to find them. After several months of traveling and hiding all over the south and southwest with Mary, Darrell discovered that Lloyd had put out a contract to kill him for stealing his drugs. Believing that his only option was to strike first, Darrell staked out Lloyd's vacation cabin, lay in wait for three days, and killed Lloyd, Lloyd's wife, and Lloyd's paraplegic grandson as they drove out into the woods on four-wheelers, firing a powerful shotgun into their heads at close range.

After he and Mary were apprehended, Darrell underwent an intense and tearful jailhouse conversion, which even cynical observers tended to credit, and proclaimed to the press that "God was his Lawyer." His faith that he would not be executed was unshaken, even when his conviction and death sentence were affirmed throughout the appellate and habeas process and the execution date was set.

Then, in a public relations gaffe, Darrell's execution was originally scheduled for the same day that Pope John Paul II, a staunch opponent of capital punishment, was to visit St. Louis. Though the Missouri Supreme Court tried quietly to reschedule the execution for a later date, the press caught on and pilloried the state for its hypocrisy. Governor Carnahan was told that the pope would ask for Darrell's pardon. At an interfaith prayer service near the end of his visit, as investigative journalist Michael Cuneo reconstructed it,

> The pope read his homily with a shaking hand and a quavering voice, closing with a ringing entreaty to all Americans: "If you want peace, work for justice. If you want justice, defend life. If you want life, embrace the truth—the truth revealed by God." There was no explicit reference in the homily to capital punishment. It was a stirring event—the comparative intimacy of the cathedral, with its byzantine mosaic-clad interior, the sumptuous music that both preceded and followed the homily, the passage from Isaiah expertly rendered by a prominent local rabbi. Everything was in perfect pitch, graceful and harmonious, with not a single note off-key. Then, a little before six, after the last canticle had been chanted and the last prayer recited, the pope struggled to his feet, gingerly negotiated the steps in front of the altar, and slowly made his way over to the front left pew where he chatted briefly with the Gores before moving on to Governor Carnahan.
>
> The two men exchanged greetings, and then the pope, his face a scant six inches from Carnahan's, said: "Governor, will you please have mercy on Mr. Mease?"
>
> And that was it. Will you please have mercy on Mr. Mease? The most direct request imaginable. The most specific request imaginable. It wasn't about the death penalty in general. It wasn't about sparing anyone else on death row. Just Darrell—nobody but Darrell.

The governor nodded, almost imperceptibly, and the pope moved on, working his way laboriously to the rear of the cathedral with his entourage in tow.[47]

The governor explained his commutation order as coming "[a]fter careful consideration of the extraordinary circumstance of the Pontiff's direct and personal appeal for mercy and because of the deep and abiding respect I have for him and all that he represents."[48]

This pardon was the result of a personal and immediate appeal. The political fallout was complex—even the antideath penalty advocates thought there were far worthier candidates than Darrell—yet Carnahan had used up all his pardon-political capital on a clearly guilty triple murderer. After Mease, the Missouri executions proceeded apace, one every month, as Carnahan fought off election-year allegations that he was soft on the death penalty. Even though Pope John Paul later wrote on behalf of another Missouri death row inmate (Roy Roberts) who had a more-than-plausible claim of innocence, "safely back in Rome now, [the pope] was much easier to ignore."[49] A year later, Carnahan was tragically killed in a plane crash and posthumously elected to the U.S. Senate over opponent John Ashcroft.

Carnahan's pardon for Darrell cannot be grounded in equity, peace, remorse, or the usual grounds of compassion, for none of these are prominent in Mease's case. Here, the pardon comes to a man of unshakeable faith (who already feels forgiven, not remorseful), without extraordinary circumstances of sympathy to recommend him, whose guilt is unquestioned. It happens because of a fluke of timing and the extraordinary personal intervention of the pope. Here, the pardon looks like grace at its most alarming, its most unpredictable, its most arbitrary, a true instance of forgiving the unforgivable. Is it divine intervention or luck? And even if the former, what place can divine intervention have in secular government? Yet, as Cuneo also points out, the crime itself can be understood as a confluence of extraordinary events; the absence of any one of several factors would have changed Darrell's decision to flee and kill. Had events unfolded differently, Darrell, an inherently likable and straightforward good old boy, might have become a preacher and not a murderer. The specter of moral luck pervades this story and makes it the most difficult case of all.

The Foundations of Pardoning: Being-With, Not Reason

The Case Against a Merciful State

Invoking the apparent fortuity and inequality of pardon decisions like Carnahan's, Dan Markel has recently argued that compassion and mercy should play no part in punishment at any level.[50] He argues that prosecutorial discretion should be overseen by ombudspersons to ensure that compassion plays no role in the charging decision,[51] that grand jury and petit jury acquittals should be subject to some form of judicial review, and that executives should also be overseen by ombudspersons and be required to give reasons for their exercise of the pardon power to ensure that only equity-based pardons are given.

Markel insists that anyone who believes in equal liberty under law must be "against mercy," though he also argues that being against mercy is a necessary consequence of retributivist principles of punishment.[52] Compassion, he argues, runs counter to three principles of liberal government: "moral accountability for unlawful actions, equal liberty under law, and democratic self-defense."[53]

First, to pardon one who is morally accountable, according to Markel, sends two wrong messages to the body politic. One, it does not take the offender seriously as a moral actor but treats the offender as irresponsible. This objection has also been voiced by other retributivists, including Michael Moore[54] and Herbert Morris,[55] who have argued for a "right" of the offender to be punished and thereby treated as an autonomous agent rather than an incompetent. Second, Markel argues that the pardon shows the state's "indifference to the legal rights of its citizens, particularly to the security of their persons and property."[56] Markel acknowledges, however, that the goal of reinforcing moral accountability for unlawful actions alone need not require actual punishment, as long as the offender is remorseful and has internalized the norms promulgated by the state.[57] And he takes the point that "indifference" to the legal rights of victims cannot be understood to require that we punish every delict, or we would have no resources for anything else.

As reinforcing moral accountability by itself doesn't justify eliminating mercy entirely, Markel goes on to discuss the principle of equal liberty under law. Here he argues, as Herbert Morris has done,[58] that crime is a claim of superiority by "taking license to which others are not entitled."[59] The state must punish in the name of equality "to reduce the plausibility of a false claim to superiority."[60] Markel believes that this argument does not explain why the *state* must punish, however, as opposed to some other entity, and therefore may still open a loophole for state mercy.

To close the final mercy loophole, Markel argues that "retribution is . . . a form of democratic self-defense."[61] The criminal, in violating the laws enacted by a democratic government, is "trying to shift where the rules of property, liability, and inalienability lie. He is usurping the sovereign will of the people by challenging their decision-making structure."[62] The crime, then, is not just against the particular victim but against the democratic state. The state must defend itself by punishing, and if it does not, it is failing to defend democracy itself.

Mercy must be completely eliminated from public decision making, then, because failing to punish even a remorseful defendant is usurping democratic rule. Under the principle of safeguarding democracy, the state must punish to maintain its nature as a democratic institution, even where no victim has been harmed or treated as an inferior by the offender. So, Markel says, even mala prohibita laws democratically enacted must be defended by punishment (as long as they do not contradict the principles of freedom and equality that are the foundation for democratic government itself).

With respect to moral accountability, many writers have elsewhere argued that "expressivist" retributivist theories like Markel's that rely on "sending a message" to the offender or polity tend to reduce to utilitarian arguments about how best to transmit messages about law and order.[63] One can argue, for example, that sending a message would be better achieved via an ad campaign, via public corporal punishment,[64] or via punishing only the most famous, only those with community ties, or only those whose associates and victims are paying attention.

One may also question the assumption that treating offenders as responsible agents means avoiding mercy. While the most attractive forms of retributivism stress that principles of dignity and respect require treating the offender as a full agent, even this requires mercy, for (1) we cannot hold finite beings responsible for all the infinite repercussions of their actions[65] and (2) because we have the obligation to treat offenders humanely, we never give them the world as it would be if their inhumane acts were universal laws, for to include offenders in the circle of humanity is itself an undeserved mercy.[66]

Markel's arguments from equality make traditional assumptions that we are already equal ex ante, before crime, in being subject to equal prohibitions by the law. As many commentators have pointed out, the prohibitions of the criminal law do not affect us or tempt us each equally.[67] For a poor person to follow the law requires greater forbearance and heroism than for a rich person. And the flaws in the argument that criminals take more than their fair share of license have been pointed out by other commentators.[68] The "license" to kill is not a license most of us desire, nor is the "superiority" claimed by the criminal over the victim one that can necessarily be readjusted by punishing or humiliating the criminal.

Finally, Markel's argument from democracy assumes that the positive laws of the state are truly "democratic"—a significant stretch of faith. Insofar as they may themselves be the result of faction and prejudice, racially biased districting, disenfranchisement of significant proportions of the population, undue influence of rich interest groups or foreign powers, small print in omnibus appropriations bills, and so forth, the argument from defense of democracy weakens. Moreover, Markel is skeptical about the exercise of discretion by prosecutors, judges, juries, and executives—concerned about bias and caprice infecting their decision making—but he doesn't bring the same skepticism to bear on the votes of legislators, who also exercise unreviewable discretion during their terms of office and have also been known to vote for reasons of bias, caprice, or corruption. Bias and caprice would seem at least equally distributed among the legislative, judicial, and executive branches, yet no number of ombudspersons would be able to correct this. And we would need ombudspersons for the ombudspersons.

Digging Out the Foundations

But these objections touch only the superficial aspects of Markel's argument. His three objections are truly foundational and point to key underlying assumptions about both ethics and good government. Again, Markel's arguments against mercy rely on three points: (1) mercy is condescending, treating us not as free and responsible agents but as pitiable victims of circumstance; (2) mercy is unjust in treating like cases differently; and (3) mercy is undemocratic in undermining or ignoring the majority's will as expressed in the criminal law. These three arguments can be related to the three restatements of Kant's categorical imperative: (1) act so that every action could be willed as a universal law (be a rational—and therefore, a free—agent); (2) treat rational nature whether in yourself or another as an end in itself and not as a means only (treat all rational beings equally); (3) act as both sovereign and subject in a kingdom of ends (enter the democracy of reason).

Not surprisingly, Kant, like Markel, rejects the pardon power for all crimes except treason. He states, "[The pardon power] ought not to be exercised in application to the crimes of the subjects against each other; for exemption from punishment . . . would be the greatest wrong that could be done to them. It is only an occasion of some form of treason, as a lesion against himself, that the sovereign should make use of this right."[69] For Kant (and Markel), any institutional arrangement, such as pardon, that challenges reason also challenges ethics, the conception of humanity, and the basic "glue" that binds together the human community in a web of mutual rights and obligations.

Kant's argument for making reason the foundation of ethics (and community) goes something like this:[70] For Kant, will is only free of causal necessity if it is an exercise of reason, for reason follows its own principles of logic and consistency, and the claims of logic are not affected by the arbitrary power of nature's relations of cause and effect. As only reason frees us from causal necessity, only reason is truly within our power, and only reason can be the basis on which we can be responsible. Hence, the first statement of the categorical imperative can be restated as "always act in accordance with reason." The good will, the ethical will, the free will is the reasonable will.

We know that we ourselves reason, or at least we have to assume we reason to deliberate, speak, and act. As reason and freedom are the same, we must assume we are free of cause and effect in order to reason (otherwise the valid result of a syllogism would not be dictated by rational necessity but by contingent cause and effect). Though reason as such cannot be "seen" or "known" as an object in nature, we do it and therefore must assume we are free. The apparent contradiction between a "scientific" understanding of humanity as caused and the "rational" understanding of humanity as free is resolved if we assume that the former is only a phenomenon of the limitations of our ability to know objects in nature. Our "noumenal" selves are free even if our phenomenal selves appear not to be.

Because I know myself as capable of reason, and reason is the only basis on which I can be held responsible, reason is an end in itself. I judge the worth of my actions by the reasons actuating them (or the "maxim of the action" or "mens rea"[71]), not by the contingent results that follow (which I cannot control). If reason is an end in itself, then it must be so whether it is my own reason or reason in another being because reason requires me to treat like cases alike. Hence, Kant derives the second statement of the categorical imperative: Treat reason whether in yourself or others as an end in itself.

Finally, Kant sees that this mutuality of reason can form community through a "kingdom of ends" in which reasonable beings come together and work out reasonable laws for themselves. These laws, based in reason, will necessarily be consistent and harmonious, forming the basis of an ethical community and an ideal state.

Kant argues that reason must recognize and respect itself. But how does one know that another being is a creature of reason? Reason is not an empirically knowable feature of the world. I cannot prove my own free will, though in reasoning, I must assume it. But I need not assume that other beings are reasoning as I am, nor can I prove their reason by empirical investigation, for I can have no way, according to Kant, to know what others are as "things in themselves" but only as I perceive them as affected by forces in the world. Psychology and psychiatry can study the causes of human behavior, but we cannot prove through these sciences that human beings are exercising reason or free will or even have the power to do so. On the contrary, we find from the perspective of the sciences that human behavior may be explained by childhood abuse, indulgence, or repression, physical damage to or chemical alterations in the brain, social isolation or conformity, genetic predilection, and so on. Although I may derive from my own reason the principle that I must respect reason wherever I find it, I cannot empirically find it anywhere. Thus, Kant's ethics (if wrongly considered as the practical basis of law) gets stuck at the point at which I must recognize other real persons as reasonable like I am—precisely the place where ethics would seem to begin.

But suppose we begin in a different place. Heidegger suggests that the foundational aspect of being human is not reason but what he calls being-in-the-world and being-with-others. We are, in his terminology, Dasein ("being there" or the ones who are open to Being).[72] This has several aspects and consequences: First, our fundamental knowledge of each other is practical, personal, and imbedded in context: a "knowing how" to be with others, not the abstracted knowledge of others as objects-of-science that hides the thing-in-itself. I know how to cajole, joke, tease, infuriate, admire, frighten, and ignore others before I know anything of psychology or psychiatry, indeed, even before I can talk. But the point is not just developmental but metaphysical. These abstracted sciences of human behavior are only possible on the basis of this prior knowledge of "how" to be with. Only on the basis of our practical knowledge can we discern and abstract the relevant categories of scientific investigation. We can pick out features from the messy "background" noise and define, for example, "childhood" or "fantasy" as relevant and sufficiently discrete categories of investigation only because we already know so much about human beings in context and in practice.[73]

Second, action and passion are not dualities but interdependent. We are able to act only because we are also "passively" open and aware. We are as we are because we already are in a world and affected by, and attentive to, that world and each other. Emotion is not an outside force pushing us around, as Kant conceives "inclination," but an experience that opens us to new possibilities of understanding.[74] Reason is not the foundation but an abstraction from the intimate, embedded, and practical knowledge of things and people that we already have.

Third, we are finite. Our knowledge is always based on a heritage we did not create and cast forward upon a future we cannot completely control or anticipate.[75] My favorite analogy for this is the common law, which tries to figure out how to treat the "case of first impression" by analogical reference to prior categories, holdings, and facts, and in deciding the new case, alters the reach and nuance of the old "rules" by adding to the analogical portfolio for the future. Language, too, works this way, giving voice to the new by reference to the old: cell phone, facsimile, Internet, Web site, Aqualung, and so on.

How do these foundational considerations play out in the context of ethical theory? Kant would resist any move that sets up the emotions as a contingent basis for morality, but Heidegger does not make the move here that Hume made (and Kant criticized). It is not our natural sympathy that makes us moral (and therefore the absence of which, through no fault of our own, that can make us blameless). Instead, Heidegger's insight is that the basis of human thought is not abstract reasoning but experience, connectedness, in-touch-ness, and the ability to perceive the world and each other. This being-with is prior to any particular emotional experience of sympathy, for example, so being-with is not just a matter of empirical contingency of whether we happen to be sympathetic or not. Instead, being-with is the core of what being human is, the basis for thinking as well as feeling, and this suggests a different starting place for ethics.

We from the first find ourselves affected by each other. And we find that we are finite, limited, and at risk. Indeed, we could not be affected (passively attentive) unless we were also finite. We are affected by and experience others as feeling, reacting, and, yes, reasoning beings. We read each others' faces, body language, eyes, words, silences, and bearing. From our earliest moments, we speak with eyes, hands, feet. A mother can understand her preverbal child as a reasoning, expressive being, even though the child lacks the ability to formulate words (or rules). We can be deceived, of course, but only because we are already attentive and connected to others who are constantly throwing us signals and meaningful gestures and words. One cannot be deceived without already conceiving, without having several meanings to untangle, several potential interpretations to unpack. The problem of being deceived by others, then, is not that we can never know the "thing in itself" that lurks in the hearts of men but that we know altogether too much about what lurks there. For Heidegger, knowing another as *mitdasein* (literally, "being there with") is simply not a problem, for we *are* Dasein—the kind of beings that share a common world and are always already with others.[76]

Because the construction of human understanding as logic, reason, or science is an abstraction made possible by the concrete ways in which we "read" each other foundationally, reason is not the glue that binds reasonable beings together as equals-in-reason to achieve a "kingdom of ends." Instead, community and our knowledge of each other come before any attempt to describe that community in scientific terms or state the contractual terms of that engagement in a rule form amenable to logical manipulation. We recognize each other as "fellow" Dasein from the outset, not through the mediation of reason's requirement of consistency. We already know how to treat each other—how to be kind or cruel, how to hurt or help, how to provoke a smile or frown. Hence, ethical obligations are not imposed through reason but precede reason. (Even Kant acknowledges this when he notes that one need not be a philosopher to be moral, but he concedes that practical wisdom precedes ethical theory.[77]) We are already tied to each other, bound to a community. Our very being, who we are, is constituted by those ties and bonds. To be sure, we can resist or break those bonds (and thereby to support some extent resist and break ourselves), but we do not need reason as the glue to connect us to each other.[78] The mutual connection is what is already there.

From this standpoint, the grounding "categorical imperatives" shift. Instead of being responsible "to the conception of laws" or to "reason," we are responsive to and for persons. Our ties, literally "obligations," are personal and particular, not originally, at least, "universal." My duty is *to* someone and my responsibility is *for* someone and only abstractly and derivatively to reason or the Universal Law. To restate the categorical imperative in its first mode from this new foundation: "Honor your responsibilities to and for others, for they make you who you are."

Equality, too, changes. It is no longer rational formal equality, treating like alike,[79] where the relevant features of likeness must be abstracted from the individual situation and totted up in a balance sheet. Each case is unique and can only be analogous, but not identical, to another. Connection is the foundation, not logical consistency. Exclusion or division is the self-negating thought here, for as I said earlier, we resist or break our bonds to others only by breaking ourselves. The second statement of the categorical imperative from this new foundation is: "To be is to belong."

The third restatement of the categorical imperative is "work through the future together on the basis of the past." To form laws together as finite creatures is not to legislate reasonable universal rules but to live law out in context, over time, based on preexisting mutual understanding and preexisting connection. Government is not founded on an imposition of abstract statements of reason on the world (though we can derivatively, based on experience, make such statements) but is founded on a working out of new connections with others in practice, on the ground, based on where and how we are and have been. Democracy itself becomes less identified with the positive legislation in the statute books than the law as it gets enforced (or not enforced), worked with (or worked around), and generally fleshed out in practice.[80] For example, we all know that laws can be dead letters, having no effect if they are too alien to the practices, and may develop their influence only incrementally.[81]

But, you may object, all of this sounds "communitarian," not "liberal." It sounds like the Borg,[82] or the totalitarian elision of "is" with "ought," not the U.S. Constitution. Markel seems right, you say, that those who wish for equal liberty under law will not find this alternative foundation sound or appealing.

But the choice here is not between liberalism and communitarianism. The thought is more foundational than that. The "being-with" that Heidegger speaks of is prepolitical. Even liberalism as we live it out is a kind of being-with; indeed, the kind of being-with that we practice for the most part in this country's institutions. Liberalism is a form of being-with that sees part of our obligation to each other as allowing practices of deliberation and debate and reason to take a central place in our responsibilities to and for each other. This deliberation *in practice* itself has highly contextual features that are not immediately explicable on the basis of an abstract rule or justification (in deliberation and debate, I may insult the president on the basis of his academic performance, but I may not insult my students on the basis of their academic performance). We also have a *practice together* of leaving each other alone in appropriate ways and times and with elaborate and embedded contextual nuances (some of you must let me bathe alone, but you need not let me do my grocery shopping alone). And part of our practice of being together suggests that you must treat me equally in certain ways and at certain times and with certain exceptions and nuances (you may not pay me less at work because of my gender, but you need not have me over to dinner the same number of times as others you know).[83]

The key implications of this new foundation that I will emphasize later are: (1) our root, richest, and most reliable form of understanding of each other and the world is through concrete practical experience (not abstract logical analysis or science); (2) as finite beings, we neither start from scratch nor reach an "end" but must always be working out law from the past and to the future in practices, incompletely articulated, and our knowledge and "power" to create our polity are neither absolute nor eternal; (3) both personally and politically, we are constituted and enabled in a host of possibilities by the personal bonds and cultural practices we start from.

The Case for the Merciful State

So how does this abstract discussion of foundations bear on clemency?

First, it excludes the kind of argument that Markel tries to make, based on formal principles of responsibility, equality, and democracy. The potential incompatibility with our *actual practices* of responsibility, equality, and democracy must be examined, of course, but it is not enough of an objection to say that clemency is contrary to abstract reason, treats like cases unlike, fails to treat others as reasonable autonomous agents, or undermines democracy because it invites unreasonable exceptions to law. In other words, arguments based on the formal *irrationality* of clemency do not touch its *foundation* because the foundation of human association (democratic or despotic) is not reason (especially not reason as logical consistency) but being-with.

So, to restate the problem, we must ask whether our practices of clemency are incompatible with our *practices* of holding ourselves responsible for and to each other, our *practices* of treating each other equally in the ways we do within the context of the criminal law, and our *practices* of aspiring to self-government in the context of our actual institutions (which are not purely democratic even in design but "mushed republican" and even, in some moments, authoritarian). Moreover, even if clemency is incompatible with some of our practices, we may still ask whether clemency can nonetheless be appropriate in light of other practices or strands of our historically extended and interwoven traditions.[84]

As pardon plays out, however, as Christopher Dole pointed out in his insightful commentary to this paper, we must acknowledge that the "hole in the law" where pardoning and mercy and forgiveness live is also where violence and repression exist. In the end, there is no guarantee that pardoning will always be done right; the power to go outside the law is murky and provisional and easily can be abused. Whether we are better off with a procrustean lawfulness inside the rules than with a malleable pardoning process outside the rules is a question that cannot be decided by philosophical argument. I can demonstrate, contra Markel, that pardons are not *necessarily* unjust or undemocratic, but I cannot demonstrate they are always *necessarily* just or appropriate. Ethical judgment, case to case, is still possible, but it is always particular and provisional and unlawful.

With this caveat, I would still urge pardon is less incompatible with our existing practices than some opponents of mercy suggest. Moreover, when we look more closely, we see that each moment or aspect of pardoning sketched earlier provides a glimpse past "reason as the ground" to the deeper ground of "being-with."

Pardons as Equity

Pardon as equity is thought to be an easy case, for it is merely better justice. But even this easy case conceals a troubling paradox. Surely innocence (the easiest case for equity pardons) is a good reason for a pardon. The difficulty is that any statement of reasons (or specification of the degree of certainty of innocence that is required to pardon) ossifies into rules and procedures that will be applied "consistently" and, therefore, in some case or other, unjustly (resulting in the punishment of the innocent). We will then need a superpardon as equity to correct the injustice of the rule-based pardon as equity. The only way to achieve the pardon as equity is to keep it ruleless and thereby lawless—making justice itself depend on the absence of legal rules.[85]

That justice cannot be done within law points out the limits of reason itself. Justice is inherently particular and contextual, not merely the consistent application of rules. In Kant's words, reason expresses a "*concrete* universal," not a generality. But for finite humans, no concrete universal is thinkable (only a God could know everything in all its particularity across all time), but we humans must slog through the muddy mess of individual cases with only incomplete rules as our temporary guides. When we do see what justice requires shining forth in the individual case, our preexisting rules will not necessarily cover the situation. We have a choice, in those circumstances, of either doing a lawful injustice or violating the law.

This illustrates why reason, in the sense of a set of logically consistent (and equally applied) rules, cannot be foundational for humans. We cannot achieve justice through rules, as they are static and general and incomplete, for we (the finite creatures who make them) are learning, growing, innovating, extemporizing, improvising, changing, and getting new glimpses of the world and each other all the time. Our ability to get these glimpses, our attunement, our attentiveness, our immersion in the world and in relationships with others, is deeper and more foundational than reason (at least as it is possible for humans to reason). Pardon as equity brings this truth to light.

From this perspective, the kinds of equity most often done in pardoning reflect our finitude and the temporality of law. Equity to redress procedural bar rules (and the procedural bar rules themselves) reflects the finitude of human process; we cannot keep relitigating infinitely even though we never have perfect and complete information. Equity to acknowledge unique mitigating factors reflects the fact that law itself is finite and its general terms, formulated in the past, cannot encompass all the changing possibilities in the world, especially when those mitigating factors may present themselves after sentencing is complete. Equity to acknowledge broader, nonlegal mitigating factors, such as domestic violence or mental illness, reflects the fact that enacted law cannot always keep up with our evolving sense of justice. Equity to acknowledge postconviction amendment reflects the fact that a conviction and sentence take an accounting at a single point in time and cannot predict or assess the future or what the offender may become. The demands of equity can never be satisfied once and for all because life, law, and knowledge of the world are always moving targets.

Pardon as equity reflects the necessary disjunction between law and justice, though it has little to do with forgiveness. It is relatively uncontroversial only because familiar concerns of innocence and extent of guilt are brought to bear on the particular case. But were we to understand this form of pardon as simply judgment itself, it might be more unsettling, for it reveals the deep indeterminacy and temporality of justice.

Pardon as Peace and Polity Making

> But the principal argument for reposing the power of pardoning in [the case of treason] in the Chief Magistrate is this: in seasons of insurrection or rebellion, there are often critical moments when a well-timed offer of pardon to the insurgents or rebels may restore the tranquillity of the commonwealth; and which, if suffered to pass unimproved, it may never be possible afterwards to recall.
>
> —Hamilton, *The Federalist* (No. 74)[86]

In the U.S. Constitution, the pardon power is granted in the same sentence as the war power. As Hamilton explains, this is no coincidence. The power to wage war must have as its necessary analog the power to make peace. Except in the case of unconditional surrender, peace requires compromise, as the law of one side cannot be imposed on the other, and the laws of war no longer apply. The peacemaking, then, must stand outside the law, and pardon provides that extralegal immunity. The pardon's role here creates a new polity, includes outlaws as in-laws, and expands the borders of legal jurisdiction through legal immunity.

As Adam Sitze's insightful account of Kant's discussion of the problem points out, however, the peace "pardon" here may be a strategic forgetfulness rather than a "grace," for a grace (or "gift") would seem to presuppose an assessment of guilt and a right to judge and punish. Moreover, Kant's "day of atonement," in institutionalizing a ceremonial forgiveness for war itself (and more generally, for the inevitable failure of humans to achieve the selflessness demanded by the categorical imperative), risks turning an unconditional, incorporeal gift into a paid-for exchange. In Sitze's perceptive gaze, Kant here signals the state's need for an unconditioned, violent, corrupted onto-theological sovereignty to serve as the necessary tool of law, bridging the gap between law and its application, law and its realization, law and the human.

Pardon as peacemaking thus allows us to glimpse a difficulty in the Kantian reason-as-foundation view. Derrida and Condorcet point out the now-familiar paradox that before a polity can be self-governing, the polity that will be voting must be specified in advance on a nondemocratic basis. This aspect of the pardon power recalls us to the foundational fact that the "being-with" must precede Kantian notions of "autonomy," for no self-government is possible without first constituting a "self." The "individual" subject of liberalism is constituted by a particular cultural context and history, already imbedded in a set of relations and practices that the "individual" has not "chosen."[87] Likewise, conquest, chance, immigration, geographic proximity, and sheer accident will bring people to live with each other and, over time, constitute a people (or set of warring peoples) that govern themselves. But the people can't choose the people. To this extent, the executive pardon's lawless character in the realm of creating or re-creating a polity through the peacemaking power can be no objection, for there is no legal or reasonable alternative.

But stopping here, as Sitze points out, we remain with a sovereign power ungoverned by any ethics, a new god on earth of totalitarianism, unless there is a possibility for right action outside law. Only through an account of a more primary being-with can such a nonlaw be found that could unify the warring positive laws of the treating states. Sitze locates such a possibility in Plato's understanding of *sungnômon*, or "the multiplication of a judgment that by definition exceeds law's limits . . . a constitutively shared or divided judgment" not amenable to the rationality of mathematical (or legal) principles. But preceding even this is the possibility of judging together at all—a possibility that can be grasped only through some thought that being-with (judging with?), and not reason, is the glue that grounds community.

Pardon as Personal Allegiance

Pardon as personal allegiance is a much harder case to make within the mainstream liberal traditions. We don't like the hierarchy it presumes; we don't like the mutual obligation it entails; we don't like the personal loyalty it presupposes. It is indeed a kind of understanding of the pardon that has faded away in most contemporary rhetoric of the institution, at least outside the context of the military. Unlike the traditional lord and vassal feudal relationship, the executive (as governor of a state or as president of the United States) seems too distant a figure to have a personal relationship of trust and future risk with and from the forgiven citizen.

But the allegiance pardon may make more sense at the more intimate levels of institutional discretion. The military has a practice of clemency that operates between commanding officer and soldier, where trust, loyalty, and mutual risk are critical and are put to the keenest tests. Outside the military, many contemporary reforms have aimed to reestablish personal loyalty to authorities in various areas of law enforcement: community policing, drug court, community or victim-offender mediation, intensive probation, or trial by (very) local juries. In all of these innovative approaches to law enforcement and practice, the emphasis is on trying to make personal connections among the police, judges, and juries, and the offenders so that the offender is responsible to the authority and the authority is responsive to the offender. David Tait has suggested that the pardon power itself should be decentralized, residing in local decision making (as it already does, unofficially at least).[88]

In these contexts, mercy is personal—part of the allegiance owed to and the protection given by an authority. But the authority is not immune from the wrong[89]; on the contrary, the authority's power is reduced by the past wrong, and the authority is both personally and in position at risk from the future conduct of the wrongdoer. Mercy here is a gift, generates gratitude, reinforces the relationship of allegiance, and takes on the risk of future dealings with the offender. Remorse on the part of the wrongdoer is in part the grief of disloyalty to the authority and demonstrates the desire to retain the bonds of allegiance. Future wrong is not only a violation of a law but, more saliently, a personal breach of trust.[90]

Repentance has always had this personal and highly emotional character, often triggered by a confrontation with another person, experienced as a bitterly painful vulnerability, and accompanied by tears. Once one takes being-with as foundation and thinks of moral knowledge as irreducibly practical, this phenomenon makes perfect sense: Our comprehension of the moral dimensions of experience arises from the emotional and imbedded ways in which we know best.

Allegiance Pardons and Responsibility To and For. Do allegiance pardons run contrary to our practices of holding each other responsible for our actions? On the contrary, we might see a place for clemency as creating or reinforcing bonds of loyalty and trust, responsibility *to* and responsibility *for* others.[91] Moreover, such person-to-person bonds are more tangible and less abstract than respect for law or laws can be. They make the obligations real to those who have them and place them in a context in which we humans are able to understand them best: the concrete and particular. When the alternative is housing offenders for a period of years in large, impersonal, institutions as an abstract "equivalent" to their crime and without any necessary contact with the victim or any other person to whom duties are owed, clemency of this kind does not seem out of balance with concern for instilling or reinforcing bonds of personal responsibility.

Consider this thank-you letter from an offender whose death sentence was commuted: "[T]his is my first opportunity for personally expressing appreciation for your act of commutation of the sentence of death given to me. Actually, I feel this expression will continue the rest of my life, as I continue to feel an obligation to show justification of your act of clemency. . . . For my part, I will want the rest of my life to at least be some proof of an amount of truth in these thoughts. It will be my hope that I will not only continue to justify your act of commutation, sir, but also give by my example some proof of the value of even a human life which was condemned."[92]

Clemency as allegiance allows remorse to play a key role because remorseful offenders understand themselves as having these concrete obligations and feel concrete pain at failing to honor them. To allow the remorseful offender to pledge his or her future allegiance and right action to another real person who can offer clemency is to reestablish the bonds of obligation that the crime broke. Abstract calls for equal justice under law or punishment as retribution save no place for remorse,[93] yet remorse seems to retain an important place in our practices, especially in the more intimate contexts of face-to-face judging considered earlier.

Derrida would object here that a remorse pardon seems earned in a way that belies its graciousness and seems to bring it closer to justice rather than forgiveness. But if it is earned, it is in a very unusual way, for remorse does not try to pay the debt incurred by the crime in any of the traditional coin of suffering or punishment. Nonetheless, remorse calls for forgiveness in a way that is not truly unconditional because forgiveness is remorse's only balm.

Derrida is right that allegiance-based pardons are not unconditional. But the characterization of pardon or forgiveness as unconditional may itself be a product of buying into a universalized understanding of the world instead of a conditioned and temporal understanding of humans as finite. For humans, nothing is unconditional—even power. It is possible that there can be a conditioned pardon that resists articulation or rule and is still not deserved.

Allegiance Pardons and Equality as Nonexclusion. Do allegiance pardons treat like cases differently? If one rapist gets ten years in prison and the next is pardoned, is not the first excluded and treated wrongly? We may presume so if that is all we know about the cases. But what if we also know that the first rapist is unremorseful, boasts of his deed, and taunts his victim, whereas the second is tearful and remorseful, voluntarily puts himself into the hands of a community mediation panel of former rape victims and their families, and after long, agonizing personal mediation, his victim accepts his word and accepts (along with other potential victim local community members) the risk that he will, despite his assurances, reoffend? Are the two still "equal"? Is the first "excluded" because he was not granted clemency too? Are we in a better place to judge the "sincerity" of the second's remorse than those who have been face to face with him?

The problem with the argument from equality is that the interaction that results in clemency may itself make the case "unequal." If our practical knowledge is irreducibly particular, personal confrontation yields knowledge that cannot be completely reduced to factors or rules. And new responsibilities to and for another may be forged even in the process of determining punishment. In a way analogous to the Heisenberg principle, the interaction itself may change the basis for measurement.

It may be, however, that there ought to be "equality of opportunity" for such a person-to-person chance at clemency; the military clemency process, for example, requires that each offender be given an opportunity to petition for clemency (though not face to face), counsel is provided, and the authority must respond.[94] Again, as a matter of procedural practicality, this would require local clemency rather than clemency by the highest executive.

It may also be argued here that not all offenders have the personality or legal representation to establish rapport with authority figures and that clemency rewards those who are charming, charismatic, articulate, likable, white, well educated, or well represented. (This may be especially troubling considering that "glibness and superficial charm" may be traits of the worst-feared psychopaths.[95]) But if such inequalities are objectionable, they are objectionable at every level of the criminal process, not just at the highest levels of clemency, from the initial interactions with neighbors (who may or may not call police), to police (who may or may not arrest), to prosecutor (who may or may not prosecute), to judge (who may or may not grant bail), to jury (who may or may not find one credible). We cannot escape the limits of our own humanity. Face-to-face confrontation is the basis for our judgments of each other. We can be wrong, but we cannot get the same understanding of the case in any other way.

The importance of face-to-face confrontation is obvious in the job application process. We rarely feel comfortable acting on a paper record without an interview or, conversely, taking a job from someone we've never met. The only remedy to discrimination and manipulation in the criminal context is the same as in the job context. It rests first on trying to find wise and experienced decision makers, aware of their potential prejudices and alert to racism, sexism, and bias. It includes some provision for information about defendants from others who know them well and has a process for checking the facts.[96]

The problem with our face-to-face knowledge, of course, is that it does not seem to extend to those who are not local. How can international justice and compassion happen if we are tied to local and insular knowledge? How can we avoid the blind patriotism of the familiar and comfortable and the xenophobia it brings if not through the universal reason of international law? Again, one can assert the primacy of reason, as Kant tried to do in his discourses on international relations. We can use reason, itself an abstraction, to bridge this gap. But the results are often disappointing because the abstract claims of equality do not engage us or move us, and acontextual conferral of abstract rights as though they were "universal"

is often a failure (as with, to take but one example, the well-intentioned but di-
sastrous nineteenth-century Allotment Acts conferring property rights on Native
Americans).[97]

Allegiance Pardons and Democracy. Does the allegiance pardon of a criminal undermine the democratic basis of the criminal law violated? Must democracy defend
itself from usurpation here?

Three related points must answer these questions. First, criminal laws, however
broadly or narrowly drafted, are nonetheless general statements of law requiring
application to individual cases. Determining what is or is not "a crime of violence"
or a "deadly weapon" or an "act of force" or a "misrepresentation" is not a matter
of plunking down the plain words of a statute on the world. Moreover, under can-
ons of judicial interpretation, mens rea and traditional justifications and excuses
(self-defense, necessity, duress, etc.) are assumed to be applicable, even when not
stated in the statute itself. De minimis violations may be disregarded. So, even a
straight application of the democratically enacted law is not an automatic application or one that looks only at the plain words of the statute. Judgment and wisdom
are necessary in making these calls, for there are no rules for the application of
rules. This is another version of the hole in the law or the Platonic "miscount"
within law itself that creates the breach between law and its actualization.

Second, as the general rule must be applied to the individual case, there is no
democratic right or expectation that any individual case must or will be pros-
ecuted. As legislative judgments multiply, the relative importance of the particular
criminal statute vis-à-vis other criminal statutes must be determined by police and
government prosecutors, not legislators. A statute that results from a momentary
legislative overreaction to a particular case may be ignored by law enforcement or
flouted so often in practice that it ceases to be enforced at all (prohibition, sodomy,
jaywalking). Law that sticks is the result of a combination of legislative pedigree,
official priority, and broad political acceptance. Democracy, then, is not just what
the legislature says but what we commit ourselves to as a whole and over time.
Voting is just one piece of democracy, understood as it is within our practice of it
rather than in the abstract.

Third, each case is unique and only comparable to another analogically. Sentencing is not a matter of totting up commensurable features, ranking them, and
then picking out the "equal" cases for equal punishment. It is hard to imagine
a metric along which mental illness, family responsibilities, remorse, and rotten

childhood, for example, could be compared as relative mitigating factors, let alone the individual constellations of salient features in any batch of real cases. These features of the case are radically incommensurable. Much of sentencing involves a much more intuitive judgment that this is a "compelling" case or that punishment is just the right thing to do, a judgment that cannot be adequately specified by a statute, however democratically enacted. If judgment is practical down to the ground, then we cannot reduce it to rule-based decision making without losing justice in the process. As Meir Dan-Cohen puts it so well: "When we are in the grip of moral truth, we are moved by its intrinsic value, rather than by its comparative advantage over other acceptable alternatives."[98]

Hence, whether an act of clemency is undemocratic will depend not on its failure to apply the law as enacted (for that happens all the time) but on its failure to accord with the values and commitments of the people over time. Recognizing remorse in the context of personal allegiance as a basis for clemency accords well with at least some of our national commitments, as the contexts mentioned earlier (military law, probation, etc.) demonstrate. Local knowledge and local decision making by one who is responsible for and at risk from the offender, careful attention to making the clemency opportunity open to all, attention to the risk of historical stereotypes and prejudice, and care in checking the facts will go a long way to making this kind of clemency stick as compatible with democratic practice.[99]

Clemency as Compassion

Finally, and hardest of all to accept, is clemency as compassion.[100] Standard jury instructions, for example, direct jurors to set aside sympathy or compassion.[101] We may have lost the sense of the medieval morality play that tears offer an experience of grace and revelation of higher truth. Yet, if one takes being-in and being-with as foundational, such a view is not nonsense. Contemporary discussion on the place of emotion in thought recognizes that our emotional tenor does indeed play a role in making certain aspects of our situation salient or even apparent in calming, focusing, or directing our thinking and in helping us make sense of what we experience.

Even in many of our actual legal practices (as opposed to our jury instructions), we insist on live testimony by witnesses in our confrontation clause, the drama of an emotionally charged trial, and stress the importance of demeanor, eye contact, body language and presence in evaluating evidence.[102] We defer to the trial court and the jury because they heard the testimony. We allow capital defendants the right to address the jury in person at the sentencing hearing without being subject to cross-examination. We do so because these kinds of person-to-person interactions cannot necessarily be completely narrated in written facts or reasons, yet they yield knowledge that is much more familiar and easier for us to interpret than abstruse statutes, complex case law, or philosophical moral discussions. Again, our primary, foundational experience of the world derives meaning from the concrete and personal: Effortlessly and without even noticing it, we distinguish the sigh of despair from the sigh of impatience from the sigh of relief. No one who has seen a trial and then read the appellate report of it could argue that the two experiences give identical kinds of knowledge, even if all the relevant facts have been included. The personal, and emotionally charged, meeting between judge and offender may yield "reasons that reason cannot tell."

The emotion of compassion may be particularly appropriate for gaining insight into the crime or character of one who is to be judged. It is an emotion that disposes one to see similarities where they may not be obvious, potentially overcoming rather than reinforcing prejudices and prejudgments. It is an emotion that concentrates one on the particular and individual, calling one's attention to detail, making the ordinary salient in its little uniquenesses. It is an emotion that humbles, closing the gap in status that may exist between judge and defendant and moving the judge away from a tendency to be inattentive, dismissive, intolerant, skeptical, lazy, or impatient (all of which are occupational hazards).[103] Compassion is an equalizer, combating the hierarchy that may exist between offenders, between victim and offender, and between judge and offender.

So it is at least possible that an interaction between a defendant and a clemency giver can and should be affected by compassion, that compassion may be triggered by, and may in turn reveal, aspects of a defendant's crime or situation that matter yet cannot be fully expressed by an abstractly stated principle or reason (and indeed, may sound inadequate when so stated, e.g., because he is old or because she is ill). The result may be a judgment that does not necessarily rest on "bias" or "caprice" but on a better understanding of the crime or defendant—one that cannot be articulated in rule form.

Compassion Pardons and Responsibility. Does compassion destroy or compromise responsibility? Compassion by a judge or decision maker may convince an offender that the "system" is not "out to get him" and that officials are not impersonal and unreachable but human and even humane. Compassion may show the offender that the judge does sympathize with his or her plight and still sees the offender as a member of the human circle rather than as a monster, outlaw, scumbag, or jerk, defined entirely by the crime. Compassion may stir an answering emotion in the offender himself, making tangible to him again the bond with others that he may have rebelled against and ultimately leading him to take responsibility for his actions rather than to deny them.

Most readers will be skeptical at this point; hardened criminals do not experience these namby-pamby, touchy-feely emotions—they are "tough customers," gaming the system, who trust no one and say anything they think you want to hear. Yet ironically, we "officially" acknowledge the power of compassion only in the context of interrogation, where it is falsely simulated as a ploy to gain a confession. It is textbook interrogation technique for the interrogator to feign a demonstration of compassion that, often enough, leads offenders to trust and stirs them to confession and even to expressions of remorse.[104] A skilled interrogator can tell when the offender is ready to "give it up." Offenders sigh, they crumple, they break, spill their guts, and often even cry. Interrogation manuals reveal the truth that offenders are anxious to find a friend, yet we use this information only strategically. We exploit an offender's proffer of trust to uncover information. But what would happen if that personal engagement and compassion were genuine instead of a ploy? Perhaps it would then reestablish responsible relationships. Again to quote a former death row inmate: "You relive your crime many times, or approach near to it in your thoughts and then back away from it in horror, appalled by it. You would turn backward. You would show your remorse—as condemned men sometimes do, one to another—the remorse you hide with your fear in your heart and mind you would show to the one with the power and the given promise to understand and not condemn you, to the one you cannot find, unless perhaps you are a person who finds him in God."[105]

Compassion Pardons and Equality.   Does compassion compromise equal treatment? Compassion draws attention to each case as unique, defeating the notion that any case is essentially like another. Compassion, however, includes the offender as a fellow human who belongs and is not excluded by his or her crime. If we rethink equality as belonging rather than as equal treatment, compassion promotes the recognition of both offender and victim as "insiders."

But what if the authority pardons out of love or friendship? Isn't it a conflict of interest to pardon someone one loves—a spouse, child, sibling, friend? And to extend the thought, can one pardon oneself?

There is something of personal love in all compassion pardons, reflecting the underlying social bond that compassion brings to the fore. But even though the authority is personally affected by the case and feels compassion, the authority (whether president or victim) must pardon on behalf of others who cannot be there to experience and judge for themselves. The claim must be that others *could* have experienced this case with compassion based on the person and the record. As with other times when our personal obligations conflict with our broader social obligations, the authority should recuse herself in judging or pardoning loved ones, for we allow her this repose to spare her from having to make tragic choices between the obligations of family and those of society.

Compassion Pardons and Democracy. Are compassion pardons undemocratic? Again, when democracy is understood as the commitments of the polity over time, it is no longer easy to argue that failure to apply the law in any particular case is ipso facto undemocratic. Compassionate clemency is only antidemocratic if the polity, over time, refuses to honor it as a value. Daniel T. Kobil[106] and James Q. Whitman[107] have argued that we live in "harsh" and "unforgiving times," but there are signs that compassion is not entirely out of the picture. Juries are more reluctant to give the death penalty; legislatures are giving attention to initiatives lowering sentences or abolishing the death penalty; and even conservative leaders are speaking out in favor of rehabilitative goals.[108] On the other hand, we are becoming much harsher in matters of immigration, asylum, and international crime. The war on drugs has given way to the war on terrorism, and in matters of international relations, we are less compassionate than we have been in my lifetime.

Moreover, in such times of suspicion and culture wars, it seems very ill-timed for me to be arguing that "local knowledge" as a basis of ethical action will yield compassion rather than more xenophobic mistrust and violence. I cannot disagree; the hole in the law yields both. Yet the way in which we daily sweep international law away as well suggests that recourse to general principles and law will not curb violence either. For example, it is at least arguable that the more vivid and particular photos of abuses at Abu Ghraib were more effective in changing interrogation and detention policies (and perhaps even in swaying the decisions of the Supreme Court) than the Geneva Conventions. The concrete effects of our fears and policies brought "in our face" can still bring us to see justice in a particular case where it is otherwise hidden in general "principles." Compassion is still possible, and compassion can even bring the outsider inside.

There is another practical barrier to the political will to be compassionate. Because compassion is based in a personal interaction, the experience cannot be easily shared or communicated to the polity. How does a decision maker allow us to judge-with, to share the experience, to feel the compassion, to be convinced that the offender is remorseful?[109] Despite reality TV, we cannot get that close. In fact, art may bring us closer than C-SPAN or Court TV can. The novelist, playwright, or movie producer can sometimes make characters real for us, make us feel compassion for them, even "convince" us of remorse.[110] However, the recourse to narrative also presents the danger that a real case will seem less real than a novelized one—we will expect the wrong cues, fail to be moved by a reality that seems thinner or more conflicted than fiction.[111] This is the challenge for the legal advocate, and whether and how judges, governors, or other pardoners can communicate the experience of compassion to a democratic constituency are open and difficult questions.[112]

Good Pardons, Bad Pardons

Assuming one could agree that some equity, allegiance, or compassion pardons are appropriate, have we justified all pardons? Have we cut away all ethical grounds for criticizing any exercise of the pardon power? Is the executive's pardoning decision one to which we must meekly submit no matter how corrupt?

Even if there is no legal recourse, moral discourse is still open. As with the Nixon pardon or the Marc Rich pardon or the pardons of white lynchers, we can say those pardons were wrong. But without law, the kind of moral discourse we have must be concrete and on the ground. Moral critique of pardons must proceed case by case.

Corruption. The pardon must be a personal act of grace exercised by a person who speaks for all who have been wronged. When an executive (or victim) is acting for personal gain,[113] he or she is not speaking for all. The easiest case of this kind is selling pardons, and as the impeachment of Oklahoma Governor J. C. Walton demonstrates, there is legal as well as moral recourse here.

But there are other kinds of personal gain. Pardoning friends or relatives seems an inappropriate personal gain, but what about not pardoning personal rivals or enemies? And how personal must it be? If an African American president were to refuse to pardon a former KKK member, would that be inappropriate? What about pardoning (or not pardoning) for political advantage? What about pardoning (or not) for personal emotional satisfaction?

Again, we cannot take the easy route of arguing that no personal considerations should ever affect a pardon. Yes, a pardon can proceed out of personal weakness and inability to make hard decisions. But a pardon grounded in a personal contact with an offender that generates compassion may also be morally acceptable as a genuine experience of connection and renewal that generates responsibility to and for. There will be hard cases as well as easy cases, and all must be judged by analogy, on the ground.

Dehumanizing Hate. Pardoning or failing to pardon out of dehumanizing hate[114] violates the foundation of being-with because it is a rejection of the bond of humanity with another. The executive, in dehumanizing either victim or offender (pardoning the white lyncher because his victim was "only" a black or refusing to pardon the black rapist because he's a "monster"), denies either the victim or the offender inclusion in the human world. But spelling out what counts as dehumanizing hate is not simple.

Justice Stevens, dissenting in *Ohio Adult Parole Authority v. Woodard,*[115] argued that "no one would contend that a governor could ignore the commands of the Equal Protection Clause and use race, religion, or political affiliation as a standard for granting or denying clemency." But Stevens's attempt to articulate what is at stake here cannot be read as requiring simple equal treatment. If one takes the view that the Equal Protection Clause requires the government to treat us "equally," then denying all petitions or flipping a coin to determine clemency would be sufficient. This does not, played out, accord with the grounding thought that government ought to respect its people and treat them with dignity.[116] In our traditions and practices, treating someone with dignity is not a simple rule but depends on context and nuance. It seems that a governor could decide not to pardon someone because the offender holds fast to, for example, anti-Semitic views, despite the fact that these views may be characterized as "political." On the other hand, it seems that a governor could take into account the (sincere and abiding) religious conversion of an offender in deciding to pardon her, despite the fact that the pardon depended on the defendant's "religious" views.[117]

Moral Luck. Justice O'Connor suggests, in *Ohio Adult Parole Authority v. Woodard,* that a governor could not just flip a coin to pardon or arbitrarily deny prisoners access to the pardon process.[118] Such "arbitrariness," she believes, would violate due process.[119]

Darrell Mease was pardoned just because he happened to be scheduled for execution on the same day the pope came to town. Is pardoning him like flipping a coin? Kevin Byrd was pardoned only because evidence in his case happened not to have been destroyed as it was supposed to have been. Is that like flipping a coin? Offenders who committed murders the day before their state legislature reinstated the death penalty will not be executed; those who committed their crimes the day after might be. Is that like flipping a coin? Offenders who commit murder on one side of the Mississippi River may be executed, whereas those on the other side of the river will not be. Is that like flipping a coin?

Moral luck pervades the system; again, it is part of being finite and in time. When do we account it arbitrary and when do we not? Again, the question is not tidy or subject to neat conceptual resolution.

Why does flipping a coin strike us as an inappropriate basis for a pardon? I would argue that it is not because it is arbitrary or random but because it is disrespectful. To make a decision with that kind of impact on an offender in such a way, using a form of decision making usually reserved for the trivial or for games, signals (in the context of our culture) that the offender's case doesn't matter. (On the other hand, one could imagine a different cultural meaning for flipping a coin that would change that meaning—if we, for example, believed that a divine power would intervene in the coin flip to tell us what justice required.)

I would argue that a similar inference of disrespect could be drawn from an executive's refusal to look at or consider any pardon applications. Even if an executive must, for extrinsic reasons (that we agree are appropriate), deny a pardon, the executive should face the case and give the offender the dignity of a personal response. For example, in Herman Melville's tale of Billy Budd, in which law (and the expedience of keeping order during wartime) wins out over mercy (and even over justice), Captain Vere explains himself to Billy before the end, privately and personally, and then treats Billy's execution with every dignity befitting an honorable soldier's funeral. Likewise, when Lincoln hears of the 303 death verdicts in the case of the Native American uprising in Minnesota, he calls for the transcripts and records because he takes seriously his pardon power and the personal responsibility it gives him for the fate of each citizen.[120] Governor Pat Brown likewise reports that on taking office, his initial inclination was not to look at the file of his first death penalty case, after being assured by aides there was nothing in it. But this decision troubled him. The next day, he called for the file and after reviewing it, ended up commuting the death sentence.

We respect leaders who face up to and take personal responsibility for these wrenching and tragic choices. This is the personal element again that I stress is so important to the conception and exercise of the pardon power: the responsibility for and to others, even when one refuses to pardon. A refusal to reach the merits at all is disrespectful.[121]

Clearly, a chief executive cannot review every criminal case personally. Death penalty cases, however, are still few enough to allow for personal attention. And offenders in other cases should have recourse to some person who can be clement. Judges at sentencing used to have that power in the federal system before the sentencing guidelines and may again.[122] Military commanders have that authority and may be clement without any review or explanation of their reasons. So it can be done (and is daily done) at the local level,[123] even if not at the gubernatorial or presidential level.

By contrast with flipping a coin or never looking at the files, the pardon in Byrd's case does not seem arbitrary, even if it was only by chance that evidence could be recovered exonerating him and even if there were other innocent inmates whose evidence was destroyed and who therefore cannot obtain the same advantage. We know that luck is often what stands between guilt–innocence and conviction (whether any fingerprint or DNA is recoverable, whether the crack investigator is on vacation, whether the neighbor happened to be looking out the window, whether memories are accurate, whether the suspect happened to be at the wrong place at the wrong time). But this sort of moral luck (good or bad) is not considered arbitrary or a denial of due process; it is simply a result of the finitude of human knowledge—a finitude we have to live with, a reasonable doubt. Pardons partaking of this same luck do not seem wrong any more than the contingencies that are part of any investigation yielding necessarily incomplete knowledge make judgments wrong. We can only do the best we can.

Likewise, pardoning Mease at the pope's request does not have the meaning of disrespect or disregard for either Mease or the other prisoners on death row that flipping a coin would have. Quite the opposite: It was out of respect that Carnahan pardoned him—respect for a moral authority other than the state.[124] Whether Carnahan should have pardoned him is still an open question, but the pardon was not arbitrary or random in the sense that it treated either Mease or others as though they did not matter.

Governor Carnahan's pardon of Darrell Mease is a hard case not because it is random but because it raises the question of whether a state can ever recognize a higher authority. Perhaps the legal system would be better if such pardons were never allowed. We certainly could not allow the pope to determine sentence in every case. Nor was there any reason to think that the pope chose Mease's case for any intrinsic reason (the pope never met Mease), so there is no argument here that there was a face-to-face interaction that changed the nature of the case. Yet, on the other hand, Carnahan's pardon is symbolic of a moment that opens the possibility of some authority beyond the authority of the state and law. Can the state recognize the possibility of grace or miracle? Or is that possibility categorically foreclosed so that grace must necessarily be understood as luck? The Mease pardon is, in my view, a hard case for these reasons. One could certainly say that such a pardon is wrong. But I have a hard time condemning Carnahan for being swayed. Would I think him a better governor if, when the pope looked him in the eye and asked him to be merciful, he refused? Religious or not, I can admire the gesture of respect here and the possibility that a governor could be personally moved by a claim of moral authority and grace. I might prefer the human (though perhaps imperfect) Carnahan who is moved to a *Biddle*-like "absolute authority" who, unmoved, rationally calculates the public interest.

What about the luck involved in getting access to a governor or authority figure? Is this luck also to be eliminated from the system? One of my colleagues landed a plum job with the Department of Justice because she happened to run into an official on the street and was able to give him directions to the metro. Many of the key events in our lives are a matter of happenstance: who we marry, what job we get, who our friends are. When is such luck an ethical problem?

Again, the answer is much more complicated than is often suggested. There will never be absolutely equal access to the pardon process. Even if everyone is entitled to have a clemency application prepared by counsel and reviewed by an authority,[125] those who have the luck to have drawn a sympathetic trial judge or compassionate prosecutor or good public defender or merciful victim and can garner their support will be more likely to succeed, and few would claim that such a pardon process was wrong or unfair. On the other hand, when the president's brother is paid to "get access" to the pardon process, we rightly bristle. Mease's case was brought to the governor's attention by the pope. Weeping mothers seemed to move President Lincoln to careful examination of several cases. Are these, too, cases of unequal access? In my view, this is the level at which we need to have an ethical discussion—finding cases in which a pardon was clearly inappropriate and then wrestling with the cases that are closer and less clear—not eliminating mercy completely nor setting out abstract rules to tame it.

What of the Law? Where does reason and law fit in if we allow room for mercy? What if we pardoned in every case? Doesn't the exception soon swallow the rule?

Law is still the way we organize our world. We need simple rules and categories to help us make sense of our complex experience. But we have to understand them as provisional and in progress. Like the categories I describe at the beginning of this chapter, like the cases in a common law analysis, they illuminate some aspects of experience and hide others. Legal categories and doctrines focus our attention, articulate the patterns we observe, give us general guidance in decision making, and preserve our understanding. But law does not exhaust the justice in any particular case.

Allowing mercy does not swallow the law (understood, again, as provisional and incomplete) because we need the law to guide and focus us. Mercy depends on law in this way: We could not identify an act of mercy unless there was law by which to judge it as merciful. But mercy is not the opposite of law—it is not meaningless or random. It is the recognition of our limitations and a reaffirmation of our mutual connection on the basis of which we try to keep making sense of the world. If a pardon is for selfish gain, is disrespectful, or spurns the human connection, it is not appropriate. And yes, at some point, letting every criminal off would itself come to mean a disrespect for both the offender and the offended. But so would punishing everyone to the full extent of the letter of the law in every case.

When We Are Wrong. Governor Brown painfully recalls the case of Eddie Wein, whom he pardoned and later allowed to be paroled, and who, once out of prison, continued in the same pattern of sexual abuse and murder that he had begun twenty years earlier. For many, cases like this are reason enough never to permit pardons. They believe we cannot take the risk.

But we must also remember that only the released who reoffend will ever be known to us. Those who die in prison or remain incarcerated, who would not reoffend if released, don't make the news. The waste and torment of their lives are never disclosed, and the good they might have done if released is never revealed. We may choose to eliminate all mercy and therefore all risk.[126] But that would condemn us all to a merciless state.

The Merciless State

> In hell there will be nothing but law, and due process will be meticulously observed.[127]

> —Grant Gilmore, *The Ages of American Law*

Imagine a world in which all public officials operate by the book, no compassion, no quarter.[128] Tom Wolfe gives us such a glimpse in the novel *A Man in Full*,[129] as he puts his proletarian everyman, Conrad, through an excruciating nightmare of lawfulness. After saving the life of a co-worker, Conrad, "the best worker in this whole fucking place," is laid off at his job at a frozen-food facility. His wife and two children were hoping to move out of a cramped apartment and into a condo, but now that is impossible. His mother-in-law is convinced Conrad is a failure. Conrad now must drive to San Francisco for a job interview at the unemployment office. According to the rules, he must take a typing test, which he fails because his hands have become so clumsy from the grueling physical labor at the refrigeration plant. When, defeated, he returns to his car, he finds another driver has pushed his Hyundai into a red zone and up onto the sidewalk, and a truck is about to tow it. His wife, kids, and mother-in-law are waiting for him; he has the only available car. But his pleas are ignored: "I told you it's too late. Once the summons is made out and the dispatcher's notified and the tow's hooked up, then it's a tow, and ain't nothing nobody can do about it once it's a tow." So, Conrad must call his wife with the bad news. But he doesn't have change for the phone, and the store has a sign that reads "no change without purchase." He buys a candy bar to get change. Then, Conrad walks across town to pay the fine. After waiting in a long line to pay his fine, he finds out that the fine is twice as much as he thought because there is a separate fine for parking on the sidewalk and for parking in the red zone. Now he needs more cash. Once again, he has to find change and call his wife. She must take a taxi to the Western Union office and wire the money. Now Conrad has to find the Western Union office. He walks across town again. He gets the $77 to redeem his car and discovers he must go all the way to the slums of East Oakland to retrieve it. He waits for a bus, but it's the wrong one. He walks six more blocks, and then he waits for another bus. It's the right bus, but he doesn't have the right change. Will the driver take a $5? "No can do." So, he again tries to find someone who will give him change. Then, he must wait for another bus. By the time he reaches the towing lot, seven hours have elapsed since he was towed, it is getting dark and dangerous on the streets, and it is only fifteen minutes before the towing lot office is to close. Sweating with anxiety and exhausted, he waits in line and comes to the front just as the office is closing. He is then told that he needs another $77 because the towing is $77 per hour or any part thereof, and his tow took one hour and ten minutes. Conrad exclaims, "This is—not right!" But the man at the counter "gave Conrad a look of glorious indifference and motioned his head toward the sign. 'There's a line here,' he said, 'There's people waiting.'"

This is the merciless state.

Notes

My thanks go out to many of my colleagues at Quinnipiac for listening to and commenting on a very preliminary version of this paper, to all the participants in the Forgiveness, Mercy, and Clemency conference for key insights and penetrating discussions, especially Christopher Dole, and above all to both Austin Sarat and Nasser Hussain for organizing such a wonderful conference, editing this book, and igniting interest and debate on these critically important topics.

1. The differences between pardons, amnesties, and commutations are not central to the investigation here. My question is whether it is ever justified to give a defendant less than he or she legally deserves, regardless of whether the penalty is forfeited, reduced, or trial is waived altogether. Amnesties present special concerns for justice, democracy, and law because truth and memory are the basis on which even forgiveness is premised, as Adam Sitze's and Bruce Robbin's contributions explore. (One cannot forgive unless one has already been permitted to show that a fault has been committed.) While I take the point, I do not give separate treatment to amnesty here. That task will have to wait.

2. See Trisha Olson, "Of the Worshipful Warrior: Sanctuary and Punishment in the Middle Ages," *St. Thomas Law Review* 16 (2004), 473.

3. Douglas Hay, *Albion's Fatal Tree: Crime and Society in Eighteenth Century England* (London: A. Lane, 1975).

4. See Daniel T. Kobil, "The Quality of Mercy Strained: Wresting the Pardoning Power from the King," *Texas Law Review* 69 (1991), 569.

5. Immanuel Kant, *Critique of Judgment*, trans. J. H. Bernard (New York: Prometheus, 2000), 16.

6. Jacques Derrida, "On Forgiveness," in *Cosmopolitanism and Forgiveness*, trans. Mark Dooley and Michael Hughes (London: Routledge, 2001), 56–60.

7. Karl N. Llewellyn, *The Common Law Tradition: Deciding Appeals* (New York: Aspen, 1960).

8. Friedrich Nietzsche, *Thus Spake Zarathustra*, in *The Philosophy of Nietzsche*, trans. Thomas Common (New York: Modern Library Edition, 1937), 71.

9. Bob Egelko, "Law Students Show Inmate Is Innocent," *San Francisco Chronicle* (Feb. 19, 2005), B-1.

10. P. E. Digeser and Joanna North rightly point out that it is more than slightly insulting to be "forgiven" for something that one did not do. P. E. Digeser, *Political Forgiveness* (Ithaca, NY: Cornell University Press, 2001); Joanna North, "The Ideal of Forgiveness: A Philosopher's Exploration," in *Exploring Forgiveness*, eds. Robert D. Enright and Joanna North (Madison: University of Wisconsin Press, 1998).

11. See also Stuart Banner, *The Death Penalty: An American History* (Cambridge, MA: Harvard University Press, 2002), 54–55, providing examples of pardons for innocence in the early years of nationhood when there was no appellate process to correct trial errors; George Lardner Jr. and Margaret Colgate Love, "Mandatory Sentences and Presidential Mercy: The Role of Judges in Pardon Cases, 1790–1850," *Federal Sentencing Reporter* 16 (2002), 212, giving many examples of trial judges supporting pardon requests when sentences required by statute seemed unjustly severe or when new evidence was discovered after trial.

12. Laurence Hammack, "Convicted Man Gets New Day in Court," *Roanoke Times* (May 15, 2005); Laurence Hammack, "Lawyer: Girl Now Says Man Did Abuse Her," *Roanoke Times* (Feb. 12, 2005).

13. See Lardner and Love, "Mandatory Sentences and Presidential Mercy," giving examples of pardons in 1790–1850 that were supported by trial judges because mandatory penalties seemed too harsh: "when these conscientious judges were confronted with harsh and unyielding laws, they didn't always wait for the president to ask them. They asked him."); Charles Shanor and Marc Miller, "Pardon Us: Systematic Presidential Pardons," *Federal Sentencing Reporter* 13 (2001), 139, arguing for systematic pardons for crack cocaine users to address unfair disparities with powder and crack cocaine sentencing structures.

14. See Richard F. Celeste, "Executive Clemency: One Executive's Real Life Decisions," *Capital University Law Review* 13 (2003), 139–140. Celeste, while governor of Ohio, granted clemency to twenty-five women who had already served at least two years on the grounds of "repeated and severe abuse," willingness to obtain treatment, and willingness to do community service on issues of domestic violence.

15. See cases discussed in David Tait, "Pardons in Perspective: The Role of Forgiveness in Criminal Justice," *Federal Sentencing Reporter* 13 (2001), 134, contrasting a jury's mercy in France in the euthanasia case of Anne Pasquiou with the Latimer case in Canada that forbade clemency at the jury or judge level in a euthanasia case where Parliament had established a mandatory penalty.

16. Austin Sarat and Nassar Hussain, "On Lawful Lawlessness: George Ryan, Executive Clemency and the Rhetoric of Sparing Life," *Stanford Law Review* 56 (2004), 1307.

17. Sarah Kershaw, "California Gang Founder Loses Death Row Appeal," *New York Times* (Dec. 13, 2005), A-27.

18. Kathleen Dean Moore, *Pardons: Justice, Mercy, and the Public Interest* (New York: Oxford University Press, 1989), 173–178.

19. Dan Markel, "Against Mercy," *Minnesota Law Review* 88 (2003), 1421; P. E. Digeser, "Justice, Forgiveness, Mercy, and Forgetting: The Complex Meaning of Executive Pardoning," *Capital University Law Review* 31 (2003), 161, 171. See also Elizabeth Rapaport, "Retribution and Redemption in the Operation of Executive Clemency," *Chicago-Kent Law Review* 74 (2000), 1501.

20. Abraham Lincoln, *Lincoln: Speeches and Writings 555–556*, ed. Don E. Fehrenbacher (New York: Library of America, 1989), 2.

21. See Daniel T. Kobil, "The Quality of Mercy Strained," 569; Charles Shanor and Marc Miller, "Pardon Us," 139, listing all the presidential pardons used to "heal sectional wounds," including pardons for various rebellions, those convicted under the alien and sedition acts, pirates who assisted in the War of 1812, Mormons involved in the Utah Rebellion, amnesty to Confederate sympathizers, participants in the Philippine insurrection, Vietnam-era selective service violators, and so forth.

22. Archbishop Desmond Tutu, "Foreword," in *Exploring Forgiveness*; Martha Minow, *Between Vengeance and Forgiveness: Facing History After Genocide and Mass Violence* (Boston: Beacon Press, 1999).

23. *Lincoln: Speeches and Writings*, 2, 416.

24. Margaret Colgate Love, "The Pardon Paradox: Lessons of Clinton's Last Pardons," *Capital University Law Review* 31 (2003), 185; Kobil, "The Quality of Mercy Strained"; P. E. Digeser, "Justice, Forgiveness, Mercy, and Forgetting: The Complex Meaning of Executive Pardoning," *Capital University Law Review* 31 (2003), 161, 168; see also P. E. Digeser, *Political Forgiveness*.

25. Lincoln, *Letters*, 572.

26. From an interview with a commander at Camp Cropper, May 25, 2005.

27. Mark S. Umbreit, *Victim Meets Offender: The Impact of Restorative Justice and Mediation* (Monsey, NY: Criminal Justice Press, 1994), 130.

28. Ibid., 132.

29. "Laws . . . cannot be framed on principles of compassion to guilt: yet justice, by the constitution of England, is bound to be administered in mercy: this is promised by the king in his coronation oath, and it is that act of his government, which is the most personal, and most entirely his own. The king himself condemns no man; that rugged task he leaves to his courts of justice: the great operation of his sceptre is mercy." Blackstone, *4 Commentaries on the Laws of England*, chap. 31.

30. Blackstone, *4 Commentaries on the Law of England*, 397–402.

31. 32 U.S. (7 Pet.) 150, 160–161 (1833).

32. 274 U.S. 480 (1926).

33. We pledge allegiance to a *flag*.

34. *Lincoln: Speeches and Writings*, 2, 577.

35. *Lincoln*, 494.

36. *Lincoln*, 663.

37. *Lincoln*, 499.

38. See Love, "Mandatory Sentences and Presidential Mercy"; Kobil, "The Quality of Mercy Strained"; Banner, *The Death Penalty*.

39. Linda Ross Meyer, "Mercy in the Military," unpublished manuscript on file with the author.

40. See Claudia Card, "On Mercy," *Philosophical Review* 81 (1972), 182.

41. Derrida, 32–38.

42. Digeser, *Political Forgiveness*; Vladimir Jankélévitch, *Forgiveness*, trans. Andrew Kelley (Chicago: University of Chicago Press, 2005).

43. Edmund (Pat) Brown, *Public Justice, Private Mercy: A Governor's Education on Death Row* (New York: Weidenfeld & Nicolson, 1989), 83–84.

44. W. G. Perdue, "Weighing the Scales of Discipline: A Perspective on the Naval Commanding Officer's Prosecutorial Discretion," *Naval Law Review* 46 (1999), 69.

45. Bibas and Bierschbach would recharacterize these as something like my allegiance pardons, to recognize offenders who give over criminal allegiances to come over to Team America. Stephanos Bibas and Richard A. Bierschbach, "Integrating Remorse and Apology into Criminal Procedure," *Yale Law Journal* 114 (2004), 85. This would be an antiutilitarian account of immunity, but insofar as the grant of immunity is contingent on (1) the fact that the person pardoned has valuable information or (2) success in prosecuting others, the immunity would still be "not on the merits." See also Alexandra Natapoff, "Snitching: The Institutional and Communal Consequences," *University of Cincinnati Law Review* 73 (2004), 645, arguing that use of informants has extremely damaging consequences for already-unstable communities, as informants continue to commit crimes with impunity and turn in only their enemies but not their friends.

46. Alwynne Smart would include in this category clemency for offenders with dependents on the ground that duties to the dependents (outside the merits of the case) would trump the duty to punish. Alwynne Smart, "Mercy," *Philosophy* 43 (1968), 345. Nigel Walker points out that her acknowledgment here runs counter to her retributivism because this idea of other duties trumping punishment looks suspiciously utilitarian. Nigel Walker, "The Quiddity of Mercy," Royal Institute of Philosophy, Cambridge (1995), available at http://www.royalinstitutephilosophy.org/articles/article.php?id=36. But I would argue that family concerns are not "extrinsic" to the case. These concerns demonstrate the level of the defendant's commitment to others and the pain that all parties including the offender would suffer because of separation, concerns that are "internal" to the case. I would categorize them as compassion pardons.

47. Michael Cuneo, *Almost Midnight: An American Story of Murder and Redemption* (New York: Broadway Books, 2004), 292–293.

48. Ibid., 296–297.

49. Ibid., 310.

50. Dan Markel, "Against Mercy," *Minnesota Law Review* 88 (2004), 1421. I concentrate on Markel's arguments here, but he is not alone in staking out this ground. See also Ross Harrison, "The Equality of Mercy," in *Jurisprudence: Cambridge Studies* (Cambridge: Oxford University Press, 1992), state has no place for mercy because it is irrational and inegalitarian; Jeffrie Murphy and Jean Hampton, *Forgiveness and Mercy* (Cambridge: Cambridge University Press, 1988), mercy appropriate only in private affairs, not in public ones.

51. Markel, "Against Mercy," 1463–1464. See also ibid., note 57: "for the fiscal year 1976, the federal government declined to prosecute 108,000 out of the 171,000 criminal matters that were referred to the federal prosecutorial force. To be sure, these declinations occur for a wide variety of reasons, including determinations based on the merits and relative scarcity of resources. But out of 108,000 declinations, one must wonder how many were products of prosecutorial compassion, bias, favoritism, and indeed even caprice."

52. More recently, Markel has argued that the death penalty is also prohibited by retributive principles. See Dan Markel, "State Be Not Proud: A Retributivist Defense of the Commutation of Death Row and the Abolition of the Death Penalty," *Harvard Civil Rights and Civil Liberties Law Review* 40 (2005).

53. Markel, "Against Mercy," 1446.

54. Michael S. Moore, "The Moral Worth of Retribution," in *Responsibility, Character, and the Emotions*, ed. Ferdinand Shoeman (Cambridge: Cambridge University Press, 1987).

55. Herbert Morris, "A Paternalistic Theory of Punishment," *American Philosophical Quarterly* 18 (1981), 263.

56. Markel, "Against Mercy," 1445. Others who have made similar arguments include George Fletcher, *With Justice for Some* (New York: Perseus Books, 1994); George Fletcher, "The Place of Victims in the Theory of Retribution," *Buffalo Criminal Law Review* 3 (1999), 51; Jaime Malamud Goti, "Emma Zunz, Punishment and Sentiments," *Quinnipiac Law Review* 22 (2003), 45; Jean Hampton, "Correcting Harms Versus Righting Wrongs: The Goal of Retribution," *University of California at Los Angeles Law Review* 39 (1992), 1659; Murphy and Hampton, *Forgiveness and Mercy*.

57. See, e.g., J. R. Lucas, *Responsibility* (New York: Oxford University Press, 1995), 107–110, arguing that a "vindicative" view of punishment as vindicating public norms can make room for mercy where a defendant is truly (and seen by the public to be) repentant.

58. Herbert Morris, "Persons & Punishment," in *On Guilt and Innocence: Essays in Legal Philosophy and Moral Psychology* (Berkeley: University of California Press, 1976), 31.

59. Markel, "Against Mercy," 1447.

60. Ibid., 1447.

61. Ibid., 1448.

62. Ibid., 1448–1449.

63. Nigel Walker, *Why Punish?* (Cambridge: Oxford University Press, 1991).

64. Lucas, who defends such a view, acknowledges that his "vindicative" theory of punishment does not rule out excessive punishment, for the degree of punishment is measured by the need to "make a point" rather than the seriousness of the crime. *Responsibility*, 93.

65. Hannah Arendt, *The Human Condition*, 2nd ed. (Chicago: University of Chicago Press, 1998), 140–141.

66. See Paul Campos, "The Paradox of Punishment," *Wisconsin Law Review* (1992), 1931; Linda Ross Meyer, "Forgiveness and Public Trust," *Fordham Urban Law Journal* 27 (2000), 1515, 1527.

67. See David Bazelon, "The Morality of the Criminal Law," *Southern California Law Review* 49 (1976), 385.

68. See Stephen Garvey, "Punishment as Atonement," *University of California at Los Angeles Law Review* 46 (1999), 1801, 1836 n. 149; Jean Hampton, "Correcting Harms Versus Righting Wrongs," 1659, 1660; Linda Ross Meyer, "Herbert Morris and Punishment," *Quinnipiac Law Review* 22 (2003), 109, 110–111.

69. Immanuel Kant, *The Science of Right* (Part 1 of the *Metaphysics of Morals*) in *42 Great Books of the Western World 449*, trans. W. Hastie (1952). Derrida interprets this passage to accord with his view that only the unforgivable can be forgiven. For Kant, the unforgivable is to undermine the authority of law itself, embodied in the person of the sovereign, so the sovereign only forgives the unforgivable. "On Forgiveness," 46–47. At the same time, however, Kant seems to be acknowledging here, as he does elsewhere, that the duty to punish is otherwise absolute, for to *fail* to punish is to fail to treat others as full persons and to *fail* in upholding law.

70. Here I paraphrase (and bastardize) Kant's argument in the *Groundwork of the Metaphysics of Morals*. My excuse is that I read Kant as legal writers have tended to do, for a certain Kant-derived approach to responsibility and ethics grounds the way "reason" is usually understood in traditional jurisprudence, leading to Kant-inspired definitions of insanity, mens rea, excuses, justifications, concepts of desert, division of authority between judge and jury, elimination of emotion from legal decision making, and so on. Kant himself is always deeper and more sophisticated than I represent him here.

71. See Meir Dan-Cohen, *Harmful Thoughts: Essay on Law, Self, and Morality* (Princeton, NJ: Princeton University Press, 2002), 236: "The core of criminal law doctrine, centered around the concept of mens rea and the variety of criminal excuses, probably comes closer than any other set of social practices to an instantiation of the Kantian conception of the responsible human subject as the noumenal self, characterized exclusively by a rational free will unencumbered by character, temperament, and circumstance."

72. See Martin Heidegger, *Being and Time*, trans. John Macquarrie and Edward Robinson (New York: Harper & Row, 1962), 74–75, 78–90: "Knowing is a mode of Dasein founded upon Being-in-the-world. Thus Being-in-the-world, as a basic state, must be Interpreted *beforehand*." Ibid., 90. For a more in-depth discussion of Heidegger's views, see

Linda Ross Meyer, "Is Practical Reason Mindless?" *Georgetown Law Review* 86 (1998), 647. See also Hubert Dreyfus, *Being-in-the-World: A Commentary on Heidegger's Being and Time, Division I* (Boston: MIT Press, 1991).

73. "The kind of dealing which is closest to us is as we have shown, not a bare perceptual cognition, but rather that kind of concern which manipulates things and puts them to use; and this has its own kind of 'knowledge.'" Heidegger, *Being and Time*, 95.

74. "Only something which is in the state-of-mind [*Befindlichkeit*] of fearing (or fearlessness) can discover that what is environmentally ready-to-hand [*Zuhanden*] is threatening. Dasein's openness to the world is constituted existentially by the attunement of a state-of-mind . . . Existentially, a state-of-mind implies a disclosive submission to the world, out of which we can encounter something that matters to us. . . . even the purest theoria [theory] has not left all moods behind." Ibid., 176–177.

75. The structure of logic and ethical deliberation itself is temporal: "But if deliberation is to be able to operate in the scheme of the 'if–then,' concern must already have 'surveyed' a context of involvements and have an understanding of it. That which is considered with an 'if' must already be understood *as something or other*. . . . The scheme 'something as something' has already been sketched out beforehand in the structure of one's pre-predicative understanding. The as-structure is grounded ontologically in the temporality of understanding." Ibid., 411.

76. "But even in this characterization does one not start by marking out and isolating the 'I' so that one must then seek some way of getting over to the Others from this isolated subject? To avoid this misunderstanding we must notice in what sense we are talking about 'the Others.' By 'Others' we do not mean everyone else but me—those over against whom the 'I' stands out. They are rather those from whom, for the most part, one does not distinguish oneself—those among whom one is too. . . . By reason of this with-like [mithaften] Being-in-the-world, the world is always the one that I share with Others. The world of Dasein is a with-world [Mitwelt]. Being-in is Being-with Others." Ibid., 155.

77. Immanuel Kant, *Fundamental Principles of the Metaphysic of Morals*, trans. T. K. Abbott (Buffalo, NY: Prometheus, 1987), 29–30.

78. Heidegger is not the only source of these points. See Larry May, *Sharing Responsibility* (Chicago: University of Chicago Press, 1992), 2–4; Dan-Cohen, *Harmful Thoughts*, 209–224, also arguing for a "constitutive" theory of self and responsibility based on slightly different philosophical progenitors. For Dan-Cohen, "for the will to serve as a responsibility base it need not be free in the metaphysical, anti-determinist sense . . . responsibility for voluntary actions simply marks them as constituents of the self. . . . Transposing voluntarist responsibility into the constitutive framework also opens up the possibility that candidates other than the will may be eligible as potential constituents of the self and therefore as bases of responsibility." 213. The piece that Heidegger adds to this assessment is an explanation of why we are "constituted" by prevailing accounts of responsibility—grounding it in being-in and being-with as the foundation of being human.

79. See Marc Miller, "The Foundations of Law: Sentencing Equality Pathology," *Emory Law Journal* 54 (2005), 271, arguing that the "formal equality" stressed in the Federal Sentencing Guidelines is not "true" equality which is more contextual.

80. See Jed Rubenfeld, *Freedom and Time* (New Haven, CT: Yale University Press, 2001), arguing for a temporally extended account of democracy.

81. This point is made well in Rubenfeld, *Freedom and Time*.

82. If you are not a Trekkie, just substitute "Borg" with "ant colony."

83. See also Miller, "Sentencing Equality Pathology," drawing on Martha Fineman's work to argue for the "inherently contextual nature of equality," and applying that insight to criticize the "formal equality" of mandatory minimum penalties and "context-free sentencing policy" of the Federal Sentencing Guidelines.

84. Digeser also suggests, from a virtue ethics kind of perspective, that other virtues may sometimes trump justice or equality. P. E. Digeser, "Justice Forgiveness Mercy and Forgetting," 167–171; Digeser, *Political Forgiveness*.

85. Sarat and Hussain, "On Lawful Lawlessness."

86. See also Margaret Colgate Love, "Of Pardons, Politics and Collar Buttons: Reflections on the President's Duty to be Merciful," *Fordham Urban Law Journal* 27 (2000), 1483, 1487; Peter M. Shane, "Presidents, Pardons and Prosecutors: Legal Accountability and Separation of Powers," *Yale Law & Policy Review* 11 (1993), 361, 403, citing Lincoln–Johnson pardons of Confederate soldiers and Truman–Carter pardons of those who violated selective service laws. Daniel T. Kobil, "The Quality of Mercy Strained," 569, 571.

87. Michael J. Sandel, *Liberalism and the Limits of Justice*, 2nd ed. (Cambridge: Cambridge University Press, 1998).

88. Tait, "Pardons in Perspective."

89. Indeed, if the authority is not at risk, then the pardon begins to look more like condonation of crime than reaffirmation of the bonds of obligation. I would insist that an authority only has the power to pardon crimes of the community in which he or she moves. An authority must be, in that respect, a potential victim. This does not mean, for example, that men cannot pardon rapists (of women) or that adults cannot pardon child abusers, for men are husbands and fathers and friends and adults are parents and grandparents and loving neighbors who are hurt by harm done to those they love. On the other hand, where communities are fractured or in a state of war, an authority of one community cannot pardon the offense against another. Examples may be the pardons of lynchers in the South or perhaps the first acquittal verdict in the Rodney King LAPD brutality cases. Based on these considerations, I have less difficulty with the argument that mercy fails to uphold victims' rights. For insofar as we are all potential victims or connected to potential victims, in granting pardon, an authority pardons on behalf of us all. See Meyer, "Forgiveness and Public Trust."

90. This form of mercy echoes our medieval past. See Trisha Olson, "Of the Worshipful Warrior: Sanctuary and Punishment in the Middle Ages," *St. Thomas Law Review* 16 (2004), 473, 508–509: "The warrior vowed to his lord loyalty and service, and the lord in return offered 'affectionate care' of his man and reward for his valor. These bonds denoted more

than mutual self-interest. They were relations of friendship, loyalty, and deference whereby feelings ran so deep that in the Anglo-Saxon poem 'The Wanderer' 'all joy . . . departed' upon the loss of one's lord. . . . To be fidelis, in turn, was to be 'law-worthy.' Undergirding medieval law was not a theory of rights, but a network of trust and deference"; Pat McCune, "Book Review," *Michigan Law Review* 89 (1991), 1661, 1671: "For medieval English people, judgment—the establishment of social order through justice—always involved mercy. Justice was joined in the minds of people involved in the courts not with an abstract notion of reason, but with the practical values of forgiveness and restoration of the balance of relationships in the community. . . . Reconciliation and forgiveness, not retribution, were for centuries the ideal means to maintain peace."

91. Stephanos Bibas and Richard A. Bierschbach, "Integrating Remorse and Apology into Criminal Procedure," 85, gesturing to a "relational" approach to criminal responsibility instead of an "individual badness" approach and suggesting opening up victim–offender mediation—even postconviction. These authors don't suggest clemency but do see an important place for apology and reconciliation in mending the social bonds that are torn by wrongdoing. Their "relational" approach to crime might be justified and supported by the foundational change suggested here.

92. Brown, *Public Justice, Private Mercy*, 15–16. I cannot resist quoting a poem from a juvenile offender published several years ago in our local *Manson Times* prison newspaper: "Mom, I'm sorry for the problems I caused you / When I was a little kid / The streets seemed to be so much fun / That I had to sneak out of the house / And do what the other kids did . . . And that's when I found out / that someone was taking over my soul / And he was the devil / He brought me money, girls, and drugs / He even gave me the mentality of a thug / It didn't last long because that thug inside of me went to steal some cars / I got caught joy riding and ended up behind bars / Now that I'm in jail, I'm realizing something I never knew before / That there was someone special in my life / That I should have never ignored . . . YOU / I'm sorry mom / Please forgive me / And thanks for not giving up." Juan Santiago, no. 233978.

93. See Linda Ross Meyer, "Eternal Remorse," in Toward a Critique of Guilt: Perspectives from the Humanities, *Studies in Law Politics and Society* 36 (2005), 139–154. F. C. Decoste draws on J. R. Lucas's account of responsibility to argue for the centrality of remorse and repentance to retributive theory. See "Conditions of Clemency: Justice From the Offender," *Saskatchewan Law Review* 66 (2003), 1, 14: "In my view, the vindicative justification [of punishment] alone supports the possibility of a kinship of this kind between justice and mercy. The fact that punishment is an 'externally imposed penance,' confronts the case where, after his conviction and before his sentence is spent, the external becomes internal to and personal for the offender; where 'compulsory penance [is] replaced by a voluntary penance . . . a sincere act of reattachment or allegiance to community values,' and where, in that sense, the offender repents his crime by renouncing the way of life and thinking that led him to act against the political morality expressed and protected in the law of crimes. . . . we must think of repentance as a 'civic' act on ground of which an offender may properly ask to be 'restored to full and legitimate membership in the community.'" See also Jonathan R.

Cohen, "Advising Clients to Apologize," *Southern California Law Review* 72 (1999), 1009; Stephen Garvey, "Atonement"; Bibas and Bierschbach, "Integrating Remorse and Apology into Criminal Procedure."

94. Linda Ross Meyer, "Mercy in the Military."

95. Benedict Carey, "For the Worst of Us, the Diagnosis May Be 'Evil,'" *New York Times* (Feb. 6, 2005), F1, F4.

96. See Margaret Colgate Love, "The Pardon Paradox: Lessons of Clinton's Last Pardons," *Capital University Law Review* 31 (2003), 185, demonstrating that Clinton's misbegotten end-of-term pardons were the result in part of failing to check the facts in the clemency petitions because of time pressures, circumventing the usual Department of Justice process, and thereby denying any appearance or actuality of equal opportunities to seek clemency.

97. For similar problems raised by land registration in Kenya, see Joel M. Ngugi, "Reexamining the Role of Private Property in Market Democracies: Problematic Ideological Issues Raised by Land Registration," *Michigan Journal of International Law* 25 (2004), 467.

98. Dan-Cohen, *Harmful Thoughts*, 130.

99. See Love, "The Pardon Paradox," 215–216, emphasizing many of these factors, including the "lull of routine."

100. Let alone something even more elusive, like grace.

101. See *California v. Brown*, 479 U.S. 538 (1987).

102. Robert P. Burns, *A Theory of the Trial* (Princeton, NJ: Princeton University Press, 1999).

103. Cf. Larry May, *Sharing Responsibility* (Chicago: University of Chicago Press, 1992), 56, arguing for a virtue of moral sensitivity that incorporates: perceptiveness toward the needs or feelings of others, caring about the effects of one's actions, critical appreciation for the morally relevant features of the situation, being moved to act to minimize harms and offenses of one's conduct.

104. Fred E. Inbau, John E. Reid, Joseph P. Buckley, and Brian C. Jayne, *Criminal Interrogation and Confessions*, 4th ed. (New York: Aspen, 2004), 242, 255: "the solicitations of a sympathetic investigator may allow the suspect to believe that if the investigator can understand the reasons for his crime, others too may be more understanding." "Much can be gained by the investigator's adoption of an emotional ('choked up') feeling about it all ... This demonstrable attitude of sympathy and understanding may be rather easily assumed by placing one's self 'in the other fellow's shoes' and pondering this question: 'What might I have done under similar circumstances?'" The interrogator as friend ploy may be more effective with younger offenders or more serious crimes, however. See Richard A. Leo, "Criminal Law: Inside the Interrogation Room," *Journal of Criminal Law & Criminology* 86 (1996), 266.

105. Brown, *Public Justice, Private Mercy*, 17.

106. Daniel T. Kobil, "How to Grant Clemency in Unforgiving Times," *Capital University Law Review* 21 (2003), 217. Kobil argues that executives should stick to retributive justifications for pardoning, as we are "confronted by a pervasive and overwhelming societal commitment to retributive principles of punishment."

107. James Q. Whitman, *Harsh Justice* (New York: Oxford University Press, 2001).

108. Justice Anthony M. Kennedy, speech at the ABA annual meeting (Aug. 9, 2003) calling for mercy, an end to mandatory minimum sentences, and revitalization of the pardon power.

109. Lucas recognizes that, within his theory, mercy based on repentance is possible but says the bystanders must also be "convinced that the change of heart of the wrongdoer is genuine." *Responsibility*, 110. My rejection of the "expressive" view of punishment avoids the conceptual problem here but not the practical one.

110. Michael Cuneo remarks, in his book on the Darrell Mease pardon, that what was missing from all the accounts of the case was Darrell himself. He sets himself the task in his book of making Darrell Mease real for us and therefore a possible object of understanding and compassion. *Almost Midnight*, 335. My experience in reading the book is that once you get to know Darrell, it is indeed more difficult to be outraged by his pardon—even if others were more deserving. See also Patrick D. Healy, "After Coming Out, a Soap Opera Heroine Moves On," *New York Times* (Feb. 24, 2005), E3, describing how conservative viewers politically opposed to gay and lesbian relationships came to feel compassion for a lesbian soap opera character after following her story so that "the lesbian girl became the moral tent pole of our show."

111. See, e.g., Cory Rayburn, "To Catch a Sex Thief: The Burden of Performance in Rape and Sexual Abuse Assault Trials," *Columbia Journal of Gender and Law* 15 (2006), 436: "When a rape is recounted through oral testimony, with limited physical evidence, it is especially prone to being underwhelming to a jury that has heard much 'better' stories and seen much more convincing accounts of rape. The fact that the television or movie rapes may have been fictional does not mean a jury's conception of rape is not actively shaped by them . . . fictional accounts can be more powerful because they are dramatized and sensationalized."

112. The issues from the standpoint of effective advocacy are well explored in Sarat and Hussain, "On Lawful Lawlessness"; Anthony V. Alfieri, "Mercy Lawyers," *North Carolina Law Review* 82 (2004), 1297; and in Daniel T. Kobil's contribution to this volume.

113. Nigel Walker lists four "easy" cases of inappropriate mercy: personal gain, favoritism, whim, and superstition (e.g., the Christmas pardon). *The Quiddity of Mercy*. Spelling these out in particular cases, however, is much harder. Is pardoning out of fellow-feeling or sympathy for "personal gain"? Is pardoning because of a religious conversion "favoritism" toward the religious? Is pardoning because of a sense of personal connection that cannot be elucidated a "whim" pardon? Is pardoning because the pope asks you to a "superstition" pardon? I do not believe it is so easy to exclude all these pardons categorically in this way.

114. Mark Strasser, "Some Reflections on the President's Pardon Power," *Capital University Law Review* 31 (2003), 141, 153, refusal to grant pardons on the basis of race or sex would clearly be an abuse of presidential power.

115. 523 U.S. 272 (1998).

116. Linda Ross Meyer, "Unruly Rights," *Cardozo Law Review* 22 (2000), 1, arguing for a dignity-based understanding of equal protection and other constitutional rights.

117. See Michael Cuneo, *Almost Midnight*, 338: "While not everyone in Darrell's home environs approved of the commutation, most of those with whom I spoke seemed unwilling to dismiss it as a mere accident of history. In the intensely religious culture of the Missouri Ozarks, there are no mere accidents. Events of every sort, but especially extraordinary ones, are believed to reverberate with divine purpose. To suggest otherwise would betray not only a lack of faith but an astonishing lack of imagination."

118. 523 U.S. 272, 289, O'Connor, J., concurring in part and concurring in the judgment.

119. Nigel Walker also argues that "merely whimsical or random" mercy is not acceptable. *The Quiddity of Mercy*.

120. P. S. Ruckman Jr. and David Kincaid, "Inside Lincoln's Clemency Decision Making," *Presidential Studies Quarterly* 29 (1999), 84.

121. I would argue that this lack of personal accountability was what bothered many federal judges when the Federal Sentencing Guidelines first were implemented. Judges rebelled against giving sentences they did not believe were just and having to tell offenders there was nothing they could do. They were also frustrated by the fact that the sentencing hearings themselves no longer included any dialogue between the judge and the offender but only legal argument about the application of the sentencing rules. The sense of responsibility to and for was gone.

122. *Booker v. United States*, 543 U.S. 220 (2005), suggests that, for now, trial courts will have more sentencing discretion than under the Federal Sentencing Guidelines, for the Court determined that it violated the right to a jury trial for facts found at sentencing to have mandatory sentencing consequences. Until Congress acts to change this ruling, the guidelines will only be advisory.

123. A state prosecutor who is adjudicating minor cases is constantly faced with questions of clemency—thinking about how to settle a case without "ruining someone's life." Interview with Susann Gill, Dec. 5, 2005.

124. And not an authority that Carnahan, a Baptist, was in any way bound to obey.

125. Which is the military practice. See Meyer, "Mercy in the Military."

126. See Austin Sarat, *Mercy on Trial* (Princeton, NJ: Princeton University Press, 2005), 32: "[M]ercy and clemency always involve risks. Taking these risks means acknowledging the limits of law and justice, and of their ability to guarantee genuine moral deliberation rather than arbitrariness, fairness rather than discrimination."

127. Grant Gilmore, *The Ages of American Law* (New Haven, CT: Yale University Press, 1977), 111.

128. No great degree of imagination is necessary here; the harsh, by-the-letter enforcement of habeas corpus or immigration law could provide many nonfictional examples.

129. Tom S. Wolfe, *A Man in Full* (New York: Simon & Schuster, 1998).

Revising the Past: On the Metaphysics
of Repentance, Forgiveness, and Pardon

MEIR DAN-COHEN

Despite important differences, the three terms listed in the subtitle have much in common. Repentance, forgiveness, and pardon—I call them *revisionary practices*[1]—all pertain to the same object, a wrongdoer, and perform the same function: the cessation of a range of appropriate negative responses triggered by a wrongful action. The three revisionary practices differ primarily in the *subject* of this reorientation: the subject of repentance is the wrongdoer; of forgiveness, the victim[2]; and of pardon, an official acting on behalf of society or the state.[3] Each of the subjects in turn correlates with a distinctive paradigmatic response to wrongdoing. Roughly speaking, by repentance the wrongdoer assuages *guilt*; by forgiveness the victim squelches *resentment*; and through pardon *stigma* is officially removed.[4] There are many differences among guilt, resentment, and stigma, but what is more instructive in the study of revisionary practices is the common thread: A wrongful act gives rise to a range of appropriate negative responses; revisionary practices bring these responses to an end. How can they do so? The question can be raised with a normative or a psychological orientation, and discussions in this area tend to oscillate between the two or conflate them. My interest in this chapter is exclusively with the former: How do the revisionary practices render the negative reactions provoked by the misdeed no longer *appropriate*?[5]

There is a simple and well-known answer, and if this answer were sufficient, philosophers in this area would be mostly out of work. What keeps them busy are the difficulties the standard answer runs into and the consequent efforts to patch them up. I don't believe these efforts have been entirely successful, suggesting that there is room for a new start.

The Standard Account and Its Problems

Of the three revisionary practices I have listed, the standard account gives priority to repentance. Though there are a number of variants, the basic idea is the same. Repentance involves a change of heart in the wrongdoer; the victim's forgiveness and the state's pardon are adequate responses to this change.[6] It is hard to dispute that some such relation does obtain.[7] But this is only a partial and imprecise story. Various attempts to complete it and bring it into sharper focus have not been an unqualified success. In discussing the standard account, I focus for the most part on repentance and forgiveness, with the understanding that unless otherwise indicated, what is said about forgiveness applies to pardon as well.

We can distinguish three versions of the standard account with different temporal orientations: present, future, and past. In a well-known paper on forgiveness, Jeffrie Murphy characterizes moral wrong along Kantian lines as an expression of disrespect toward the victim. The main significance of repentance, he maintains, is that it negates an inference from the past wrongdoing—namely, that the wrongdoer still disparages the victim. Since the repentant wrongdoer is not "*now* conveying the message that he holds me in contempt," my forgiveness is deemed appropriate.[8] In contrast to this present-oriented approach, Norvin Richards highlights a future perspective. Repentance amounts to the fixing of a dangerous defect, "like repairing that part of a house which contributed to an accident." The path to forgiveness is open because "there has been a replacement of (part of) what was responsible for the suffering with something which promises to be harmless."[9] Neither the present- nor the future-oriented approach is adequate. Since the revisionary practices put an end to reactive attitudes that are otherwise deemed appropriate, any account must imply or presuppose a view about the point of the reactive attitudes themselves. The present-oriented view of forgiveness implies that resentment toward the wrongdoer is a reaction to his or her *ongoing* disparagement, whereas on the future-oriented view resentment is sustained by the *threat* the wrongdoer poses.[10] In these implicit accounts of resentment (and by extension, the other reactive attitudes), the past wrongdoing plays merely an evidentiary role, creating a rebuttable presumption regarding the wrongdoer's present attitudes in the one case or future propensities in the other. Since we could in principle form judgments about these attitudes or propensities apart from the past wrongdoing, that historical action is, strictly speaking, neither necessary nor sufficient for the reactive attitudes to take hold. The present- and future-oriented accounts of forgiveness as responsive to the wrongdoer's change of heart thus miss or understate the essential rather than merely evidentiary role played by the past wrongdoing as the source of reactive attitudes.

But if guilt, resentment, and stigma are essentially past oriented, how can repentance undo them without erasing the past? Two main lines of argument purport to provide an answer. According to the first, the past action does play an ineliminable role in shaping our attitude to the wrongdoer; nevertheless, subsequent behavior, most notably repentance, casts new light on the past wrongdoing and changes its significance in the overall assessment of the offender, who may turn out not quite so bad as we thought. Forgiveness and pardon express this reassessment.[11] The problem with this argument is that it does after all amount to denying or at any rate considerably weakening the premise that the reactive attitudes are concerned with the wrongful act as such. Although the wrongful act is here acknowledged to play a substantive role in forming the reactions to the wrongdoer, requiring that it be assessed within a broader diachronic perspective dilutes the significance afforded to the act. To see that this dilution is unacceptable, consider that a broader time frame, a backward-looking one, is already available when the wrongful act is committed: The act can be assessed against the background of the offender's record up to that point. And yet we commonly resent a wrong done to us by someone acknowledged to be a good or acceptable person overall, just as that person may experience guilt and remorse for a single moral failure despite an otherwise flawless record.[12]

The second line of argument that retains the reactive attitudes' past orientation makes a more radical claim: The change wrought by repentance may be so profound as to count as a change of identity. Since the repentant individual is not the same one as the wrongdoer to whom we bore a grudge, the offender's transformation deprives the reactive attitudes of their object. But this apparently easy solution fails as well. Even putting aside qualms about discontinuous personal identity, a serious and often-noted objection remains. If we allow that as a result of the change in identity there is no one to resent or attach stigma to anymore, we must also recognize that for the very same reason there is no one to forgive or pardon either. Just as resentment loses its object, so do forgiveness and pardon.[13]

The change brought about by repentance cannot be so radical as to count as a change of identity, nor can it be merely a change of mind. The idiom often used, "change of heart," though perhaps apt, is vague and uninformative. The kind of change required is better indicated by Jeffrie Murphy's observation that through repentance a person may "sever himself from his past wrongdoing."[14] But what does it mean for a person to sever herself from her past, and how can she do it? Suppose, however, that such a severing is actually accomplished. This brings up a further query in the form of a familiar paradox. If the change of heart does amount to the wrongdoer's successfully distancing herself from the evil deed, what role is left for forgiveness? Resentment is rendered inappropriate; so forgiveness is no longer called for or indeed possible since forgiveness consists in the overcoming of *appropriate* reactive attitudes, not inappropriate ones.[15]

Forgiveness presents additional difficulties of its own. According to the standard account, the essence of forgiveness is the overcoming of (appropriate) resentment or other negative feelings toward the offender. By thus focusing on the forgiver's internal economy of emotions and attitudes, this account leaves out, and unexplained, the wrongdoer's stake in the matter. Why should the wrongdoer desire forgiveness? To be sure, forgiveness may be a prelude to restoring an amicable relationship between the parties, and the wrongdoer may be interested in that. But this need not be the case; an amicable relation may never have existed or its resumption may not be in store, without this detracting from the importance the offender assigns to forgiveness.[16] Nor is the wrongdoer's interest just a matter of not having others entertain negative feelings and attitudes toward her. If, for example, resentment were to cease due to the victim's memory lapse, the wrongdoer's relief would be naturally tinged with disappointment at being deprived of something valuable. The vital interest the wrongdoer has in the victim's active and intentional forgiveness implies that forgiveness has some distinctive impact on the wrongdoer and on her life. Correspondingly, in deciding whether to grant or withhold forgiveness, the victim seems to exercise some kind of power over the wrongdoer. The standard account sheds no light on these facts.

The existing accounts also leave the precise link between repentance and forgiveness unclear and unsettled. It is generally agreed that repentance has a privileged role in regard to forgiveness; the point in dispute is whether it is necessary. Here again, conflicting considerations bear. Ordinary perceptions weigh against positing repentance as a necessary ground for forgiveness. Forgiveness in the absence of repentance seems possible and indeed particularly noble. A philosopher is surely not in a position to legislate it out of existence. The difficulty is how in the absence of repentance we can distinguish forgiveness, with its positive connotations, from an objectionable condonation of the wrongful act. An adequate account would have to solve this difficulty by explaining both why repentance is a standard but not a strictly necessary ground for forgiveness and how forgiveness without repentance need not slide toward condonation.[17]

Finally, the standard account runs up not only against these difficulties but also, and perhaps even more significantly, against a vague and inchoate yet deeply felt yearning that defines our pretheoretical attitudes in this area. The past sometimes weighs heavily on us, and we desire to shake free of it; we wish for a new start. Revisionary practices appear from this point of view as answering to this yearning.[18] Here pardon provides the most compelling metaphor, that of erasing a nasty event from one's record. But when the record consists in the actual sequence of life's events, in our histories and biographies, how can it be amended? How can we pluck an event out of the past and expunge it? And if we cannot, are we to conclude that the aspiration underlying revisionary practices is incoherent and occasional glimpses of success a mirage?[19]

Revising the Boundaries of the Self

The preceding comments are not exhaustive. I hope, nonetheless, that they provide a fair representation of a range of difficulties and puzzles so as to vindicate my initial claim that there is room for a fresh start. A plausible place to begin is with the self—the subject as well as the object of the practices we explore. It is natural, in other words, to pose at the outset the following question: What conception of self is presupposed by revisionary practices and makes best sense of them? Though conceptions of the self abound, one metaphor—that of *boundaries*—has become dominant and runs through many otherwise disparate approaches. My main claim is that this locution and this imagery, seriously taken, hold the key to the account we seek. One way to take the boundaries metaphor seriously is to trace it to its original and most natural habitat: the political domain. The first step in the account I propose accordingly consists in observing some prominent features of boundaries among states and in demonstrating how these features, when transposed to the case of the self, help overcome the difficulties and solve the puzzles we observed. However, the transposition must be defended and clarified. This will be the burden of the following step. The result is an account that may be summarized as follows. Reactive attitudes such as guilt and resentment presuppose the offender's responsibility for a wrongful act. Revisionary practices redraw the wrongdoer's boundary so as to leave the offense outside, thereby releasing the wrongdoer from responsibility and rendering any negative attitudes toward the wrongdoer based on the past misdeed no longer supportable.

The Political Analogy

I turn now to the political analogy, and a simple example is all we need. Imagine that the state of Arcadia has near its border a pollutant that causes environmental damage to the neighboring states. As a matter of course, Arcadia bears responsibility for this pollutant: It is required to take measures to reduce the damage, to compensate the affected states, and so on. It is equally obvious that this responsibility would expire if, say, by treaty or by war, Arcadia's border were redrawn so as to exclude the offensive site.[20]

Five features of this example are noteworthy. First, the example illustrates the general idea of how a border change can affect responsibility by removing a responsibility base. Second, the political scenario makes vivid the constructive and hence indispensable role played with regard to the reallocation of responsibility by the process or action by which the boundary is changed. Many good reasons for retracting Arcadia's border may have existed prior to the change, and these reasons may have prompted the actions, peaceful or belligerent, for making the change. But the reasons themselves, no matter how compelling, are not self-executing. Arcadia's responsibility for the pollutant would persist in face of such reasons until and unless the change in the border is actually made.

Third, consider more precisely how the change in the border is brought about. I mentioned a treaty and a war as agents of a border change. But how can they bring it about? Since the change is normative, the answer too must be normative: Some events and some parties have the normative power to affect a state's boundary in the sense that the happening of these events or certain actions taken by these parties simply *mean* or *count as* a border change.[21] Why do they mean this, or to whom do they so count? What are the source and the scope of this power? The fourth feature is that neither as a matter of logic nor of political practice must these questions have a clear and uniform answer. There is room among states not just for border disputes but also for disputes about the proper means of settling them, without there being a supreme authority able to settle all such disagreements. There is accordingly room for indeterminacy in the location of a state's border, with different parties accepting different territorial versions of one and the same state.

Finally, note the delicate balance between continuity and change in the hypothetical scenario. To say that Arcadia's boundary has been redrawn implies a change substantial enough to relieve Arcadia of responsibility but not so substantial as to threaten the state's continued identity. Though the region containing the pollutant is no longer part of Arcadia, the state of Arcadia does persist as a viable subject so that saying *it* is no longer responsible for the pollutant is not an empty or a paradoxical claim.

When applied to the self, these five features of the political example offer solutions to the puzzles and difficulties raised by revisionary practices. First and most important, the suggestion is that repentance, forgiveness, and pardon are ways of redrawing the wrongdoer's boundary so as to exclude the wrongful action, thus relieving the wrongdoer of responsibility for it. By doing so, these practices render guilt, resentment, and stigma—the ordinary incidents or ramifications of this responsibility—inappropriate. Second, these practices are constructive in the sense that the effects on the wrongdoer's boundary and responsibility are brought about by the practice itself rather than by any antecedent reasons there may be for activating the practice.[22] This explains the offender's interest in forgiveness for its own sake, apart from any additional effects it may have on the offender's relation with the victim, as well as the sense in which granting or withholding forgiveness is an exercises of normative power over the offender: the power to redraw a particularly consequential segment of the offender's self.

The third feature of the political analogy helps explain the role played by the different subjects: the wrongdoer, the victim, and the state. By engaging in the respective practice, these subjects exercise their normative powers to modify the wrongdoer's boundary. Where do these powers come from and how do they relate to each other? Though roughly speaking the answer must rest on the special interest in the wrongful act of each of the three subjects, the fourth feature of the political analogy teaches that these powers are contestable and vague so that the resulting boundary line may be indeterminate and ill-defined. Consequently, the connection among the three practices is contingent and loose: Repentance does not necessitate forgiveness, nor the other way round; similarly with regard to pardon. Different versions of one and the same self may coexist. It is an advantage of this account, moreover, that while insisting on the practices' logical independence, it highlights their interconnectedness as well. Though disparate drawings of the same self's boundary are possible, there is considerable pressure for convergence exerted by two main factors. One consists in the reasons that trigger any of the three practices.

Since on the present view these are reasons for redrawing the wrongdoer's boundary in a particular way, the reasons that prompt one of the revisionary practices would invite the other practices as well. The other factor concerns the significance of the very fact that a party that is putatively empowered to do so has drawn a boundary in a particular way. As in the political arena, in matters of the self there is also an advantage in uniformity and agreement regarding the location of the boundary line and consequently a tendency to recognize or ratify a boundary simply because it already enjoys some normative support.

Finally, the fifth feature of the political case illuminates the kind of change in the wrongdoer that the revisionary practices involve. As we saw earlier, we need to find a conception of change strong enough to support and explain the cessation of negative attitudes toward the offender without being so strong as to disrupt identity. Redrawing a state's boundary to exclude a chunk of land is a vivid illustration of this middle ground.

The Self and Its Past

An account of revisionary practices along lines suggested by the political analogy seems attractive. But is the analogy apt? Two worries come immediately to mind. First, is the self sufficiently similar to the state in relevant respects to sustain such an analogy and make it fruitful? Second, even if we accept the analogy between self and state in general, extending it to revisionary practices may appear misguided. The change we described in the case of Arcadia is spatial, concerning Arcadia's territorial shape, whereas the corresponding change in the case of revisionary practices is temporal, involving the self's diachronic shape. Spatial changes are a commonplace. Isn't using them as a model for changes regarding past events to blithely ignore or beg the difficult questions that trigger our interest in revisionary practices in the first place?

I consider the second worry first. It is based on the observation that there is a difference between time and space in respect of change: We can rearrange objects in space but not events in time. Excluding the pollutant from Arcadia's geographic scope is easy, but that is quite unlike excluding a wrongful act from the self's temporal scope. The gist of my response is to deny the premise—namely, that the political example involves a change that is spatial in a sense that contrasts in point of feasibility with the ostensibly temporal changes that revisionary practices bring about. Here is why. The alteration in Arcadia's border is indeed a geographic and hence a spatial change: Arcadia has been cut down and reduced in size; its territory has shrunk. The alteration thus appears to resemble what happens when a tree is reduced in size by having its branches trimmed or a rock by having part of it lopped off. But the appearance is misleading. Reducing the size of a tree or a rock does indeed consist in these physical operations, the trimming or the lopping, and in the material reconfigurations they bring about. Reducing Arcadia's size, by contrast, involves no such physical operations and no material change. Everything on the ground, so to speak, remains just as it was. Specifically, the pollutant does not change its location, and its emissions continue to affect the same region as before. What then does the change of boundary consist in? How does it exempt Arcadia from responsibility?

To answer these questions, a more basic question must be posed: Why is Arcadia held responsible for the pollutant in the first place? The common reply would be that the pollutant is on Arcadia's territory and forms part of it. Though this reply is valid and plays an indispensable pragmatic role in our ordinary dealings with the kinds of issues that Arcadia's border change illustrates, it hides more than it reveals. At a deeper explanatory level, a more informative answer is available. Put somewhat roughly, it is this. Rather than it being the case that a state is responsible for X because X is within its boundaries, it is the other way round: X is said to be within the state's boundary and counts as part of that state insofar as and in the sense that the state bears responsibility for it. To say about the pollutant that it is in Arcadia is not to specify its geographic location in the same sense as pointing out that it is, say, a hundred miles south of the Rockies. It is instead to indicate a normative, jurisdictional property, one that alludes to a complicated network of institutional and other normative arrangements that can be summarized, if somewhat crudely, by the statement that Arcadia is responsible for that pollutant. We can now provide a single answer to the two questions we posed about Arcadia's boundary change. The answer to the question what is a boundary change and to the question how it releases Arcadia from responsibility is one and the same: A border change ultimately just *is* a reallocation of responsibility concerning the pollutant.

How are we to reconcile the two replies I've contrasted—the common, pragmatic one, which views the fact that the pollutant is within Arcadia's borders as the ground of Arcadia's responsibility for it, and the theoretical, explanatory one, which reverses this statement? Correspondingly, how can a reallocation of responsibility over the pollutant be explained by a border change when border changes just are or amount to reallocations of responsibility? Doing full justice to the difficult issues that arise would take us too far afield, but the gist of the matter can be briefly indicated by considering a variant on the original example. Imagine that in Arcadia's case the usual incidents of the border line do not converge on a single geographic location: Some people are allowed to enter Arcadia's territory at one point, while others may enter elsewhere; customs are paid at some putative "entry points" but not at others; Arcadia bears only partial responsibility for certain goings on in some scattered territories, whereas others are responsible for the remaining goings on and the remaining regions; and so forth. Obviously, at some point, such arrangements would drain talk of a *border* of all meaning, and at about that point, any talk of *Arcadia* would be empty too.

The impracticality of this alternative arrangement, at least in the world as we know or think we know it, is also apparent. Such impracticality serves as a backdrop for understanding the pragmatic role of reifying *border* and *state*. Though a state's border is nothing but the reflection of such normative arrangements as I have mentioned, it provides various norms and attitudes with an indispensable focal point, thus allowing for an easy consolidation of what would otherwise be both cognitively and practically an unwieldy jumble of such norms and attitudes. Correspondingly, border-changing practices such as treaties are devices for inducing in one fell swoop the modification of an entire battery of norms and attitudes that are considered the common incidents of the border's location, a modification which in principle, but probably not in actuality, could be wrought piecemeal, without recourse to the orienting or unifying idea of a border or its change. So when we cite, as we commonly do, the location of the border or changes in it as the ground for judgments of responsibility, we simply take advantage of the orientation and unification that these ideas provide.

I have stressed the relationship of borders and their changes mostly to the allocation of responsibility, but it should be recognized that usually more is at stake. Other factors, such as various people's attitudes and attachments regarding the territory in question, are significant too. But taking account of these additional factors, though doubtlessly complicating matters, does not affect my main point. To see the point more clearly, we need to distinguish between two senses of *spatial*: *in space* and *pertaining to space*. Trimming trees and breaking stones are spatial in the first sense since they involve essentially the redistribution of matter *in space*. Redrawing a country's boundary, by contrast, is spatial in the second sense; it is changing the network of normative relations, as well as other understandings and attitudes, *pertaining to* a particular piece of land. Now a similar distinction applies to *temporal* as well. In one sense, a temporal change would require an alteration in the sequence of events. It is a fundamental tenet at least of our common-sense metaphysics, that unlike the corresponding spatial changes, temporal changes of this kind are impossible. A second sense of temporal, however, is that of *pertaining to* or *concerning time*. Changes in the significance we attach to past events, in our attitudes toward them, and most important for our purposes, in their normative ramifications are temporal in this second, innocuous sense.

We can now identify with precision the faulty premise of the objection to the analogy between the self's temporal change and the state's geographic change. The objection implicitly views the spatial border change, and correspondingly the temporal change wrought by revisionary practices, as involving the first sense of the respective adjectives, whereas they actually involve the second sense. The bearing this has on the argument must by now be clear. Just as redrawing Arcadia's border does not require any rearrangement of material objects but consists instead in a reduction in the spatial scope or field of application of some norms and attitudes, specifically with regard to the pollutant, so also in redrawing the self's temporal boundaries revisionary practices need not interfere with the sequence of events; all they need to accomplish is a contraction in the temporal scope or field of application of some norms and attitudes, specifically with regard to the past misdeed.

These considerations help overcome one metaphysical obstacle to analogizing revisionary practices to Arcadia's border change; but an additional obstacle remains. This is the first worry I mentioned earlier: Is the self such that its boundaries and shape are the product or reflection of such things as norms, practices, and attitudes? A dominant conception of self leads to a negative answer. This is the view of human beings as natural kinds, not relevantly different from trees and animals. The question where a tree ends or whether a cat caught a mouse has a determinate answer that no amount of fiddling with norms and attitudes will affect. On this conception, the same must be true of people as well. To remove this obstacle, this conception of self would have to be modified or debunked, but this is not my present aim. Instead of removing the obstacle, I only try to circumvent it by pointing to another widely held conception of self, or rather a family of such conceptions, with which the political analogy and the boundary metaphor are associated and in terms of which attaching to revisionary practices the significance I do makes better sense.

Many thinkers have spoken of the self in dramaturgical, narrative, or semiotic terms.[23] These imageries and metaphors dovetail with another broad theme. The view that "man has no essence" and must create his own originated at least as far back as the fifteenth century,[24] but has been given new impetus and significance in the twentieth, forming a common ground for some of the most influential and otherwise diverse schools of thought of the recent past, such as existentialism, postmodernism, and communitarianism. Two main variants on this theme that are particularly relevant to our present concerns can be discerned: one emphasizing the idea of *self-constitution* and the other of *social construction*.[25] Both purport to describe how as human beings we create ourselves, with the *we* interpreted either distributively—each individual is the author of his or her own identity—to yield the first variant, or jointly—social practices, discursive and otherwise shape our selves—to yield the second. In either case, the self-creation takes place in the medium of meaning: The self is the product of the web of meanings we spin around various objects and events, most importantly the human body and its career. This is of course a very cursory sketch of these conceptions of self, but I trust that they are familiar enough for the sketch to be recognizable. And no matter what details define and distinguish the various variants, it seems plausible that for all of them, norms, practices, and attitudes are precisely the kinds of materials that constitute selves and circumscribe them.[26] So although vast differences between the constitution of a state and of a self no doubt exist, the way is nonetheless clear to an instructive analogy between the two. Specifically, judgments of individual responsibility, as well as other personal norms and attitudes, which we commonly validate by reference to the constituents and the boundaries of the predicate self, are also the kinds of factors that shape the self and delineate its boundaries.[27]

However, removing the metaphysical obstacles to an account of revisionary practices as changing the temporal boundaries of the self gives only qualified support to this account. Even if the account does not encounter insurmountable metaphysical obstacles, is it true to the facts? It will be specifically objected that revisions in the self's temporal boundary, though conceivable, do not ever occur. For example, if asked point blank whether she had done the wrongful act, the offender would have to avow that she had despite having repented the act and having been forgiven and pardoned for it. To be sure, under these conditions the matter is unlikely to arise. It is inappropriate for the truly repentant to dwell on the past misdeed, and the hypothetical interrogator's bringing up the nasty event would be deemed unfair and obtuse. Still, the mere possibility of such an avowal seems to belie the claim that revisionary practices accomplish anything approaching the removal of the misdeed from the ambit of the wrongdoer's self.

To defuse this objection we need only take a closer look at the facts. These, as I had the objector recount them, are complex. One fact, the one that gives the objection its bite, is the counterfactual avowal. But an equally salient fact is that the avowal is for the most part counterfactual or hypothetical, prompted, if at all, by an inappropriate question certain to provoke indignation and disdain. However, if the misdeed were forever inscribed in the offender's past, as the objector implies, the latter aspects of the situation would be puzzling. Admittedly, an inquiry into the truth may sometimes be considered tactless or tasteless, but why would it meet, as it does in this case, with severe aversion? How can dredging up the past strike us not just as uncouth but also as unfair? Obviously, important norms are here at play, colloquially rendered by expressions such as "let bygones be bygones," designed to discourage an appeal to the past by rendering such an appeal highly inappropriate. Barring a rude violation of these norms, the offense will not come up, and the various attitudes and other ramifications ordinarily associated with it will have been effectively extinguished. These are powerful facts that need to be accounted for no less than what happens when the norms are breached and the past exhumed.

The proposed account offers a straightforward explanation for all these facts. A serious wrongdoing invariably casts a long shadow over the offender's life in the form of lasting negative attitudes and other consequences. When, due to the operation of the revisionary practices, the shadow disappears, we ought to conclude that its source in the wrongdoer's life has been removed. But this is only half the story. The possibility, no matter how remote, that the past misdeed may still surface must be accounted for as well. The key is a point I made earlier concerning the indeterminacy of Arcadia's border change: Various parties can draw a state's border in different ways without there being a single overriding authority or fact of the matter to choose among them or reconcile them once and for all. A similar indeterminacy, the product of a plurality of competing versions, pertains to the self's temporal shape. Revisionary practices give rise to a new version of the self from which the wrongful act is excluded. When this version is inhabited and enacted, it replaces the older one as superior or more authoritative. As long as this version is adhered to, as by and large it will be, the misdeed is indeed excluded from the self and does not cast a shadow. But the new version does not obliterate the other one; it only supersedes it. So if one insists, cruelly or obtusely, on unearthing the older version and on resorting to it, one is not strictly speaking mistaken but merely cruel or obtuse.[28]

Limits of Revision

Many believe that forgiveness has its limits and that certain acts are unforgivable: The enormity of evil may defy our capacity to overcome resentment.[29] Without disputing this view, I note that it does not, and does not purport to, provide any principled reasons against forgiving even the most egregious crimes; it only underscores people's inability to do so. Since forgiveness is generally thought to be a good thing, this inability appears to be a regrettable external limitation. Moreover, this approach opens up a gap between repentance and forgiveness. The psychological limitations on of forgiveness need not have their counterpart in the case of repentance, and at any rate, the limitations in both cases are unlikely to be the same. Consequently, cases may arise in which an offender truly repents an offense with no prospect of forgiveness. The tighter the link between forgiveness and repentance, the more disturbing this state of affairs would be.[30] My proposed account contrasts with the standard one in both of these respects. First, rather than focusing on the victim's psychological limitations, the constraints my account implies reflect the normative significance of the wrongdoer's identity. Second, since the constraints focus on the wrongdoer, who is the common object of all the revisionary practices, they apply not only to forgiveness but also and to the same extent to repentance and pardon. The magnitude of evil plays a role here as well, but its significance is different from the standard account, and additional considerations come into play.

The constraints on revisionary practices can be best understood in light of an earlier observation. In discussing Arcadia's border change, I have highlighted the balance between continuity and change that this case illustrates: To remove the pollutant from Arcadia's territory is to release Arcadia from responsibility while retaining its integrity as the object of these changes and as the beneficiary of the release. Since in my view revisionary practices redraw the temporal boundaries of the self, the redrawing cannot be so extensive as to effectively destroy the offender's self or amount to a change of identity. The wrongdoer's identity conditions thus set the limits of revision. Though specific conceptions of self and varying conditions of identity will have different implications on the permissible scope of

revisionary practices, the general point is straightforward. Considerations of identity preclude revision when the wrongdoing looms so large within the offender's
self that removing the wrongdoing would not result in a viable or recognizable
version of that self.[31]

The severity of the wrong done clearly retains its relevance within this account.[32]
Doing major harm ordinarily requires greater effort and resolve than inflicting minor harm, and the features of mind and character on which such an act depends
are likely to be pervasive and central. It may not be possible, therefore, to effect a
neat excision of an egregious misdeed without destroying the offender's identity
in the process.

My account also draws attention to constraining factors other than the magnitude of evil. Without trying to be exhaustive, I will mention three. One concerns
the way wrongfulness is to be measured. If the offender harmed many individuals,
the standard view will tend to assess wrongfulness distributively. People's capacity
to overcome resentment is likely to be more sensitive to the wrong experienced by
each of them. Consequently, victims may find it possible to forgive their individual
injuries without regard to aggregate harm. In my approach, by contrast, the aggregate harm dominates. Since we're primarily interested in the overall significance of
the wrongful behavior in the *wrongdoer's* life, the sum total of harmful actions is a
more suitable measure. The second factor is the duration of the wrongful behavior
within the offender's life. Revision is less appropriate and less likely to satisfy the
identity conditions in the case of a lifelong hit man than in the case of someone
who killed the same number of people in one shooting spree early in life. Even if
the crimes are equally heinous, committing them as part of an enduring career
makes them a more central source of meaning and a defining characteristic of the
life story as a whole. The third factor concerns the distinction between "personal"
and "impersonal" activities, such as those done in an official capacity. Since the
latter typically call for, and perhaps are defined by, a large measure of detachment
and compartmentalization, they are relatively confined within the offender's self
and kept secluded from the rest of it. Other things being equal, it is easier to re-
create a viable version of a self with impersonal wrongs removed than in the case
of someone who commits wrongs in a personal capacity.

One final comment. I earlier noted that the limitations that are commonly
thought to apply to forgiveness are for the most part a matter of the victims' psychology, specifically their finite capacity to overcome resentment. This appears
as a brute fact and, given the value of forgiveness, an unfortunate one. Are the

constraints imposed on revisionary practices by the offender's conditions of identity any different? Aren't they also regrettable shackles on what could be a gentler and more lenient world? This is a nagging thought, so it is important to underscore the fundamental difference between these two sets of limitations. Unlike the victim's psychology, the offender's identity is essentially implicated in the operation of revisionary practices from the start. To see this, recall that the reactive attitudes such as guilt and resentment play a decisive role in defining a person's responsibility and that by doing so they participate in the construction of a self. Now revisionary practices are involved in this construction by setting limits on the scope or operation of the reactive attitudes. But their ability to do so is in turn limited by the identity-based constraints. The main point is this: Constructing a self, like anything else, must accord with some imperatives. In building a house, you cannot build the roof first. Such imperatives aren't just constraints on the enterprise but are just as much its enabling conditions. The identity-based constraints to which revisionary practices are subject form a part of a single set of imperatives that guide and enable the construction of selves. The reactive attitudes, the limitations imposed on them by revisionary practices, and the identity-based constraints that limit revisionary practices' capacity to terminate reactive attitudes are all interlocking parts of one and the same enterprise, the enterprise of creating a self or, which comes down to the same thing, being one.

Notes

For their helpful comments, I would like to thank my friends and colleagues Bruce Ackerman, George Fletcher, Chaim Gans, Ruth Gavison, Paul Hoeber, Niko Kolodny, Andrei Marmor, Seana Shiffrin, and Steve Sugarman, as well as the participants in the Bay Area Forum for Law and Ethics (BAFFLE), in a session at the APA—Eastern Division Annual Meeting, in the Law, Philosophy and Political Theory Workshop at Berkeley, and in the symposium on which this volume is based.

1. By speaking of *practices*, I only mean to imply that some public criteria exist as to what counts as repentance and so on. It doesn't follow that the practices themselves must consist in public acts. For example, internal, subjective acts of contrition may in principle satisfy the criteria for repentance, though in such a case these acts would obviously have to be communicated for repentance to play its usual interpersonal roles (e.g., as a reason for forgiveness).

2. This is the dominant view and clearly the paradigm case, but borderline cases sometimes arise, complicated by the occasional difficulty of establishing who counts as the victim

of a wrongdoing. See, e.g., Trudy Govier and Wilhelm Verwoerd, "Forgiveness: The Victim's Prerogative," *South African J. Phil.* 21 (2002), 97.

3. It is quite common to view pardon as a form of official forgiveness. See, e.g., Joram Graf Haber, *Forgiveness* (Savage, MD: Rowman & Littlefield, 1991), 60–61. The proximity between forgiveness and pardon is also suggested by the French word *pardoner*, meaning "to forgive," a usage that has a colloquial echo in the English expression "pardon me."

4. This corresponds to the three types of reactive attitudes distinguished by Peter Strawson in "Freedom and Resentment," in *Freedom and Resentment and Other Essays* (Methuen, 1973): *personal, self-reactive,* and *vicarious.* The view of forgiveness as the overcoming of resentment probably originated with Bishop Butler, see Joseph Butler, "Upon Forgiveness of Injuries," in *The Works of the Right Reverend Father in God, Joseph Butler, D.C.L.,* ed. Samuel Halifax (New York: Carter, 1846), 106–107, and has been reinforced by Strawson's influential paper, in which resentment is seen as the paradigm reactive attitude and thus the natural focal point of discussions of forgiveness. This is not to deny, however, that other negative attitudes exist and that complete forgiveness ought to suppress those as well. See on this point Norvin Richards, "Forgiveness," *Ethics* 99 (1988), 77, 79; and Robert C. Roberts, "Forgiveness," *Am. Phil. Q.* 32 (1995), 289.

5. Related to my normative focus is another qualification—namely, that I discuss a decisively idealized conception of revisionary practices both in the sense of a (Weberian) ideal type and in the sense of something worth aspiring for. I believe that both of these idealizations are consonant (in the respectively appropriate ways) with widely spread ordinary perceptions and aspirations, but I will not try to buttress this belief.

6. See, e.g. Haber, *Forgiveness*; John Wilson, "Why Forgiveness Requires Repentance," *Philosophy* 63 (1988), 524; Zoltan Balazs, "Forgiveness and Repentance," *Public Affairs Q.* 14 (2000), 105, 120–124; Richards, "Forgiveness," 88. Authors differ, though, on how tight the connection is between repentance and forgiveness. As I point out later, my proposed account aims to accommodate this difference of opinion.

7. Hard, but not impossible. For a rather extreme dissent, see Margaret R. Holmgren who maintains that "the appropriateness of forgiveness has nothing to do with the actions, attitudes, or position of the wrongdoer," in "Forgiveness and the Intrinsic Value of Persons," *Am. Phil. Q.* 30 (1993), 341, 342.

8. Jeffrie G. Murphy and Jean Hampton, *Forgiveness and Mercy* (Cambridge: Cambridge University Press, 1988), 26 (emphasis in the original).

9. Richards, "Forgiveness," 88.

10. Both of these moments are combined in a sophisticated version of these accounts offered by Pamela Hieronymi, on whose view "*resentment protests a past action that persists as a present threat,*" in "Articulating an Uncompromising Forgiveness," *Phil. and Phenom. Research* 62 (2001), 529, 546 (italics in the original; note omitted).

11. This is the gist of Jean Hampton's position. "The forgiver comes to see [the wrongdoer] as still *decent, not* rotten as a person, and someone with whom he may be able to

renew a relationship." In Murphy and Hampton, *Forgiveness and Mercy*, 83. On her view, repentance provides the main reason for such a change in the forgiver's conception of the wrongdoer, though Hampton also allows for forgiveness "for old times' sake."

12. The distinctive role played by the wrongful act is sometimes exaggerated and distorted by the recommendation, associated most famously with St. Augustine, that one hate the sin but not the sinner. Despite the noble sentiment (and the august provenance), the recommendation is incoherent. We can't conceive of an action in abstraction from an actor. To see correctly the role played by the wrongful act in regard to the reactive attitudes, we must distinguish between their *ground* and their *object*. Resentment is addressed to the offender as its object, but its ground is the misdeed, not the person as a whole; we resent the actor *qua* the author of the wrong.

13. For a critical discussion of the change-of-identity approach, see Haber, *Forgiveness*, 95–98; Joanna North, "Wrongdoing and Forgiveness," *Philosophy* 62 (1987), 499.

14. In Murphy and Hampton, *Forgiveness and Mercy*, 26.

15. See Aurel Kolnai, "Forgiveness," *Proceedings of the Aristotelian Society* 74 (1973–1974), 98–99.

16. Contrast in this regard Joanna North's view that "Forgiveness is a way of healing the damage done to one's relation with the wrongdoer," "Wrongdoing and Forgiveness," 503, with the observation by Tara Smith that "one person can forgive another even when they have had no relationship to continue," in "Tolerance and Forgiveness: Virtues or Vices?" *J. Applied Phil.* 1 (1997), 31, 37.

17. Cf., e.g., R. S. Downie, "Forgiveness," *Phil. Q.* 15 (1965), 128, esp. 130; Martin P. Golding, "Forgiveness and Regret," *The Philosophical Forum* 16 (1984–1985), 121, 130; Jean Harvey, "Forgiveness as an Obligation of the Moral Life," *International J. Moral and Social Stud.* 8 (1993), 211; and Berel Lang, "Forgiveness," *Am. Phil. Q.* 31 (1994), 105.

18. Cf. Hannah Arendt, *The Human Condition* (Chicago: University of Chicago Press, 1958), § 33.

19. As indeed some firmly believe. It has been said, for example, that "repentance consists in our setting ourselves against a past reality and absurdly attempting to efface that reality from the world." Haber, *Forgiveness*, 94. See also Lucien Jerphagnon, "Repentance," *Phil. Today* 3 (1959), 176, for a discussion of several approaches to this general theme.

20. In light of the analogy to revisionary practices that I wish to draw, two clarifications of this example are in order. First, the border change obviously does not relieve Arcadia of obligations that have already accrued prior to the change. My point is only that pursuant to the change, no new obligations will accrue. Second, it is immaterial whether after Arcadia's border changes, the pollutant is joined to another state or winds up in some unowned territory. The latter possibility is less likely on a globe that is mostly divided among states, but this is a contingent, and indeed a relatively recent, state of affairs.

21. On the significance of "counting as" as fundamental to social phenomena in general, see John Searle, *The Construction of Social Reality* (New York: The Free Press, 1995), esp. 43–51.

22. This point is sometimes conveyed by describing some revisionary practices as *performative*. Compare, e.g., Haber, *Forgiveness*, 6–7, and Lang, "Forgiveness," both of whom conceive forgiveness in this way, with Downie, "Forgiveness," who denies that forgiveness is or requires a performative but believes that pardon does. Since I speak more broadly, and vaguely, about revisionary *practices*, and thus don't limit myself to speech acts, the more general designation *constructive* is more apt than *performative*, and I need not enter the debate regarding the applicability of the latter to any of the revisionary practices. See also in this connection my comment in note 1.

23. The dramaturgical perspective is most famously associated with the work of Erving Goffman, e.g., *Encounters* (Indianapolis, IN: Bobbs-Merrill, 1961), 85–152, and *Frame Analysis: An Essay on the Organization of Experience* (Chicago: Northwestern University Press, 1974). For sources that canvass the literature on the two other approaches I mention, see Charles Taylor, *The Sources of the Self* (Cambridge: Cambridge University Press, 1989), and Marya Schechtman, *The Constitution of Selves* (Ithaca, NY: Cornell University Press, 1989), on narrative conceptions; and Norbert Wiley, *The Semiotic Self* (Chicago: University of Chicago Press, 1994), on the semiotic conception.

24. In a well-known text by Giovanni Pico della Mirandola, *Oration on the Dignity of Man*, trans. A. Robert Caponigri (Washington, DC: Regency Gateway, 1956).

25. The connection between the self-constitution idea and the political analogy is made explicitly in J. David Velleman, "The Self as Narrator," in *Autonomy and the Challenges to Liberalism: New Essays*, ed. Joel Anderson and John Christman (Cambridge: Cambridge University Press, 2005), 56. See also Tamar Schapiro, "What Is a Child?" *Ethics* 109 (1999), 715.

26. Cf. Max Scheler's view of repentance as involving not a change of the past but of the meaning with which we endow the past, e.g., in "Repentance and Rebirth," in *On the Eternal in Man* (Hamden, CT: Shoe String Press, 1972), 35. Scheler's views on this subject are discussed in Peter H. Spader, "A Change of Heart: Scheler's *Ordo Amoris*, Repentance and Rebirth," *Listening* 21 (1986), 188. In a similar vein, Pamela Hieronymi stresses the social meaning of the wrongful act as well as of repentance and forgiveness, linking the social meaning to the bearing of revisionary practices on the offender's identity. "Articulating an Uncompromising Forgiveness," 549–551.

27. Although the conceptions of self to which I allude are broadly speaking hospitable to my approach, they do not settle without further argument, which I cannot attempt here, all the issues that the version of "ascriptivism" to which I subscribe gives rise. I spell out this view somewhat more fully in "Responsibility and the Boundaries of the Self," *Harvard L. Rev.* 105 (1992), 959; a revised version appears as chap. 7 of my *Harmful Thoughts: Essays on Law, Self, and Morality* (Princeton, NJ: Princeton University Press, 2002). For an earlier relevant debate, see H. L. A. Hart, "The Ascription of Responsibility and Rights," *Proceedings of the Aristotelian Society, New Series* 49 (1949), 171; P. T. Geach, "Ascriptivism," and George Pitcher, "Hart on Action and Responsibility," both in *The Philosophical Review* 69 (1960), 221–225 and 226–235, respectively.

28. Let me mention briefly two other questions that may arise. One concerns the relationship between revisionary practices and punishment. My account implies that the revisionary practices are inconsistent with a continued insistence on punishment so that they must either occur subsequent to punishment or as a substitute for it. For the contrary view, see, e.g., Jeffrie Murphy, in Murphy and Hampton, *Forgiveness and Mercy*, 33. See also Anthony Duff's view that the purpose of punishment is to induce and express repentance, in *Trials and Punishment* (Cambridge: Cambridge University Press, 1986) chap. 8–10, and "Punishment and Penance—A Reply to Harrison," *The Aristotelian Society* Supp. Vol. 62 (1988), 153–167. The second question concerns the status of the revisionary practice itself relative to the reconstituted self. For example, if due to my repentance I am no longer the author of the wrongful act, there is nothing to which my act of repentance can latch on or be about. Does that mean that I am deprived of credit for having repented and am otherwise precluded from counting the process of contrition itself as part of my life? I can see three responses. The first is to acknowledge that a successful process of repentance does result in having the entire episode, including the repentance, excised from the self. Credit for repenting is indeed lost together with the guilt for the offense. The second option is to draw a line between the wrong done and the revisionary practice, removing the former from within the boundary of the self but retaining the latter. What makes this seemingly incoherent suggestion viable is the narrative conception of the self. Since a story need not contain an answer to every question that its plot invites, it is possible for a process of repentance to be part of a narrative while leaving unanswered the question of what was the repentance for. The third possibility, and the one toward which I most incline, is to deny that the revisionary practice must either be within the boundary of the self or outside it. Rather, the practice is itself the marker of the self's boundary. On this view, to ask with respect to a revisionary practice whether it falls within or without the self's temporal boundary is like inquiring with respect to Arcadia on which side of its border the border itself lies.

29. See, e.g., Golding, "Forgiveness and Regret," 122.

30. This has led some to play down the psychological difficulties and to deny any limitation on forgiveness. See, e.g., Trudy Govier, "Forgiveness and the Unforgivable," *Am. Phil. Q.* 36 (1999), 59.

31. Despite the surface similarity, my point differs fundamentally from the position critiqued by Trudy Govier. Using the example of Pol Pot, Govier examines the possibility that "in such a case the moral person is defined by his acts over so much of his lifetime—that ultimately we cannot draw a moral distinction between these terrible things to which he committed so much of his life and the person that he is." Ibid., 68. Govier rejects this line of reasoning, arguing that "We go too far if we insist that some people have become so indelibly evil that there is no possibility of their moral change . . . Many persons do change, and even some persons who have been guilty of appalling evil do change," 69. But this is essentially the future-oriented conception of revisionary practices and, by implication, of the reactive attitudes, which I criticized earlier on. This approach does not take seriously

enough the significance of the ongoing presence of the past atrocities in the person's life and identity quite apart from any subsequent changes in the person's attitudes or values. A future-oriented change of heart does not by itself explain why reactions to these features of the person's identity become no longer appropriate.

32. Cf. Lang, "Forgiveness," who lists this and some other factors as bearing on whether an action is in principle unforgivable. I am not quite clear what theory is supposed to unite these considerations in his view.

Comparative National Blaming: W. G. Sebald on the Bombing of Germany

BRUCE ROBBINS

In an article entitled "Israel, Palestine, and the Campus Civil Wars," published in December 2004 in the online journal *Open Democracy*, British historian Stephen Howe wrote: "There is a good rule of thumb for social arguments, now applicable to almost any subject and circumstance. It goes simply: whoever first mentions the Nazis loses the argument."[1] I ask you to consider this one-liner in conjunction with another, not as clever but again emerging from debate about the Middle East. It describes a common response on the Israeli street to political reproaches from foreigners about Israel's treatment of the Palestinians: "Nobody's better than we are, so they should all shut up."[2]

These slogans differ, of course, in how much shutting up they encourage and how much immunity from hostile commentary this silence seems intended to se-cure. At a certain level of abstraction, however, the two slogans can perhaps be said to share the same purpose: to throw a critical light on the rhetorical practice that I call, for want of a more precise term, *comparative national blaming*. (A utilitarian alternative might be "the calculus of national accountability for infelicity," but I can't see that catching on.) Both sentences seem to object in particular to the use of national comparison to seize, as the saying goes, the high moral ground, with the invocation of fascism as absolute evil, for example in Christopher Hitchens's repeated post-9/11 references to "Islamo-Fascists," being merely a special instance of such seizure. But is this an exercise that can only be conducted from a moral ele-vation? It might seem that criticism of one nation's conduct could be legitimately illuminated by reference to another nation's conduct without anyone being obliged to produce a certificate of spotless rectitude. All likeness is inexact, but is this a suf-ficient reason for prohibiting references to the Union Carbide disaster at Bhopal as the Hiroshima of industrial accidents or discouraging parallels between today's Guantánamo prison camps and the Soviet-era gulag? On what grounds exactly should Toni Morrison be prevented from dedicating *Beloved* to the 60 million, thereby linking the victims of the Middle Passage to the Jewish victims of the Holocaust? Yet the second and more popular of my initial slogans, expressing a defensive national pride that is surely not confined to Israelis, refuses even a moderate version of national comparison. If one is permitted neither (1) to take sides on a questionable action or situation by identifying it with an earlier, unquestioned figure of wrongdoing (the Nazis) nor (2) to refer to national differences that also involve relative historical inequalities, whether of scale, of degree of guilt, or whatever, then national comparison itself seems ruled out—except to the extent that it always remains implicit in "nobody's better than we are." If forgiveness is what follows and undoes a prior act of blaming, then this discursive state of affairs might be tentatively described as generalized presumptive forgiveness.

In the United States, the assumption on the street would probably be that "we're better than anyone else." Within the limits set jointly by this assumption and by our overwhelming ignorance of the rest of the world, national comparison thrives. Perhaps the only place where it does not thrive is the humanities, where the anti-comparison position has made a surprising amount of room for itself. Although Howe's no-Nazi rule of thumb, which seems representative of the reigning academic common sense, seems intended merely to curb attributions of essential and irredeemable evil, it makes its point by implying that the Holocaust, a product of such evil, is unique in that respect. Accordingly, the sufferings of its victims must therefore remain beyond or above all comparison. But this logic has proved wildly popular and therefore impossible to quarantine. In effect, the uniqueness of the Holocaust has been universalized. After all, whose national suffering is not, in its own way, unique? Whose national particulars cannot claim to be inherently incomparable? If it does not shut down completely all efforts to compare, the incomparability position certainly burdens them with considerable anxiety.

Benedict Anderson takes the title of his book *The Spectre of Comparisons* from José Rizal's masterpiece *Noli Me Tangere*, where it refers to the Filipino hero's inability to "matter-of-factly experience" the municipal gardens of Manila without simultaneously comparing them with the (original, primary) gardens he has seen in Europe (2).[3] This double vision is "incurable" (2), Anderson says, but with such regret as to suggest that if so, then countries like the Philippines will never enjoy, as they have every right to, a genuine cultural autonomy. The search for a cure, a means of exorcizing the specter of comparisons, thus continues to motivate. It is commonly taken for granted across the humanities disciplines that because any comparison demands a common standard and because any (supposedly) common standard will in fact favor the interests of some over the interests of others (a frequent example is the discourse of human rights), comparison is imperialistic by its very nature.[4] Although the academic rhetoric of praise and blame is far too deeply ingrained not to find other ways of expressing itself, one might say that, where international comparison is concerned, the academy has cordoned off a zone of universal blamelessness, dramatically distinct from the strident national name-calling assumed to be going on outside. Within this zone, the one critical act likely to be blamed is national blaming itself.[5]

I begin with these two quotations, which call attention to the apparent but precarious division between academic and nonacademic common sense on the comparing of nations, first of all because they frame the large questions that underlie this chapter (without unfortunately finding satisfactory answers within it). How is comparative national blaming actually done? What might it look like if done better or done right? Can we, should we, give up on it? These questions are urgent in themselves, but they also provide an essential background to the issues of forgiveness, mercy, and clemency dealt with in this volume. Common-sense notions of justice and fairness, which flow into the law, pressure it, and sometimes expose its shortcomings, have of course their own shortcomings for which the law in turn tries to compensate. Nowhere are both sets of shortcomings more obvious than in judgments of events beyond the borders of the nation. In the international realm, a realm to which the adjective "Hobbesian" seems almost as firmly attached now as fifty years ago, the law itself has only a fragile hold. The mass media, not notorious for their responsible attention to domestic matters, seem still more unreliable on foreign affairs. Yet this realm provides us with case after case, past and present, in which the vocabulary of accusing, forgiving, and forgetting, however inappropriate, will nonetheless be asked to do what it can do—that is, to mediate between international politics and an individual scale and sense of what is and isn't right. When pundits advise us not to play "the blame game," a phrase insinuating our well-established agreement that the game itself is blameworthy, should we take their advice? Can countries forgive? Can they be forgiven? Surrounded as we are by statements about what Elazar Barkan calls "the guilt of nations," we have no choice but to find out more about the general cultural resources instructing us on these matters.[6] And if comparison reveals a significant difference here between opinion on the street and the credentialed wisdom of the experts, we need to know that as well.

I also find these opening quotations compelling points of reflection because they respond to a situation in the Middle East that is—if you will permit me an insidious but to me unavoidable moment of national comparison—*like* that of the United States after September 11, 2001, a situation in which a claim to victimhood is put forward by a population seen widely from without as victimizers rather than victims. This rhetorical likeness is also one source of uneasy fascination in W. G. Sebald's book *On the Natural History of Destruction*—in the original German, "The Air War and Literature"—which I will discuss at some length.[7]

The topic of the two lectures that comprise this book was again a silence that was also a refusal to blame: silence about the sufferings of German civilians in cities devastated by Allied bombers in World War II, a catastrophic experience that Sebald argues took half a century even to begin working its way into the national consciousness or the national literature. The most evident explanation for this silence, the explanation Sebald mentions once early on and then returns to at the end of his text, is again a practice of national comparison: a comparison with the sufferings Germany caused. It is this comparison, however implicit, that plausibly leaves the Germans, despite more than half a million dead, unable to believe in their absolute victimhood and hence unable to narrate or perhaps even to remember. On the last page, Sebald notes "the fact that the real pioneering achievements in bomb warfare—Guernica, Warsaw, Belgrade, Rotterdam—were the work of the Germans" (104). "The majority of Germans today know, or so at least it is to be hoped, that we actually provoked the annihilation of the cities in which we once lived" (103). If there was never an "open debate" in Germany about the strategic or moral justification for the Allied bombing, he says, it was "no doubt mainly because a nation which had murdered and worked to death millions of people in its camps could hardly call on the victorious powers to explain the military and political logic that dictated the destruction of the German cities. It is also possible . . . that quite a number of those affected by the air raids, despite their grim but impotent fury in the face of such obvious madness, regarded the great firestorms as just punishment, even as an act of retribution on the part of a higher power with which there could be no dispute" (14).[8] What better motive for silence than the conviction, as Christopher Hitchens puts it in his review of the book, that "well, what goes around comes around" (186)?[9]

This hypothesis is intriguing, to begin with, because it's so obviously not what a majority of Americans decided after 9/11. If not, then why not? What would it take for Americans now to respond the way Germans did after 1945? Am I breaking

Stephen Howe's rule in conceiving this question? But the hypothesis also invites further and more serious scrutiny because Sebald himself does not appear to believe it. If he did believe it, why would he have written thousands and thousands of words accusing the Germans of their failure to remember? Why did he go on to treat the silence as something like a crime, and an unsolved one? According to Volker Hage in his 2003 book on literary reactions to the air war, *Zeugen der Zerstörung* (*Witnesses to the Destruction*), German critics have often insisted, against Sebald, that the German silence was self-conscious and entirely appropriate: "if one measured the suffering of the perpetrating nation against the horror that Germany and its henchmen had brought to the conquered peoples of the East and above all those sacrificed to the design of racial elimination," then, as one of them put it, "Perhaps the silence concealed a shame that is more precious than any literature" (118–119).[10]

In what he modestly describes as unsystematic notes, Sebald offers several very different interpretations of the German silence. Sometimes he suggests, restricting all blame to the bombers, that these "true stories . . . exceeded anyone's capacity to grasp them" (23). The word *capacity* is stressed. "The death by fire within a few hours of an entire city, with all its buildings and its trees, its inhabitants, its domestic pets, its fixtures and fittings of every kind, must inevitably have led to overload, to paralysis of the capacity to think and feel in those who succeeded in escaping" (25). The magnitude of the experience seems, like Kant's mathematical sublime, to defy all comparison, making a demand for representation that cannot be refused, on the one hand, while at the same time and by the same token, that very magnitude makes adequate representation impossible. The absolute horror of the firestorms, the inhuman scale and speed of the death and destruction, simply exceeded the capacities of the human senses and/or the categories of the human mind. As in media discussions of so-called "compassion fatigue," the size and shape of the human container are considered to set more or less absolute limits to how much suffering can be taken in and digested before people turn off or tune out.

According to Andreas Huyssen, this account of the German response to the bombing is less than totally accurate: "there always was a lot of *talk* about the bombings in postwar Germany."[11] Another problem with Sebald's hypothesis might be called its technologism. Like Walter Benjamin's parable in "The Storyteller" of how the technology of long-distance killing in World War I undermined the "experience" of the soldiers, hence also their ability to tell stories, it suggests that technology, whether expanding our destructive powers or expanding the scope of our senses, necessarily collides with the capacities of the individual rational mind, conceived as fixed and finite. The ability to kill from further and further away, so that the combatants finally need not see each other at all, is of course a real truth about the history of modern warfare. Yet the conclusions drawn from it seem to rely on implicit contrast with a universal "face-to-face" norm or model of comprehensible, communicable violence. And this model lends itself to all sorts of ethical and political confusions, among them (1) a naturalizing of local and national belonging at the expense of long-distance affiliations and commitments, as if the latter were less natural and less real and (2) the delusion that physical proximity acts as a kind of natural brake or impediment to violence. The canonical wisdom on bombing is articulated in Eric Hobsbawm's history of the world from 1914 to 1991, *The Age of Extremes*. Hobsbawm describes "the new impersonality of warfare, which turned killing and maiming into the remote consequences of pushing a button or moving a lever. Technology made its victims invisible, as people eviscerated by bayonets, or seen through the sights of firearms could not be. . . . Far below the aerial bombers were not people about to be burned and eviscerated, but targets. Mild young men, who would certainly not have wished to plunge a bayonet in the belly of any pregnant village girl, could far more easily drop high explosives on London or Berlin, or nuclear bombs on Nagasaki. . . . The greatest cruelties of our century have been the impersonal cruelties of remote decision, of system and routine" (50).[12] By flattering the mildness of the mild young men, this indictment of technologically mediated impersonality as such cries out for the sarcasm it receives from media critic Thomas Keenan, encountering a version of it in a recent online discussion of the war in Iraq: "Yeah, I think we all share a longing for the good old days when killing was up close and personal, when you really had to see your enemy ('whites of their eyes,' and all that) before the slaughter could begin, when war was real and effective, not this inefficient but easy virtual game stuff. Like, um, in April and May and June of 1994, when those interahamwe guys . . . in Rwanda set the current world record for temporally-concentrated killing, 800,000 to 1,000,000 people dead in 100 days."[13] Or to take another sort of example, when the ancient Israelites killed all of the neighboring Midianites except the nubile virgins, one cannot say the genocide was hindered by the primitiveness of their weaponry. It's possible to negotiate between these two positions, for example by insisting, as in Mahmood Mamdani's book on Rwanda and Joanna Bourne's book on "face-to-face killing in 20th century warfare," on how much ideological work has become necessary to turn everyday mildness into face-to-face murder.[14] Still, the automatic ethical effects supposedly caused by the military technology of remoteness seem as questionable in relation to bombing as in relation to video games.

The remoteness-makes-cruelty-easier argument, which seems obscurely linked to the proposition that being bombed makes narrative difficult, often comes accompanied by just that ironic corollary to which Keenan alludes: the suggestion that bombing doesn't actually work. This may well have been the case in World War II, as Sebald claims (correctly, according to most authorities).[15] It was certainly the case in Vietnam and again—from the perspective of "winning the peace"—now in Iraq. But there is something strange in the repeated yoking of remoteness both to psychological ease and to strategic ineffectuality. There are blatant historical cases like the Gulf War or the ousting of Saddam Hussein or the many other colonial wars documented by Sven Lindqvist in his *History of Bombing* where, for better or worse, bombing *did* work, at least in the sense of achieving its aims. We seem to be in the presence here of a counterfactual but deeply embedded cultural narrative.

Sebald suggests at first that the bombing, strategically irrelevant, was pursued nonetheless as an attempt to break the "morale" (17) of the Germans, and it was also seen as "essential for bolstering British morale" (18). Then he goes further. The bombing was not merely a piece of bad planning based on nothing more solid than phantasmatic projections of future "morale." It was not merely a strategic mistake, something the Allies hoped would shorten the war but didn't. It was irrational in its very essence. Sebald quotes with approval Elaine Scarry's conclusion from *The Body in Pain*: "the victims of war are not sacrifices made as the means to an end of any kind, but in the most precise sense are both the means and the end in themselves" (19–20). In effect, this is an alternative explanation for the failure of German memory.[16] If the bombing was fundamentally irrational, if it did not even respond to the strategic self-interest of the Allies, if in that sense it was incomprehensible, then its incomprehensibility would of course also make it harder for the victims to fix the bombing in narrative or in memory. And it would become that much easier to nudge the bombing and the Holocaust closer to equivalence.

This oblique commitment to incomprehensibility would also explain why Sebald lays the responsibility of remembering on literature rather than some other form of discourse, while simultaneously making it impossible for literature to fulfill this responsibility. He asks literature not merely to preserve "traces of pain," as eyewitness accounts might do just as well, but to make the pain "comprehensible" (10), to tell us "what it all actually meant" (4). Telling us what it all actually meant entails something much more strenuous. Indeed, for Sebald, it is self-contradictory and ultimately unattainable. He speaks of literature as an attempt "to make sense of the senseless" (49)—a characteristically no-win formulation that somehow leaves him free to accuse anyway, even though "sense" itself, could it be achieved, might then be understood as proof of literature's failure to do justice to the event or to *be* literature. Logically enough, he accuses every literary text that did treat the bombing of doing so badly, and badly precisely to the extent that it is, indeed, literary: because it uses plot, style, self-conscious artifice, and so on rather than simply recording the observed facts.

The cultural narrative that subtly turns the inefficiency of bombing into the irrationality of bombing is a strangely comforting one, I would suggest, for it allows the *system* to replace the *individual* as the source or site of a fundamental irrationality, and thus—this seems to be the intent of Scarry's overeager embrace of the irrationality of war as well—it manages to save the rationality of the individual. In preserving the freedom to remember or not, it also preserves a responsibility to remember, and with the responsibility it allows leverage for Sebald's indignation that they did *not* remember. Psychoanalysis, which of course rejects such assumptions about the fundamental rationality of the individual, is not one of Sebald's preferred modes of explanation. Though he occasionally refers to "repression," for example, quoting Enzensberger's theory that the "mysterious energy" behind the German economic recovery came in part from repression of their "total degradation" (12–13) in the bombings, he more often seems to prefer a humanistic vocabulary that suggests a greater degree of individual freedom to remember or not. In that freedom, as I said, lies a mandate for Sebald's indignation. Sebald comes closer than Enzensberger to saying, indignantly, that his postwar compatriots wanted to forget merely to concentrate on making money.

Here I open a brief parenthesis concerning national comparison in general. Clearly, one of its functions is to affront. Explaining the bipartisan French vote in 2004 for Jacques Chirac to stop the far-right nationalist Jean-Marie Le Pen, Perry Anderson writes, "The second round duly gave him a majority of 82 per cent, worthy of a Mexican president in the heyday of the PRI. On the Left Bank, his vote reached virtually Albanian proportions" (14).[17] Albania and Mexico are terms of abuse, yes, but there is no obvious inaccuracy here to which a Mexican or Albanian chauvinist might legitimately object. (For contrast, consider Michael Moore's visual references to "the coalition of the willing" in *Fahrenheit 9/11*.) Objection might perhaps be made to the assumption that France really is, or ought to be, different in its expectations of democratic diversity from Mexico and Albania. Is Anderson expressing a sort of Great Power arrogance? If so, he is also, and unexpectedly, holding open a zone of free will. Playing on the presumed incongruity between French and Albanian versions of democracy, he appeals to the possibility of doing a better job than the French, at least, seem to be doing. If you are proud enough to think that your democracy works better than Albania's, he tells the French, then prove it—you can. In the same mode, he tells the English that if the French could make a bourgeois revolution, then they can too; comparison reveals that it can be done, for somewhere it *has* been done. Anderson, whose structural, antihumanist, somewhat deterministic version of Marxism makes him constitutionally skeptical of all appeals to the will, finds in the language of national comparison an oblique, somewhat backhanded means of expressing exhortation, which is to say implying the existence of freedom, hence accountability—his equivalent of Sebald's indignation at his fellow Germans.

The link between Sebald's equivocations as to the cause of the German silence and his defense of the rational individual appears in an early passage when he speaks of the so-called "literature of the ruins" as "probably influenced by preconscious self-censorship—a means of obscuring a world that could no longer be presented in comprehensible terms" (10). If the world could no longer be presented in comprehensible terms, then one would think it was already obscure enough. What was there to be gained by seeking to obscure it further? It's as if Sebald wants to blame the survivors (they were surely trying to gain *something*) without being quite sure on what grounds the blame is deserved. The next two lines compound this ambiguity. "There was a tacit agreement, equally binding on everyone, that the true state of material and moral ruin in which the country found itself was not to be described. The darkest aspects of the final act of destruction, as experienced by the great majority of the German population, remained under a kind of taboo like a shameful family secret, a secret that perhaps could not even be privately acknowledged" (10). This "not to be described" (in German, "nicht beschrieben werden" [18]) does not suggest something by its very nature "indescribable," as one might think, so much as a self-imposed imperative *not* to describe—an imperative that, like any other imperative, one could choose either to obey or not to obey, and might be blamed for not obeying.

Yet this same passage also gives an indication that the forces involved might *have* to be obeyed, might be too unquestionably overpowering for even the staunchest will to withstand.[18] The German term translated above as "ruin" is *Vernichtung*, more literally "destruction" or "annihilation" but also "extermination," the very word (I quoted it a minute ago from the Hage book) that has stuck to the Nazi "extermination camps." This is a strong verbal hint of equivalence between what was done by the Nazis in the extermination camps and what was done by the Allies in the German cities. It attributes the silence of the German survivors in the cities to a trauma of memory no less cataclysmic than that suffered by the survivors of the camps.

Here Sebald is breaking Howe's "he who mentions the Nazis first" rule. Or perhaps I should say that he is breaking *down* that rule—playing the game of comparative national blame so as to undermine the absolute and incomparable authority of the Nazi example. As I suggested earlier, it remains unclear whether this authority is something that Howe himself, while eager to reject a rhetorical figure of instantly legitimized hatred, is also eager to preserve.

How should we feel about this comparison? We would certainly be within our rights if we protested, worrying for example about how comparison threatens to devalue the privileged term and thus about an apparent step toward the "normalization" of the Holocaust. But perhaps a better response would be to take seriously the comparison of Allied bombing to German camps and, like Sven Lindqvist, follow it out. "In both cases," Lindqvist writes, "it was a question of a well-organized mass murder of innocent people, sanctioned at the highest level but contrary to international law. . . . [Here I'm leaving out some details.] But the difference between the German and the British war crimes is . . . also very clear. In the first place, the order of magnitude in the two cases is completely different. . . .The allied bombing offensive against Germany claimed about half a million civilian lives. That is less than the margin of error surrounding the Germans' crime. In the second place, the victims of the Germans were almost completely defenseless . . . Up to the conclusion of the war, Germany's cities defended themselves energetically; the graves of 56,000 British airmen testify to that fact . . . And in the third place, the British had no plans for a conquest that would require the killing of Germans in order to make room for British settlement . . . The air attacks against Germany stopped as soon as the German armed forces had surrendered. The German war crimes, on the other hand, were committed for the most part after the surrender of their opponents" (97).[19] Reading this instructive page, one wishes that Sebald had focused less on "the experience itself," horrific as it was, and more on national comparison. For comparison, risky as it is, does not necessarily end in the equivalence of all suffering.

But wait—maybe the equivalence of all suffering is precisely where we *want* to end. The warm welcome Sebald's lectures have received outside Germany undoubtedly owes a great deal to what might be called the human rights consensus. By "human rights consensus" I mean, in this context at least, a general willingness to extract civilian suffering from its historical (national, causal) contexts, from all narratives of provocation, collective responsibility, just retaliation, or "what goes around comes around." If we have come to feel—I concede it's a genuine "if"— that remembering what the Nazis did in the Holocaust and to cities like Guernica should not stop us from remembering the sufferings inflicted by the Allies on German civilians, the obvious reason would be that we have ceased to identify German civilians sufficiently with the Nazis or even as Germans. We have come to think that they can and must be detached from their national belonging, at least for this purpose, that they must be protected from it and treated instead as abstract individuals. If human rights has become a new secular religion, as is sometimes proposed, this might be described as an essential precept of the new creed.[20] Each human rights violation, we now believe, is absolutely unique and must be looked at alone, without regard for mitigating circumstances, guilty histories, yesterday's actions by today's victims, comparisons of any sort. The discourse of human rights radically amends the Israeli street wisdom with which I began: Nobody's country is any better than anybody else's country, and therefore *no one* should shut up. Everyone has a right to speak about their own as well as everyone else's country, no matter what their own country may have done. Belonging to a given country is morally irrelevant. The nervous backward glance at one's own national history and the guilt or shame it carries should be no impediment to speech or indeed to action.

It's worth noting that Sebald's success in resuscitating the memory of how Germany's cities were destroyed owes something to the passage of time, which (in contrast to what is usually said about time in Sebald) here seems to indicate not melancholy decay but, more happily, the lifting of a burden, the removal of a blockage.[21] But time does not work this miracle alone. Sebald also gets direct support from human rights cosmopolitanism as I've just described it. His defense of the abstract rational individual is consistent with a nonnational, radically individualist, and relatively guilt-free worldview, a worldview he would perhaps have been more exposed to in England than in Germany. Speaking for myself, I can't imagine ever stepping entirely outside this worldview, and especially not on the subject of saturation bombing. And yet I think it's also necessary to consider its possible limits, limits that are relevant both to an understanding of Sebald and to an understanding of the world since 9/11, and that may lead us back after all to the practice of national comparison that human rights cosmopolitanism would seem to be trying to supersede.

To articulate the human rights position is to be aware immediately that it is not quite Sebald's position, or not all of it. In various ways, in this text and others, Sebald tries quite hard to seek out a connection between the bombing and his own infant life to show that "this catastrophe . . . left its mark on my mind" (viii). Like references to the "great American novel," his complaint that no one has written "the great German epic" of this period can only be read as the demand for a certain affirmation of nationhood. Notorious self-exile and fervent cosmopolitan that he was, Sebald also seemed to be trying to negotiate some new mode of belonging to Germany.

This is not an effort with which anyone, even a would-be cosmopolitan, should want to interfere. There is no excuse for the Allied commanders who, knowing they were bombing civilians and facing evidence that they were doing so to no rational end, nevertheless imposed national belonging on Germany's civilians from above. Yet national belonging, whether imposed or negotiated, can never be far from the mind of anyone trying to prevent or redress or even win recognition for atrocities like these. Here we cosmopolitans may have something to learn from the wisdom of the street, which (like the psychoanalysis of national trauma) takes for granted on manifestly insufficient evidence that nations can be treated as if they were persons and hence are capable of such actions as forgiving, showing mercy, and apologizing. Consider some of the progressive political causes that cannot possibly succeed without an *increase* in the sentiment of national belonging. Efforts to win agreement about reparations and restitution (for U.S. slavery, say, or for our treatment of Native Americans) often founder on the issue of national belonging, especially across time. They run up against a refusal to acknowledge, on the part of descendants of the perpetrators, that they do belong in a sufficiently powerful sense so as to justify present sacrifices in compensation for acts that they themselves did not commit. And they run up against a refusal to acknowledge that the descendants of the victims deserve to receive reparations for harms done not to them directly but only to their ancestors. The cohesiveness and continuity of national belonging are stretched even more drastically in the case of recent immigrants who are asked to accept (in the form of taxation, for example) part of the guilt for crimes against slaves or native inhabitants even though neither they nor their ancestors were present when the crimes were committed.[22] Radical individu-alism in the human rights style, which asserts that nothing done by the collectivity ought to have any weight for you unless you yourself choose it as your own, will discourage people from acknowledging the benefits they inherit, without having lifted a finger, on the basis of someone else's primordial crimes. Yet white Ameri-cans continue to benefit from a racialized structure of property ownership that goes all the way back to slavery. Immigrants who come to former settler colonies like the United States, Canada, and Australia benefit directly from the land that others took away from the indigenous people. The crimes and benefits constitute an unconscious belonging that only political effort can perhaps render conscious and eventually channel into compensatory policy.

All these devious tracks of causality are relevant to my own life, but I should perhaps confess that the causal line leading to this chapter is also more direct and more personal. During World War II, my father was the pilot of a B-17, or Flying Fortress, the largest bomber the Army Air Corps possessed. His squadron flew out of the area of southeastern England where Sebald would later visit and describe the lonely remains of the bases. When he took his plane over Germany in 1944 and 1945, he wanted above all to get back all in one piece, and I don't think he could afford to be overscrupulous about where his bombs fell. In trying to hit his assigned targets, which he told me were industrial targets, he certainly wasn't try-ing to give the postwar U.S. economy the huge relative advantage that he would discover when he got home in 1946, an advantage that would ease the way to pre-cipitous upward mobility for him and to a much easier childhood for me than he or my mother had had. But in this sense, among others, my childhood, like Sebald's, is part of the bombing.[23] One might say the two childhoods are two tiny points on the enormous circle of the same event.

I say this with a mixture of pride and shame. In its emotional logic, at least, acknowledgment of benefits received as the result of an earlier generation's acts of violence and injustice would seem to resemble the more traditional acknowl-edgment of indebtedness to the heroic deeds and virtuous sacrifices of founding fathers. (In my own father's case, at least, it's probably too late for me to disentangle the two.) In insisting on a debt to those who came before, both will inevitably seem to restate a position—the premise of a debt too large ever to be repaid—that is essentially theological. To see oneself as an accomplice after the fact to theft and other crimes is the functional equivalent, that is, of seeing oneself as born into a state of sin and requiring divine grace. Ideally, one would like a less theological foundation for the need to temper the law with forgiveness, for the risky regress of looking *before* as well as *at* any individual's actions and thus diluting or dispersing personal responsibility for them, for the imperative to hold the law open, allowing at least intermittent entry to the sorts of extralegal supplement with which the contributors to this volume are concerned.

My argument here has been that this debt explains why national belonging cannot be simply disavowed, and thus also why we cannot wholeheartedly embrace the blithe cosmopolitan individualism of the human rights consensus, which would encourage us to condemn the Allied bombardment of Germany simply, without giving any thought to the German actions that preceded it. (How much and what kind of difference that thought should make are questions too complex for me to take on here.) It is worth pointing out that such debts are not necessarily shared with fellow nationals alone; like our strongest loyalties, they do not magically disappear the moment we step across the nation's borders. So if this argument leads away from cosmopolitanism in one sense—in its hesitation toward the individualist impulse of human rights discourse—it leads back to cosmopolitanism in another sense. In its insistence that stepping outside one's nation to criticize and/or apologize for it, thereby acknowledging a transnational or cosmopolitan standard, it seems to require a prior psychological identification with the nation, a sense of national belonging. It seems entirely plausible, to take the case most pertinent to this chapter, that Sebald refused to accept the possibility that his fellow Germans blamed themselves for the Allied bombing and that he refused at the same time the practice of comparative national blaming, in part because of a failure or deficiency in his own sense of national belonging. Pursuing the parallel, it would seem to follow that if we want to make Americans more cosmopolitan, we may have to start by first trying to make them better Americans.

As I said at the outset, this chapter has been largely inspired by the fraught, controversial parallel between Americans since 9/11 and other possible claimants to the title of victimhood who accepted—more (like the Germans since 1945) or less (like the Israelis since 1948)—the responsibility for having victimized others. A great deal more might be said, of course, about each of these parallels. Andreas Huyssen has written very powerfully against the abusive mobilization of German memories of the Allied bombardment even in the excellent cause of opposing recent American bombing campaigns.[24] As for the United States, the rage for retribution that led the American public to accept its government's invasion and occupation of Iraq, even in the glaring absence of any evidence of Iraqi involvement in the 9/11 attacks, would seem to indicate that American mechanisms of national blame are functioning only too well. But this is not to say that what Americans need is a more fervent commitment to forgiveness.

"Forgiveness is a power held by the victimized," Martha Minow writes, "not a right to be claimed."[25] To decide in advance that peace must be privileged over justice, reconciliation over truth, is to exercise a form of moral absolutism every bit as oppressive as the familiar claim to victimized innocence. To live in the world as a responsible political agent is to forego the dubious certainty that one can foreknow such things about each and every situation that will present itself. There is no permanent title to the high moral ground. Thus, Minow suggests, in my view correctly, that "[p]erhaps forgiveness should be reserved, as a concept and a practice, to instances where there are good reasons to forgive" (17). Theological and, for that matter, deconstructive arguments for forgiveness, which share an insistence on forgiveness in the absence of good reasons to forgive, usefully insist on the inadequacy of those reasons that are offered and accepted, whether for forgiveness or for blame.[26] But surely, there would be no rejoicing in either camp if reasons were taken as good at the level of the individual but not at the level of the nation, so that individuals could be blamed but nations could not—if nations were taken to enjoy a sort of corporatelike limited liability that, grounded in the supposed incommensurability of scale between moral individual and impersonal state, prevented questions of responsibility from ever being asked. The word we use to insist on the connection between those scales is *politics*. Politically speaking, the state of the world does not permit us the luxury of a universal, preemptive absolution where national blame is concerned.

I have suggested here that to blame our own nation, as modern Americans have no ethical choice but to learn to do, modern Americans must forego the pleasures of detachment, pleasures that human rights individualism has made dangerously accessible and that overlap with the presumed ethical superiority of forgiveness. To be forgiven, and perhaps eventually also to forgive others, we must first acknowledge that we belong.[27] In the concluding chapter of *The Spectre of Comparisons*, Benedict Anderson proposes an effectively low-key mode for such an acknowledgment: not national pride but national shame. One can see the difference between nationalism and religion, he says, "if one tries to transform 'My Country, Right or Wrong' into 'My Religion, Right or Wrong.' The latter is an inconceivable oxymoron. How could Islam for Muslims, Christianity for Christians, Hinduism for Hindus possibly be Wrong?" (360). But one's country can

153

be Wrong. And this conviction coexists with—indeed, is made possible by—the complementary conviction that one's country can and should be made Right. The country can be blamed because, like the individual, it is a site of some quantity of free will. Anderson declares his desire to propagate the slogan "Long Live Shame!" (362). There are worse slogans.

Notes

1. Stephen Howe, "Israel, Palestine, and the Campus Civil Wars," *Open Democracy* (December 14, 2004). The passage continues: "By that measure, *all* sides in polemics over the middle east have long since lost: comparing each other to Nazis has become the routine, shop-soiled and ever-devaluing currency of dispute."

2. Quoted in John Leonard, "Motherland" (review of Amos Oz's *A Tale of Love and Darkness*), *New York Times Book Review* (December 12, 2004), 16–17.

3. Benedict Anderson, *The Spectre of Comparisons: Nationalism, Southeast Asia, and the World* (London: Verso, 1998).

4. See, for example, Charles Bernheimer, ed., *Comparative Literature in the Age of Multiculturalism* (Baltimore and London: Johns Hopkins University Press, 1995). In his introduction, entitled "The Anxieties of Comparison," Bernheimer writes: "The more literatures you try to compare, the more like a colonizing imperialist you may seem. If you stress what these literatures have in common—thematically, morally, politically—you may be accused of imposing a universalist model that suppresses particular differences so as to foster the old humanist dream of man's worldwide similarity to man. If, on the other hand, you stress differences, then the basis of comparison becomes problematic" (9).

5. The famous debate between British Marxist historians E. P. Thompson and Perry Anderson might be seen as, among other things, a reflection on the practice of comparative national blaming. In his essay "The Peculiarities of the English" (1965), reprinted in *The Poverty of Theory and Other Essays* (London: Merlin, 1978), Thompson accuses Anderson and Tom Nairn of making illegitimate use of "an undisclosed model of Other Countries" (37), or what he refers to as "inverted Podsnappery" (36). Podsnap, in Dickens's *Our Mutual Friend*, is the patriot who proclaims that "No Other Country is so Favoured as This Country." Thompson imagines Anderson and Nairn as answering the question of how other countries do as follows: "They do—we are sorry to be obliged to say it—in Every Respect Better. Their Bourgeois Revolutions have been Mature. Their Class Struggles have been Sanguinary and Unequivocal. Their Intelligentsia has been Autonomous and Integrated Vertically . . . Their Proletariat has been Hegemonic" (37). In his defense, Anderson might have insisted on the difference between using a national model and not disclosing that model. In *English Questions* (London: Verso, 1992), which reprints the original essays of the early 1960s to which Thompson was objecting, Anderson accepts "the justice of [Thompson's]

criticism" (4) and discloses the model: "The standard is provided by France" (5). Anderson acknowledges that he was excessively influenced by Gramsci, whose comparison of advanced France with belated Italy inspired Anderson's own comparison of a mature France with a premature England. Whatever the failings of the French model, there surely exists a better case in favor of national comparison in general than Anderson, a master of the art, seems willing for the moment to make.

6. Elazar Barkan, *The Guilt of Nations: Restitution and Negotiating Historical Injustices* (New York and London: W. W. Norton, 2000).

7. W. G. Sebald, *On the Natural History of Destruction*, Anthea Bell, trans. (New York: Random House, 2003); the German edition is *Luftkrieg und Literatur* (München: Carl Hanser Verlag, 1999).

8. Even in the immediate aftermath, Germans may well have agreed with Churchill, Sebald writes, that there was "a higher poetic justice at work" (19).

9. Christopher Hitchens, *Atlantic Monthly*, 291: 1 (January–February 2003), 182–189.

10. Volker Hage, *Zeugen der Zerstörung: Die Literaten und der Luftkrieg Essays und Gespräche* (Frankfurt: S. Fischer Verlag, 2003). "Das 'Schweigen der Betroffene' . . . sei zu begrüssen, wenn man das Leid des Tätervolks messe an den Entsetzen, 'das Deutschland mit seinen Schergen über die unterworfenen Völker im Osten und, das vor allem, über die Opfer des rassistischen Vernichtungs-Wille' gebracht habe . . ." "Das Schwiegen verbarg vielleicht eine Scham, die kostbarer ist als alle Literatur." My translation. On the troubled German reception of Sebald's book, see Mark Anderson, "The Edge of Darkness," *October*, 106 (Fall 2003). For another judicious contextualization of this debate, see Noah Isenberg, "Dresden Mon Amour. Realism or Revisionism? Germans Revisit the War," *Bookforum* (Summer 2005).

11. Andreas Huyssen, *Present Pasts: Urban Palimpsests and the Politics of Memory* (Stanford, CA: Stanford University Press, 2003), 147.

12. Thus, the supposed ease and geometrical clarity of bombing, seen from the bomber's aerial point of view, could be counterposed to the difficulty of remembering bombing, from the point of view of the victims on the ground.

13. Available from the author, Department of English, Bard College.

14. Mahmood Mamdani, *When Victims Become Killers: Colonialism, Nativism, and the Genocide in Rwanda* (Princeton, NJ: Princeton University Press, 2001); Joanna Bourne, *An Intimate History of Killing: Face to Face Killing in 20th Century Warfare* (New York: Basic Books, 1999).

15. Hitchens writes: "Few historians or strategists now argue that the bombing made much difference if any to the outcome of the war" (189). See also Robert Pape, *Bombing to Win* (Ithaca, NY: Cornell University Press, 1996); Daniel Byman and Andrew Waxman, *The Dynamics of Coercion: American Foreign Policy and the Limits of Military Might* (Cambridge: Cambridge University Press, 2002); and Andrew Stigler, "A Clear Victory for Air Power: NATO's Empty Threat to Invade Kosovo," *International Security*, 27: 3 (Winter 2002–2003). Thanks to Jack Snyder for these references.

16. This romantic tendency in Sebald, visible also in other works, seems sometimes to be complaining more about the modernization that followed the bombs than about the bombs themselves, as when he speaks, for example, of "a second liquidation . . . of the nation's own past history" (7).

17. Perry Anderson, "Union Sucrée," *London Review of Books* (September 23, 2004).

18. And if they were, of course, then the individual would be redeemed from the shame of having chosen not to remember.

19. Sven Lindqvist, *A History of Bombing*, Linda Haverty Rugg, trans. (New York: New Press, 2000).

20. I discuss related complexities of human rights blaming in "Temporizing: Time and Politics in the Humanities and Human Rights," *boundary 2*, 32: 1 (Spring 2005), 191–208.

21. Time seems Sebald's enemy, elsewhere in his writing, in that it makes atrocities into classics, whitens the bones, dilutes the moral absoluteness of suffering.

22. In *Nation and Identity* (London and New York: Routledge, 1999), Ross Poole writes interestingly, for example, about the issue of whether recent Australian immigrants from Europe and Asia can and should be induced to share responsibility for white crimes against aboriginals, even though they obviously weren't there to participate in the crimes.

23. As it happens, the Army Air Corps did not engage in the deliberate bombing of civilian populations in Germany. See A. C. Grayling, *Among the Dead Cities: The History and Moral Legacy of the WWII Bombing of Civilians in Germany and Japan* (New York: Walker, 2006), 12.

24. Andreas Huyssen, "Air War Legacies: From Dresden to Baghdad," *New German Critique*, 90 (Fall 2003), 163–176.

25. Martha Minow, *Between Vengeance and Forgiveness: Facing History After Genocide and Mass Violence*, Foreword by Judge Richard J. Goldstone (Boston: Beacon Press, 1998), 17.

26. See, for example, Jacques Derrida, *On Cosmopolitanism and Forgiveness*, Mark Dooley and Michael Hughes, trans. (London and New York: Routledge, 2001).

27. Of course, no one belongs only to the nation, and the diversity of debts to other collectivities loosens the individual's responsibility to each. Acknowledging debts to the nation, even debts that cannot be liquidated, need not entail treating the nation as a single, Alcoholics Anonymous-style higher power.

Keeping the Peace

ADAM SITZE

The Indiscernibility of Amnesty and Pardon
as a Problem for the Philosophy of Law

It is nothing short of a miracle, Carl Schmitt claims in his 1950 text *The* Nomos *of the Earth*, that Western jurisprudence found itself able to successfully resolve the basic problem faced by every legal order: the containment or bracketing of war.[1] The conceptual basis for this bracketing, Schmitt argues, is Western jurisprudence's ability to distinguish the just enemy (*justus hostis*) from the foe (*inimicus*).[2] War against the just enemy does not aim at the eradication of evil or at the punishment of a thief, gangster, or traitor; it entails neither moral nor legal guilt.[3] Like a duel or feud fought between equals, it is a formal act, an exchange of blows between legal persons, each of whom respects, in the other, a certain set of determinable rights.[4] Only on the basis of the concept of the just enemy is it possible to bring hostilities to an end in a peace treaty,[5] for where the enemy is construed as evil or criminal, there is no longer any way to place limits on the enmity that is war's essence. War against an unjust enemy entails absolute enmity and, as such, cannot be brought to a close in a peace treaty: It demands the absolute victory of one party over the other.[6] Schmitt will therefore insist that the late nineteenth and early twentieth century criminalization of aggressive war, which categorized the enemy as unjust, will not end war. It will merely internationalize war into global civil war, in which military campaigns are reduced to the equivalent of police actions,[7] even as its authorization of unlimited enmity opens the door for a war that can no longer be concluded in a peace treaty. Where the concept of the just enemy dissolves, the enemy becomes a pest or wolf that, by its very nature, is a threat to humanity.[8] Where international law becomes disconnected from its source in Western jurisprudence, wars of extermination and annihilation become not only possible but also necessary.[9]

It is thus imperative, Schmitt believes, for the jurist to safeguard the sovereign's capacity to name a just enemy. Schmitt claims that a naming of this type not only rationalizes and humanizes war between states (because it limits enmity and makes peace treaties possible) but also quells war within states (because the naming of a just enemy permits the constituents of a state to recognize one another as friends).[10] In the same stroke that the naming of a just enemy enables the bracketing of war, it thus also institutes the reality of the political itself.[11] In an epoch where the ascendancy of administrative law, humanitarian norms, police action, the pursuit of economic interest, and above all, the concept of the social threaten to dissolve the very possibility of a just enemy, Western jurisprudence has a clear duty. To oppose the desertion of the political, it must oppose the notion that aggressive war is a crime. If law is to have any chance at bracketing or containing war, jurisprudence must first of all save war from legal and moral repression.

Schmitt's arguments in *The* Nomos *of the Earth* are, without doubt, extreme. Their relation to Nazism and German nationalism has been amply discussed in recent years,[12] and there is no need to directly repeat the sum or substance of these discussions here. My interest in Schmitt's *The* Nomos *of the Earth* is that, precisely in its extremism, it throws into relief a subtle but exigent problem in the philosophy of law. That problem, which shall be the focus of this chapter, is *the relation of indiscernibility* that pertains between *the sovereign power to pardon* and *the theory and practice of amnesty*. There is no better way to introduce this problem's full force and paradox than to outline the way that Schmitt's text, taken on its own terms, is incapable of posing it.

The political philosophical basis of this problem is plain enough. Just as the sovereign right to take life partakes in the sovereign right to wage war so that public law treats the criminal as an internal enemy against whom the state may justly make war,[13] so too does the sovereign right to spare life partake in the sovereign right to make peace. "Pardon," Hobbes writes, "is nothing but granting of Peace."[14] It is this same logic that permits Alexander Hamilton, in *The Federalist* (No. 74), to argue that if rebellions are to be quelled by well-timed offers of amnesty, the right to pardon must be vested in a single, sovereign person.[15] Hobbes and Hamilton are not outliers: Handbooks legal and lay regularly define amnesty as though it were synonymous with the right of pardon.[16]

This synonymy has at least two roots; the first pertains to the problem of enmity. Because Schmitt follows Hobbes in understanding the essence of war to be not physical violence or pitched battle but enmity itself,[17] Schmitt considers the

central question raised by the bracketing of war to be "whether enmity can be contained and regulated, that is, whether it represents relative or absolute enmity."[18]
As Nicole Loraux has shown, one of the purposes of amnesty in its classical form
was to accomplish precisely this containment and regulation. By enjoining the
participants in Athens' internal war to promise not to recall past wrongs, the Athenian amnesty of 403 B.C. aimed at unraveling the "knot of hatred" that remained
after the city's factions made war upon one another.[19] The opposite of amnesty, in
the Athenian oaths as in Aeschylus's *Oresteia*, is thus not so much *memory* as *fury*.[20]
Pardon has a similar aim. In his 1967 text *Le Pardon*, Vladimir Jankélévitch sets
forth an argument about rancor that is at once contrary to Schmitt's politics and
yet still Schmittian in its epistemology. "Rancor arouses cold war, which is a state
of exception," Jankélévitch writes, "and pardon, be it true or false, does the opposite: it lifts the state of exception, liquidates what rancor maintained, and resolves
vindictive obsession. The knot of rancor unravels."[21] When Jankélévitch concludes
that pardon "is an intention of perpetual peace,"[22] he implies that pardon satisfies
not only Kant's first preliminary article for peace among states (peace demands *the
end* of hostilities, not merely their *suspension*) but also Hobbes's "Fundamentall
Law of Nature" ("to seek peace, and follow it"[23]). If pardon can be considered synonymous with amnesty, it is first of all because pardon, like amnesty, is designed to
unravel the enmity that is the essence of war.

But this synonymy also distorts the relation between pardon and amnesty: It
erases their difference with regard to legal and moral guilt. In its modern iteration
in international law, the purpose of amnesty is to conclude war between states
without also criminalizing the defeated party: Amnesty clauses directly contradict
the doctrine of just war as set forth by Christian theologians and Roman law.[24]
The inclusion of an amnesty clause in a peace pact implies that the conclusion of
the war cannot and should not assume the form of a judgment on legal or moral
guilt. It is neither an accident nor a superficial detail that the rise of the order of
sovereign states in Europe between the fifteenth and seventeenth centuries coincided with a marked increase in the number of peace pacts grounded in amnesty
clauses.[25] The just enemy, on which Schmitt considers the *Jus Publicum Europaeum*
to be founded, is precisely that enemy whose defeat is an occasion for amnesty and
not punishment or extermination: Amnesty is a constitutive part of the concept of
the just enemy.[26] In both its classical sense as a technique for diminishing absolute
enmity into a mode of legal and political dispute and in its modern sense as a synecdoche for the peace treaty itself, *amnesty is the concrete, institutional condition of
possibility for the temporal containment of war.*

Pardon, however, presupposes the very legal and moral guilt that amnesty precludes.[27] Where pardon is understood in a generic sense as the remission of deserved punishment, then even the use of mutual pardon to conclude war will not rule out a determination of the legal or moral guilt of the defeated party. On the contrary, the granting of mutual pardons to conclude war implies that war is potentially *un*pardonable, which is to say, criminal and immoral. To the extent that a peace pact mixes the moral theological concept of pardon with the juridical political concept of amnesty, or construes amnesty as pardon, it will thus have preserved precisely the possibility that aggressive war is deserving of punishment. It is part and parcel of what Schmitt calls Hugo Grotius's "unsteady and uncertain" writings on international law[28] that Grotius's discussion of amnesty entails a mixture of this type. Grotius argues that, to reconcile all contending claims at the conclusion of war, a general amnesty should be declared and the victor should exercise moderation by granting clemency and pardon.[29] Contra Schmitt, Grotius's unsteadiness on this point reflects more than merely the informal assumption of every sovereign power to have right on its side.[30] It raises critical questions about the juridical status of guilt and responsibility in the peace pacts that concluded hostilities during the epoch of the *Jus Publicum Europaeum*. Why is it, for example, that the increase of amnesties in the peace pacts of this period was accompanied by the disappearance, from those same peace pacts, of the language of reciprocal forgiveness for war?[31] Is it perhaps because the ostensible relation of synonymy between pardon and amnesty is actually, on the contrary, what Kierkegaard might call an either–or?

It is not lost on Schmitt, of course, that, as Samuel Pufendorf suggested in 1688, the sovereign power of pardon is an example of the more general sovereign power to suspend law.[32] Schmitt acknowledges as much both in his 1922 text *Political Theology*, where he mentions the power to grant pardons and amnesties as an example of the " 'omnipotence' of the modern lawgiver," [33] and in his 1934 text *On the Three Types of Juristic Thought*, where he clarifies why the Calvinist teaching on grace is an example of decisionist thinking.[34] Yet it is far from clear whether Schmitt can fully account for the possibility of an either–or between pardon and amnesty internal to the bracketing of war. To be sure, when Schmitt criticizes Articles 228–230 of the Versailles Treaty, his complaint is not merely that the treaty's concept of "war crimes" recriminalizes war and erodes the miraculous accomplishments of Western jurisprudence and so forth, but also that it fundamentally alters the very idea of amnesty, which Schmitt calls a "basic legal institution." [35] With the ratification of these articles, Schmitt argues, "amnesty was destroyed by a discrimination against the vanquished." [36] But despite Schmitt's own argument that it is *amnesty* that is destroyed with the dissolution of the concept of the just enemy, and despite Schmitt's own understanding of jurisprudence as that discipline charged with the duty to safeguard the unity, consistency, and sources of law [37]—up to and including that most fundamental of legal problems, the bracketing of war—Schmitt at no point in *The* Nomos *of the Earth* raises amnesty to the status of a serious problem for jurisprudence. Why?

The most obvious reason is Schmitt's emphasis on the spatial origin of legal concepts. [38] The division of European soil into territories with firm borders is, in Schmitt's view, more than any peace pact the concrete, institutional basis for the bracketing of war in the epoch of the *Jus Publicum Europaeum*. [39] Yet Schmitt's emphasis on space in his text is so strong that it turns into exactly the simplistic antithesis of space and time against which he warns. [40] Even as Schmitt praises Hobbes's "systematic clarity and conceptual power," [41] he breaks completely with Hobbes's argument that war consists in "a tract of time, wherein the Will to contend by Battell is sufficiently known: and therefore the notion of *Time*, is to be considered in the nature of Warre." [42] Schmitt's *displacement of time into space* not only leads him to offer spurious arguments about the desirability and inevitability of European colonization, [43] but it also leaves him unable to understand the problem of the bracketing of war with any systematic clarity or conceptual power. Were Schmitt to heed Hobbes and avoid lapsing into an antithesis of space and time, he would be obliged to regard the destruction of amnesty not merely as an epiphenomenon but as a fundamental ontological problem on a par with the just enemy or land appropriation. He would be obliged, in other words, to ask what it means for amnesty to be the concrete, institutional condition of possibility for the temporal containment of war. Instead, even though the destruction of amnesty at Versailles is at the very core of Schmitt's anxiety (1919, for Schmitt, heralds the dawn of the epoch of criminalized war), amnesty remains entirely absent as a concept worthy of jurisprudential inquiry (it is not an ontological problem but merely one among many ontic facts). Amnesty is the *dead center* of *The* Nomos *of the Earth*.

Schmitt's silence on amnesty is no mere oversight. Nor is it a simple corollary of Schmitt's spatial orientation (the jurisprudential analogue, say, of Heidegger's argument that the *polis* is the originary site of human history [44]). It is rather a symptom of an incommensurability internal to Schmitt's inquiry: Schmitt is unable both to systematically consider amnesty as a problem for jurisprudence and to remain loyal to the discipline of jurisprudence as he understands it.

This becomes clear when we consider the second and more fundamental root of amnesty's indiscernibility with pardon: their shared ontological problematic. Pardon, writes Jankélévitch, is a response to a basic question: "how does one go about it so that what happened never happened?" [45] This question has a long intellectual history. In his *Nicomachean Ethics*, Aristotle writes:

> There is no will with regard to the past. This is why no one wants Troy to have been sacked, since no one decides what happened but only what will be and is possible; what has happened cannot have been. This is why Agathon is right in saying: "This only is denied even to God, / The power to undo what has been done." [46]

The question Aristotle here poses reappears throughout the history of modern philosophy. Kant turns to it in *The Critique of Judgment* to exemplify the predicament of impossible desire, [47] and Heidegger raises it in his 1951 lectures on Nietzsche to argue that the spirit of revenge derives from representational thought's inability to deliver itself from the "it was" of the past. [48] Modernity's confusion of war and peace, Heidegger suggested, cannot be thought without first asking, in a manner that resembles the Christian doctrine of forgiveness, what it means to overcome the will's inability to will the past. [49] Giorgio Agamben, meanwhile, understands Aristotle to be asking a question about the "impossibility of realizing the potentiality of the past." [50] Because sovereign power, in Agamben's view, is in essence that which "maintains itself in relation to actuality precisely through its ability not to be," [51] Aristotle's question about the past's ability not to be will register, for Agamben, as a distinctly political problem of sovereign power. [52]

Agamben's insight is borne out by the history of modern political philosophy. The more precise is a given political philosophical inquiry into *the power* of pardon or amnesty, the more clearly *the impossibility* of undoing what has been done emerges as their common, constitutive limit. When Hegel defines the right to pardon, he argues that a pardon "proceeds from the sovereignty of the monarch, since it is this alone which is empowered to realize the spirit's power to make undone what has been done [*das Geschehene ungeschehen zu machen*] and to destroy a crime by forgiving and forgetting it." [53] In his 1749 *Jus Gentium*, Christian Wolff states that "the effect of decreeing amnesty is that acts wrongfully done are to be considered as though they had not been done." [54] In his 1758 *Law of Nations*, Emmerich de Vattel argues that amnesty causes the damages of war to be "regarded as having not happened [*non-avenus*]." [55] Jankélévitch, meanwhile, suggests that pardon is a miraculous, gratuitous event: "By the grace of pardon, the thing that has been done has not been done."⁵⁶ Yet in this, Jankélévitch merely repeats the standard Kierkegaardian poetics that supplies Schmitt with his most crucial categories,⁵⁷ without also comprehending the precise sense in which pardon and amnesty are limit-concepts for the philosophy of law. The enduring insight of Jankélévitch's suggestion that pardon "is an intention of perpetual peace," on the other hand, is that it condenses into a single rigorous phrase a problematic that governs modern political philosophical thinking on sovereign power, yet is only vaguely intimated within that same tradition: *The sovereign right of pardon exercises a power the ontological problematic of which is indiscernible from the amnesties through which sovereign states enact their right to make peace.*⁵⁸

This shared ontological problematic points to the first and simplest reason Schmitt is unable to explicitly pose amnesty's temporal bracketing of enmity as a problem for jurisprudence. To think through amnesty in any systematic, consistent, or unified manner would require Schmitt to recognize that the division between amnesty and pardon is a division internal to the same basic power. Yet to recognize this indiscernibility is necessarily also to acknowledge, at the very heart of the institution that grounds the temporal bracketing of war, *another* indiscernibility: that between *the just enemy* (who is nothing other than a noncriminal partner in amnesty) and *the unjust enemy* (whose guilt for war is either pardonable or unpardonable). This has an important implication. If there is, at root, no systematic way to discern pardon from amnesty, then the possibility for the criminalization of aggressive war will not only be inscribed in the peace treaties that ground the temporal bracketing of war but will also remain a permanent possibility for the very sovereign powers to whom Schmitt entrusts that bracketing. If the sovereign right to make peace is indiscernible from the right of pardon, then it is precisely *the principle of indivisible sovereignty itself* that will guarantee the confusion of criminal law and international law that so troubles Schmitt. The vanishing point between the sovereign power to pardon and the theory and practice of amnesty is, in this respect, also the vanishing point of the *Jus Publicum Europaeum* itself.

From this flows a second reason Schmitt cannot raise amnesty as a problem for jurisprudence. Schmitt believes that Western jurisprudence's bracketing of war is miraculous because that bracketing founds a set of conceptual oppositions that, taken together, provide a bridge over the abyss of global civil war.⁵⁹ The most important of the distinctions held in place by the bracketing of war is that between *polemos* (war between states) and *stasis* (war within a state).⁶⁰ Where this distinction does not hold, military valor vanishes into grunt police work, politics is swarmed by the socioeconomic, the partisan, agent of *stasis*, takes the place of the soldier-citizen, and the polemico-political essence of Western history and destiny is forgotten.[61] Yet insofar as Schmitt presupposes that *amnesty* is the legal institution that is supposed to safeguard this distinction, Schmitt will be faced with the precise opposite of the Heideggerian–Hölderlinian cliché that "where the danger is, the saving power grows also." For where the salvation of the *polemos-stasis* distinction is entrusted to amnesty, *the saving power will have been the danger itself.*

This is because the Athenian amnesty of 403 B.C., which has supplied modern jurisprudence with its paradigm for amnesty at least since Wolff,[62] emerged primarily as a technique to resolve *stasis*. To contain wars between states on the basis of amnesty is then implicitly to construe *polemos* as *stasis*.[63] Now, on the one hand, this poses no problem to Schmitt at all. When Schmitt praises the familial bond or fraternal equality that pertains in the community of feudal European sovereign states,[64] he presupposes that Europe is bound by an alliance of blood into a single racial entity. Understood in a generic sense, *stasis* signifies fratricide or a shedding of blood among a population that shares the same blood.[65] To reconcile wars between European states as though they were family feuds is then consistent with the worst of the worst in Schmitt. Schmitt may misrecognize the conditions of possibility for the *Jus Publicum Europaeum*, since he attributes to an exclusively spatial order of land an alliance of blood that is implicit in modern amnesty's construal of *polemos* as *stasis*. But nothing here would challenge his fundamental presuppositions about the essence of European unity. Yet, on the other hand, amnesty's construal of *polemos* as *stasis* would also require Schmitt to pose the question of global civil war in a much different manner. Were Schmitt to raise amnesty as a serious problem for jurisprudence, he would have to recall some characteristics of the paradigmatic amnesty of 403 B.C. that would contradict his presumption that amnesty is commensurable with his understanding of the bracketing of war.

There are at least three. First, the Athenian amnesty *did not* exclude criminal punishment of the defeated party. Quite the opposite: It entailed a death sentence for the Thirty Tyrants as well as for an unnamed Athenian democrat who violated his oath not to recall past wrongs.[66] Second, the Athenian amnesty *cannot* be reduced to a resolution of a war between brothers. The victorious democratic faction that restored peace to Athens was comprised of not only women and slaves but also the very strangers who are supposed to be the object of *polemos*.[67] Loraux will therefore argue that the participation of strangers in the reconciliation of Athens "transgressed the opposition between *stasis* and *polemos*, the norm of all organized political life, thus creating an exceptional situation."[68] Third, even though amnesty kept the peace in Athens and in Europe, amnesty is neither an Athenian nor a European invention. Just as Husserl claimed that Thales's invention of geometry was only posed as a properly *epistemological* problem by the Greeks,[69] so too does Schmitt's own phenomenological history of the *Jus Publicum Europaeum* suggest that the Egyptian invention of international law, up to and including amnesty, was only understood in a finally complete, self-conscious, and systematic manner by Western jurisprudence.[70] But if Schmitt's text is any indication, the success of that endeavor is very much open to question. For if Schmitt were to raise amnesty as a problem for phenomenological history, the characteristics of the paradigmatic Greek amnesty would oblige him to ask whether the desert or abyss of global civil war is called into being not by *a failure* to bracket war but by *that very bracketing itself*. Schmitt would be obliged to pose, as a problem for jurisprudence, the question whether the dominant legal institution for the temporal bracketing of war is not in some sense *programmed* to confuse *polemos* and *stasis* and, in so doing, to hasten the advent of the global civil war it appears to prevent.

The reason Schmitt cannot pose amnesty as a problem for thought, despite its being within the provenance of his inquiry into the bracketing of war, is thus plain: any systematic and consistent inquiry into the paradigmatic amnesty would exceed, from within, the discipline of jurisprudence as Schmitt conceives it. Jurisprudence, for Schmitt, is just as much an ascetic discipline (involving fidelity to *polemos* as the ontological essence of the West) as an academic discipline (involving claims of scientific rigor, unity, and consistency). Because amnesty is at once the legal institution that contains war and safeguards Europe from the abyss of global *stasis* and, in its paradigmatic iteration in Western jurisprudence, a concept that not only treats wars between states precisely *on the model of*, or even *as, stasis*, but also, as such, throws the *polemos-stasis* distinction itself into question, any serious inquiry into amnesty would require Schmitt to part ways with his ascetic argument that the duty of jurisprudence is to serve as the guardian of Western essence. Schmitt's text shouts through gritted teeth about the criminalization of the defeated party, but the political unconscious for this tone of barely contained fury is not as perfectly obvious as it might seem. The paradox of *The* Nomos *of the Earth* is that Schmitt's bitter opposition to the forgetting of the political is itself governed by the dynamic Loraux felicitously calls "the forgetting that founds the political."[71] Ignorant about its ignorance of the basic problem of every legal order, Schmitt's text offers neither a *philosophy* of law nor a philosophy of *law*.

The Political Theological Refrain

What would it mean to take the indiscernibility of pardon and amnesty seriously as a problem for the philosophy of law? This chapter offers a primarily genealogical response to this question. I begin by returning to Kant's writings of the 1790s. These writings are requisite because of the paradigmatic status of Kant's discussions of perpetual peace and the sovereign right of grace[72] and because of Schmitt's claim that Kant's political writings undo the *Jus Publicum Europaeum* by reintroducing into international law a moral theological concept of the unjust enemy.[73] Yet there is no way to understand what Kant says about peace and pardon without first posing the *readability* of Kant's text as a problem for thought. The very textuality of Kant's "Perpetual Peace," I argue, implies an important lesson about Kant's understanding of amnesty. After juxtaposing Kant's "Perpetual Peace" to Wolff's argument that silence is the element in which amnesty subsists, I suggest that the interest of Kant's "Perpetual Peace" is that it *observes* the amnesty *in its very form*: Kant's text *obeys amnesty's imperative not to speak of past wrongs* even as it *speculates on amnesty's insufficiency for lasting peace*. Only by posing the readability of Kant's "Perpetual Peace" as a problem, I conclude, do we become able to understand the limit or *parerga* from which its critique of amnesty is issued. That limit is the political theological concept of grace.

By tracing the relation of amnesty to grace in Kant's writing, I continue, we find a paradigm I shall call the *political theological refrain*. In *State of Exception*, Agamben observes that the Greek concept of *kharis*, or "grace," provides the root for the concept of the "charismatic leader"[74]—that is to say, the authority whose decisions are grounded not in written law but only in the animate law of his or her *persona* and who derives the halo of his or her sovereignty, as well as his or her capacity to suspend law, primarily from what Portia would call the "twice blest" quality of his or her mercy.[75] Opposing this paradigm in the name of democracy would be straightforward were it not that *kharis* is also at the root of a specifically Eucharistic concept of community, in which a fraternal equality instituted through the brothers' sacrifice and incorporation of the father's hypostasized body presupposes remembrance of and mercy for this shared crime as the condition of possibility for community as such.[76] The *salus* of this community—its salvation, safety, health, well-being, welfare, or security, its immunity from risk, accident, or damage—is guaranteed not so much by what Freud would call its "expiation fantasies" as by the police powers that keep the peace wherever law is suspended.[77] Commentaries

on and critiques of Agamben's writings on sovereignty have tended to assimilate
Agamben's thought into liberal narratives of the excesses of an unchecked executive branch or into neoconservative narratives of liberalism's latent tyranny. But
this reception of Agamben is structured by a symptomatic silence. There is no way
to undo the decisionism implicit in the sovereign right of grace without also undoing the paradigm of salvational democracy—the aspirational principle of a completely immune community—of which decisionism is merely the concentrated
expression. By "political theological refrain," I will then refer to *the repetition in effect whenever this undoing remains incomplete.* Whenever criticisms of charismatic
authority turn into little more than affirmations of Eucharistic equality, I argue,
we disavow the basic ontological problematic of political sovereignty and repeat
the refrain we ostensibly oppose.

To find a way out of this refrain, I turn in the second part of this chapter from
Kant to Plato's *Laws.* Because Kant declared Plato's *respublica noumenon* "the eternal norm for all civil organization in general,"[78] we are obliged to reread Plato if
we wish to read Kant on his own terms. Keeping in mind Jacques Rancière's view
that Book III of Plato's *Laws* "contains within it all that is theological in politics,"[79]
and recalling that it is to Plato that Schmitt turns to thematize the friend–enemy
distinction in the first place,[80] I reread Plato's *Laws* from the same angle as I do
Kant's political writings. The very form of Plato's text, I argue, implies a substantive understanding of amnesty. Particularly because Plato participated, by his own
account, in the same *stasis* the Athenian amnesty of 403 B.C. regulated,[81] there is
no way to understand the *Laws'* account of amnesty without reading the *Laws* itself as a text constituted in and by a political dispute over amnesty. By reading the
Laws against itself, and by tracing the place and function of amnesty within it, I
suggest, we find that the political theological refrain, which is by no means limited
to the Platonism of the West,[82] emerges in Plato's *Laws* first and foremost as part
of a calculation designed to suppress *stasis.* This same calculation underwrites not
only the *Laws'* foundational formulation of the rule of law[83] but also its account
of two of the concepts from which the sovereign right of pardon will eventually
be derived—namely, *epieikeia* and *sungnômon.* Each of these concepts points to a
way out of the vicious circle of *stasis* and hence, too, toward a certain concept of
peace. Each also marks a limit to justice construed as calculation, retribution, and
exchange of blows. Plato's *Laws* thus offers an unexpected chance to rethink the
origins of one of the most rote concepts in political theological discourse on the
right of grace: *immeasurability.*

My genealogical claim regarding this immeasurability is that it emerges first and foremost as a way to resolve the problem that Rancière would call "the miscount."[84] If, as Alain Badiou suggests, the state is founded not on a social bond but on the prohibition of unbinding, then amnesty will be one of the basic sources for state power. Amnesty, as precisely a measure designed to unravel the hatred that binds, in this sense raises an originary political ontological problem that political theology *then* misrecognizes as the problem of grace. From Plato's *Laws* we learn that the political theological refrain does not so much "pass the peace," as the Pauline salutation *ea chairein* implies,[85] as *keep peace to itself* or *institute a monopoly on peace* by claiming that *there can be no peace without* kharis. Political theology's most powerful effect, in this respect, is to make *the power to undo what has been done* conditional upon *participation in a soteriological economy of hypostasis, deliverance, and salvation*, even and especially where, as in Schmitt, that participation takes the form of tracing political peace to its forsaken theological origins.[86] Political theology claims to protect or preserve the very idea of peace from oblivion at a moment when peace and war have become one and the same thing.[87] But to keep the peace in this manner is to keep another peace from coming into its own.

A Hermeneutic of the Irreparable

In his 1798 "The Strife of the Faculties," Kant calls the "Platonic ideal" of a *respublica noumenon* "the eternal norm for all civil organization in general," one that "averts all war" and which humanity is therefore obliged to adopt as a system of government. Amnesty has a silent but pronounced place and function in this ideal. Kant mentions it in the one-sentence paragraph that concludes Section 58 of his 1797 *The Metaphysics of Morals*. After laying out the elements of which peace treaties should consist, he writes, "[i]t is implicit in the very concept of a peace treaty that it includes an amnesty."[88] Kant's reference here to the "implicit" is itself a tacit reference to the passages on amnesty in Wolff's *Jus Gentium* and Vattel's *Law of Nations*. When Kant grounds his discussion of the peace treaty in a distinction between force and law, he follows Wolff and Vattel in their break with Grotius's limited endorsement of penal war.[89] Kant argues that despite the victor's desire to act with the pretensions of a judge when setting down the conditions for the peace treaty, the treaty should not assume the form of a verdict.[90] Where there is no law, there can be no punishment. Because independent states relate to each other in a lawless state of nature that amounts to de facto war even if it is not war de jure,[91] and because there are no courts of justice and no lawsuits in this state of nature,[92] it would be a categorical error to confuse the military right to retaliate with the legal rights of retribution and punishment.[93] "For punishment can only occur in a relationship between a superior (*imperantis*) and a subject (*subitum*), and states do not stand in that relation to each other."[94] The amnesty implicit in the peace treaty should be arranged as equitably as possible,[95] but even though amnesty may therefore resemble clemency, it nevertheless remains distinct from the right of clemency in principle: The ruler who remits a deserved punishment presupposes a sovereign right to punish no victorious state can assume.[96] Because no legal relation pertains between states and because force is the only court capable of deciding disputes between states, the victorious state should negotiate its peace treaty with the defeated party on the basis of its superior force and its superior force alone: It should drop the question of wrong altogether.[97] The victor should not propose compensation for the costs of war because this would imply that the defeated party had fought an unjust war, and it should not enslave or remove the civil freedom of the subjects of the defeated party for the same reason, though it does have the right to an exchange of prisoners "without regard for their being equal in number."[98] The peace treaty, in short, must undo the law of force without recourse to the force of law.

What precisely is the place and function of amnesty in all of this? According to Wolff, "the effect of decreeing amnesty is that acts wrongfully done are to be considered as though they had not been done; from which immunity for them naturally arises."[99] Although Grotius certainly does not disagree that a peace treaty should sink the cause of war into oblivion,[100] Wolff and Vattel are obliged by their opposition to penal war to go further. Because amnesty is for them, as for Schmitt, incommensurable with the punishment of the defeated party, they are compelled to rely on amnesty *alone* to restore the sovereign peace after war. Wolff and Vattel consequently consider amnesty, understood in the style of the Peace of Westphalia as complete and lasting oblivion, to be implicit in any and all peace treaties, even and especially if that peace treaty should happen to remain silent on the matter of amnesty. Wolff's remarks on this point are particularly intriguing.

> Since in a treaty of peace neither party convicts the other of wrong, and since when peace
> has been made as regards that cause for which the war was waged, war cannot again be
> renewed, consequently the war and whatever is done in it is consigned to perpetual
> oblivion and everlasting silence, and since an amnesty is complete and lasting forgetful-
> ness of wrongs and offences previously committed; in a treaty first of all there must be

an agreement for an amnesty, and this is contained in every treaty of peace as such, even if there should be no agreement for it.[101]

This passage at first seems simple: It appears to be nothing more than a gloss on the maxim *in amnestia substantia pacis consistit*. Wolff here seems to suggest simply that amnesty is a synecdoche for the text of the peace treaty, which is to say, that part of the peace treaty that represents the essence of the treaty as a whole. The last clause of Wolff's passage, however, poses a problem for reading. How can amnesty *be there in the text of the peace treaty* even if it is *not there in the text of the peace treaty*? What is amnesty, such that it can come into being not only through *an agreement to take part in silence* but also through *a silence that needs no agreement to take effect*? If the substance of peace consists of amnesty, what is the substance of amnesty itself?

This problem only becomes sharper in what follows. Not only is amnesty the unsaid condition for any and all peace treaties, Wolff argues, but all that remains unsaid in a peace treaty falls under the category of amnesty.

> Those things concerning which nothing has been said in a treaty of peace remain as they are. For, since neither of the contracting parties is convicted of injustice or wrong, the property which has been occupied in war is generally considered as occupied as if by right, and in like manner the things which have been done on either side are understood to have been done as if without wrong, and to this result especially contributes the fact that there is an amnesty in every treaty of peace as such.[102]

If amnesty is a synecdoche for the peace treaty, Wolff here seems to argue, then the unspoken will be a metonym for amnesty itself: The unspoken will be that part of amnesty's complete and lasting forgetfulness of past wrongs to which the textual operation of amnesty as a whole may be reduced. This amounts to a rule for the reading of peace treaties. Amnesty, for Wolff, is in effect that principle of intelligibility according to which *what is not said* in the text of a given peace treaty may be read as a trope not only for *what peace is* but also for *what peace ought to be*. The reason amnesty can be implicit in the text of the peace treaty, even if it is not the object of an explicit agreement, is that amnesty is not merely one among many clauses of the peace treaty. It is more fundamentally *the hermeneutic principle that governs the readability of the text of the peace treaty as a whole*. It is the principle that hears, in that text's omissions, gaps, ambiguities, and indeterminacies, the fullness of peace itself. In place of a legal or moral judgment that ends war with a determination of guilt, amnesty brackets war through an *apophantic judgment—*

a judgment that determines *what is* and *what ought to be* on the basis of a fundamentally interpretive act, by speaking and listening *as if* past wrongs had not occurred.[103] Amnesty in Wolff entails a textual dynamic we may call *a hermeneutic of the irreparable*: It is a method for the interpretation of peace treaties that, presupposing the impossibility of providing a remedy for war, operates by hypostasizing the unspoken of peace treaties into a substantial statement, namely that the ravages of war may be understood as a fundamental repose, as the rule of law itself.[104]

This helps explain why, in the seventeenth and eighteenth centuries, in a period of noncriminal war when—presumably, amnesties would have been at their most powerful—amnesty clauses instead disappeared from the texts of European peace treaties altogether.[105] The reason amnesties could disappear from peace treaties without also enabling the recriminalization of war is that amnesty was never merely one among many clauses in the first place. Precisely because amnesty in its modern form is a synecdoche for peace, and because the unspoken in a given peace treaty is a metonym for amnesty, amnesty could subsist as the substance of a peace pact without also appearing explicitly as a clause in the peace treaty itself. The gradual concealment of amnesty in the text of the peace treaty is then in no way antithetical to its being in force. On the contrary, the fact that amnesty remained unspoken during the very heyday of bracketed or contained war suggests the specific way in which amnesty was central to the maintenance of the *Jus Publicum Europaeum*: It was that principle of intelligibility, in the interpretation of peace treaties, that permitted the sovereign peace to be in force without also being in significance.

Amnesty as a Problem in Kant's "Perpetual Peace"

> The State is not founded upon the social bond, which it would express, but rather upon un-binding, which it prohibits.
>
> —Alain Badiou, 1988

Kant will critique Grotius, Pufendorf, and Vattel by name in "Perpetual Peace," but he remains silent on Wolff. Where then does Kant's program for peace stand in relation to Wolff's account of amnesty? How, if at all, might Wolff's correlation of amnesty and the unspoken require us to reread Kant's text? The sixth and final of Kant's 1795 "Preliminary Articles of a Perpetual Peace Between States" obliges states to wage war "in accordance with principles that always leave open the possibility of leaving the state of nature among states (in external relation to one another [rather than internally, through a social contract]) and entering a rightful constitution."[106] For a peace treaty to leave open the possibility for states to act as though the relations between them were lawful, it must do away with the causes of hostility without also having recourse to law's judgment.[107] Codifying an unequal relation of force as a legal relation, which is to say a relation defined by a kind of reciprocally binding formal equality,[108] would foreclose on this possibility. This is the risk Wolff runs by taking the result of war *as* law, *as if* it had settled the question of wrong and right. How then does Kant propose to avoid this risk in his discussion on the peace treaty?

Whereas Wolff's discussion of the peace treaty begins with an explicit discussion of amnesty's power of forgetting, Kant's discussion of perpetual peace begins with a discussion of the archive's power to keep written records beyond any living memory. The first of Kant's "Preliminary Articles of a Perpetual Peace Between States" is that "no treaty of peace shall be held to be such if it is made with a secret reservation of the material [*des Stoffs*] for a future war."[109] On this basis, Kant draws a distinction between mere truces, which only suspend hostilities in specific cases,[110] and peace *as such*, which involves "an end to all hostilities."[111] Kant will provide two tests by which we can judge the unconditionality of peace. Neither test will mention amnesty, even though both will bear directly on what Wolff writes about amnesty.

The first test is given by the archive. "Causes for a future war," Kant writes, "extant even if as yet unrecognized by the contracting parties themselves, are all annihilated by a peace treaty, no matter how acute and skilled the sleuthing by which they may be picked out of documents in archives."[112] The archive tests the strength of the peace because it provides an extreme case of a material secret reservation. A true peace would be one that so completely negates the reasons for war that it would not be haunted by the reappearance of writings that have never before seen the light of day. *Even* the archive could not revive war. But what is the power of the archive such that it could threaten peace? The verb tense of the archive is not the past perfect, but the future perfect: Its power is to keep secrets beyond all memory, secrets that will have been forgotten until their reappearance undermines the peace. Because these secrets are written, and hence remain beyond the limits of any living memory, they are not kept out of any ill will on the part of those who sign the peace treaty. They instead mark a constitutive limit for knowledge, a limit imposed by time itself. Archival documents define a class of secret reservations that could not have been made public at the moment those parties signed their peace treaty; they indicate what the contracting parties could not possibly have known when endorsing the peace treaty's promises with their signatures. The archive thus tests the perpetuity or everlastingness of true peace. Kant's test of the archive turns to the written trace of enmity to test the temporal limits of amnesty's power of oblivion.

Kant's second test is even more radical. Because archival documents can, in principle, be made public, their secrets do not violate the transcendental formula of public right—namely, that "all actions relating to the rights of others are wrong if their maxim is incompatible with publicity."[113] The second and most radical test of perpetual peace, by contrast, will pose the problem of a reservation so secret, and so lasting, that it will almost no longer be material. "A mental reservation (*reservatio mentalis*) regarding old claims to be worked out only in the future—which neither party may mention just now because both are too exhausted to continue the war—with the ill will to make use of the first favorable opportunity for this end belongs to Jesuitical casuistry and is beneath the dignity of the ruler[.]"[114] Since mental reservations cannot, as can archival documents, be nullified through publication, the only hope that they will not revive war is that the ruler for whom they will always remain possible will understand that they contradict the hallmark of moral law, namely, "dignity" [*der Würde*]. The very temporal index of mental reservations (their being bound constitutively to the past, as a kind of resentment) provides the strongest safeguard against their revivification, for they by definition lie beneath the timeless, sovereign friendship of which the kingdom of ends is a rational prophecy: If a king were to hold onto ill will, time would run against the king.[115] Mental reservations are then *like* the secret material reservations held in the archive because each only appears for the first time after the peace treaty is signed. But *unlike* an archival document, mental reservations violate the formula of transcendental right *in their principle*. The very idea of a "public mental reservation" is a contradiction in terms: If a reservation has been published in some form, it will have taken on a material form and will no longer qualify as a mental reservation. Once clothed in language, a reservation by definition becomes unreserved: It becomes unable to resist lending itself to quotation, dispute, debate, and even war. Mental reservations cannot then both be openly declared and remain mental reservations. They are incommensurable with publicity in their principle; they are unjust.[116] If they are to persist in their being, mental reservations must be kept not only secret but also silent. Above all, the monarch who holds mental reservations while also signing a peace treaty will commit perjury. Kant's second test is designed to judge the material limits of amnesty's power as a written oath (its limits, in other words, in *extensio*).

Implicit in the radicality of this second test is that the "ill will" [*bösen Willen*] Kant associates with mental reservations partakes in the "radical evil" [*das Radikal Böse*] he discusses in his 1793 article "Religion Within the Boundaries of Mere Reason." There Kant defines radical evil as the "intelligible deed" or act of thought by which the human race incorporates maxims contrary to the moral law into the ground of its power of choice or will.[117] Kant understands evil as the notion that nonmoral maxims (in particular, those related to self-love) could provide a sufficient ground for the power of choice.[118] Even if maxims so grounded do indeed produce actions that, in their outward effects, appear in every way consistent with the moral law, they still remain evil, for they are based in a subordination of the moral law to nonmoral maxims.[119]

There is therefore a very specific sense to the "ill will" Kant mentions in "Perpetual Peace" in connection with mental reservations. The relation of ill will to radical evil implies, to begin, that ill will refers to the maxims of self-love, namely, jealousy and rivalry—those unjust desires that, according to Kant, ground the "secret or open hostility to all whom we consider alien to us."[120] Kant classifies these desires as "vices of culture" as distinct from the "bestial vices of gluttony, lust and wild lawlessness."[121] The distinction is important, not least because the vices of culture produce the hostility that Kant, following Hobbes, treats as a synonym for war itself.[122] Whereas bestial vices derive from the human race's nonreasoning animality (its desires for self-preservation, for the propagation of the species, for community with other human beings), the vices of culture are a product of reason and, in particular, of comparison. Comparison gives rise to hostility because its reasonable premise—the assumption of equal worth—turns into an unreasonable form of competition. The assumption of equal worth entails not only the anxiety that we are not equal to others who may in some way be ascendant over us but also the preventive measures we take to procure ascendancy first.[123] The competitiveness that results from this assumption may be commensurable with sympathy and reciprocal love.[124] It may also contribute to purposive *Kultur* because the "unsocial sociability" it produces will be one of the means by which nature will drive the human race forward to its goal, a universal cosmopolitan existence.[125] And it may even produce the merciful effect of peace in a nonmoral way, since the "spirit of commerce" to which it gives rise is the best insurance against the risk of war.[126] But despite all of this, the assumption of equal worth will remain radically evil: It will never ground a concept of human dignity as such.[127] Even though self-love cannot offer a maxim that could take the place of the categorical imperative, the human race continues to think, act, and hope as if it could do just that.

Where does amnesty figure into this schema? Kant's passages on commerce derive, in a general sense, from Plato's distinction between two modes of friendship: properly political amity, on the one hand, and the suspension of enmity that is merely the side-effect of commercial exchange, on the other. For Kant and, as we shall see, for Plato too, amnesty will fall into the latter category. Yet the opening passages of "Perpetual Peace" also raise a more direct question about Kant's relation to Wolff's hermeneutics of amnesty. Whereas the opening passages in "Perpetual Peace" refer to a peace treaty threatened by archival documents and unspoken mental reservations, *The Metaphysics of Morals* states that an amnesty is implicit in the very idea of a peace treaty. "Perpetual Peace" thus construes the unsaid as a domain where writing threatens the amnesty that, according to *The Metaphysics of Morals*, goes without saying in the peace treaty. Kant's "Perpetual Peace" implies a critique of amnesty.

To begin explicating this critique, we may refer briefly to the essay Kant's title cites, namely, the Abbé de Saint-Pierre's 1713 *Projet Pour Rendre la Paix Perpétuelle en Europe*. Saint-Pierre's text establishes an analogy between the subject and the state and argues that the best possible world would be that in which the sovereign states form a world republic.[128] This analogy does not originate in Hobbes; its profile is already apparent in Plato's *Alcibiades* and *Republic*.[129] Kant makes an interesting use of this analogy in "Perpetual Peace." He turns to it in a way that not only conspicuously marks its limits but also leaves open the possibility for its reversal. By tracing this opening, we will be able to begin to understand the limit from which Kant's critique of amnesty is written.

Kant cites Saint-Pierre's analogy at the conclusion of his "Second Definitive Article of Perpetual Peace," only then to sharply curtail it.

> In accordance with reason there is only one way that states in relation with one another can leave the lawless condition, which involves nothing but war; it is that, like individual human beings, they give up their savage (lawless) freedom, accommodate themselves to public coercive laws, and so form an (always growing) *state of nations* (*civitas gentium*) that would finally encompass all the nations of the earth. But, in accordance with their idea of the right of nations, they do not at all want this [since, as Kant will write later, "the craving of every state (or of its head) is to attain a lasting condition of peace in this way, by ruling the whole world where possible"[130]], thus rejecting *in hypothesi* what is

correct *in thesi*; so (if not all is to be lost) in place of the idea *of a world republic* only the *negative* surrogate of a *league* that averts war, endures, and always expands can hold back the stream of hostile inclination that shies away from right, though with constant danger of its breaking out. (*Furor impius intus—fremit horridus ore cruento.*)[131]

Kant's citation of Saint-Pierre implies a twofold understanding of the distinction between *stasis* and *polemos*. On the one hand, Kant affirms that distinction: Because of the imperial cravings of states to establish peace through force, a world republic cannot come into being in the same way as a republic. The transition from lawlessness to law in the one cannot run parallel to an identical transition in the other, and Saint-Pierre's program cannot hold. The resolution of *polemos* in a world republic remains qualitatively distinct from the resolution of *stasis* within the republic itself. Yet, on the other hand, Kant's citation of Saint-Pierre's analogy also points to *a reversal* and *an undoing* of this same logic. If sovereign states are analogous to subjects, are not subjects analogous to sovereign states? If states' imperial desires to institute peace through force will prevent a world republic from coming into being, won't those same desires (which, on the terms of Kant's moral law, could *only* be considered pathological) threaten the republic's own sovereign peace? Doesn't the impossibility of resolving *polemos* between states also imply the impossibility of resolving *stasis* between citizens who desire peace? Won't Kant's sharp curtailment of Saint-Pierre's program for peace leave open the possibility of a critique of the origins of the state's own sovereign peace?

Kant takes up a critique of this type in a well-known passage of *The Metaphysics of Morals*. But while Kant argues in "Perpetual Peace" that "all actions relating to the rights of others are wrong if their maxim is incompatible with publicity," the passages on the origins of public law in *Metaphysics* seem to violate precisely this formula. In the section of *Metaphysics* that concludes with "The Right of Punishment and the Right of Pardon," Kant begins by laying down a law limiting inquiry into the origins of the state's authority.

This passage is significant for two reasons. First, and most basically, the prohibition it sets forth can be assimilated to the standard psychoanalytic account of censorship only at the cost of distorting its relation to sovereign power. For Kant's prohibition does not merely *censor* such inquiry. It more precisely *bans* it. Kant declares inquiry into the past wrongs of the state to be both impotent and unactionable. In accordance with the principles Kant sets forth in his 1784 "What Is Enlightenment?" and later in his "Conflict of the Faculties,"[132] Kant in effect proposes in *The Metaphysics of Morals* that Enlightenment critique should maintain itself in relation to the sovereign state *in potentia*: Critique should rigorously observe its limits and should not become an actual legal judgment. Practical philosophy's inquiry into first principles poses the question of its limits, in other words, in a way that promises to keep the sovereign peace.

Yet of what exactly does that sovereign peace consist? Here it becomes important that Kant's prohibition entails a relation to the problem of amnesty or, more to the point, to the indistinction of *polemos* and *stasis* that is forgotten in amnesty's modern iteration. To follow Saint-Pierre's analogy beyond the limitation that, according to Kant, the desire of states has placed upon it is to find that *Kant's prohibition against the recollection of public law's past wrongs stands in the same relation to the social contract as amnesty stands to peace pacts between states*. The classical amnesty that Wolff turns into a principle for resolving *polemos* between states reappears, in Kant, as a way to ban critique of the origins of the state itself.

> A people should not *inquire* with any practical aim in view into the origin of the supreme authority to which it is subject, that is, a subject *ought not to reason subtly* for the sake of action about the origin of this authority, as a right that can still be called into question (*ius controversum*) with regard to the obedience he owes it. For, since a people must be regarded as already united under a general legislative will in order to judge with rightful force about the supreme authority (*summum imperium*), it cannot and may not judge otherwise than as the present head of state (*summus imperans*) wills it to. Whether a state began with an actual contract of submission (*pacta subiectionis civilis*) as a fact, or whether power came first and law arrived only afterwards, or even whether they should have followed in this order: for a people already subject to civil law these subtle reasonings are altogether pointless and, moreover, threaten a state with danger. If a subject, having pondered over the ultimate origin of the authority now ruling, wanted to resist this authority, he would be punished, got rid of, or expelled (as an outlaw, *exlex*) in accordance with the laws of this authority, that is, with every right. A law that is so holy (inviolable) that is already a crime already to call it in doubt *in a practical way*, and so to suspend its effect for a moment, is thought as if it must have arisen not from human begins but from some highest, flawless lawgiver; and that is what the saying "all authority comes from God" means. This saying is not an assertion about the *historical basis* of the civil constitution; it instead sets forth an idea as a practical principle of reason: the principle that the presently existing legislative authority ought to be obeyed, whatever its origin.[133]

Whereas Wolff's account of the amnesty of 403 B.C. is predicated on a forgetting of the indistinction of *polemos* and *stasis* in that amnesty, Kant's account of amnesty leaves him able to pose just that indistinction as a problem for thought: Unlike Wolff, Kant considers amnesty in relation to both *polemos* and *stasis*. But Kant's capacity to analyze this relation is limited by his fidelity to Wolff's account of amnesty on another point. When Kant argues that the authority of the state must, for purely practical reasons, be thought to have emerged *as if* from God, Kant adds a political theological supplement to the apophantic judgment Wolff situated as the agency of amnesty's forgetting. The very idea of political theology—the purely practical principle that the edifice of the state ought to be marked by height or elevation, ought to be sacred or in some way immune from the community it safeguards—thus emerges in Kant's text not as an autonomous principle but only as a means to compel respect for the state's ban on the recollection of past wrongs.

We might then be tempted to say that amnesty is to political theology what a foundation is to a keystone, but this would not clarify the precise place Kant gives to amnesty, as ban, in the architecture of the sovereign peace. Amnesty is not so much the castle's foundation as the hollow interior within that foundation. *Amnesty is a keep.* It is the state's innermost, strongest, and most secure space, the crypt where the state's most valuable and vulnerable possessions, up to and including the secret traces of its originary crimes, may be safely stored. That the state be able to remain immune from its own origins in and the desire to establish peace through war is essential to the sovereign peace it keeps. The holiness of its sovereignty is, in this sense, merely the hypostasization of its capacity to remain unscathed by the *parrhesiasts'* recollection of its past wrongs. The philosopher who knows this to be true but who does not say so is precisely a keeper of the peace, someone who *observes the amnesty*, not only by *keeping watch over it* and *standing guard against inquiries that threaten to violate it* but also by *letting it become the law that governs his own speculative discourse.*

On this read, the point at which Kant most clearly observes the amnesty in "Perpetual Peace" is the point where he cuts short his account of Saint-Pierre's analogy. At the threshold where Kant conspicuously abandons the implications of this analogy, so as not to recall the *stasis* or unbinding on which the state is founded, his own philosophical discourse becomes indiscernible from amnesty's ban on recalling past wrongs. To observe the amnesty, to keep the peace it institutes, is to keep up the appearance of political theology and to keep the truth-tellers away from the state's archive. If the archive is a test of perpetual peace, it is not only because it is one and the same thing as the state's *arkhê*, its starting point and commanding principle,[134] but also because it houses traces of the anarchy and anomie the state at once fears, claims to oppose, and keeps to itself as its own most intimate law.

Whereas true peace would be so solidly founded as to withstand even the publication of archival documents, which is to say the reappearance of secret traces of the past in the future, the already founded state would be vulnerable, downright fragile, on exactly this point.[135] The multitude or mob that inquires into the state's *arkhê* would have to remain practically silent, especially if, as Kant predicts, that inquiry were to yield a discovery of past wrongs.[136] Traced beyond the limitation placed upon them by states' desires, the unswerving lines of Saint-Pierre's analogy point to *either* the impossibility of true peace *or* the necessity of calling into question the state's very principle. Even though Kant would seem to resolve this antinomy by conceding that "the positive idea of a world republic cannot be realized," his clear-cut swerve from Saint-Pierre's analogy, as well as his remark that international right has been consigned only to the obscurity of the archives, suggest the very opposite.[137] Despite, or perhaps because of, Kant's capacity to critique the amnesty, he says nothing that would unbind the sovereign peace.

The Murmurous Silence of the Keep

> Your grace was kind enough to wish to ease the complaints of residents
> on the Schlossgraben concerning the stentorian singing of prayers by
> hypocritical inmates of the jail. I do not think they would have any cause for
> lamentation—as though their spiritual rehabilitation were in jeopardy—if
> they were required to modulate their singing so that they could hear them-
> selves even with the windows shut and without yelling with all their might.
> They can still obtain the jailer's testimony (which seems to be what they are
> really concerned about) to the effect that they are very God-fearing people,
> for he will hear them all right and in essence they will only be retuned to
> lower the pitch of the note by which the pious citizens of our good city feel
> themselves to be sufficiently awakened in their homes. A word to the jailer,
> if you should wish to summon him and make the foregoing a permanent
> rule for him, would remove an annoyance from one whose peace you have
> often been so kind as to promote and who is ever with the greatest respect
>   your most obedient servant
>   I. Kant
>   —Immanuel Kant, July 1784 Letter to Theodor Hippel, mayor of Königsberg and
>   self-styled humorist, thanking Hippel for his efforts to silence the loud prayers
>   of prisoners held in Königsberg Castle, which lay within earshot of Kant's
>   newly constructed house

What a joy to lie pressed against the rounded outer wall, pull oneself up, let oneself slide down again, miss one's footing and find oneself on firm earth, and play all those games literally upon the Castle Keep and not inside it; to avoid the Castle Keep, to rest one's eyes from it whenever one wanted, to postpone the joy of seeing it until later and yet not have to do without it, but literally hold it safe between one's claws, a thing that is impossible if you have only an ordinary open entrance to it; but above all to stand guard over it, and in that way to be so completely compensated for renouncing the actual sight of it that, if one had to choose between staying all one's life in the Castle Keep or in the free space outside it, one would choose the latter, content to wander up and down there all one's days and keep guard over the Castle Keep. Then there would be no noises in the walls, no insolent burrowing up to the very Keep itself; then peace would be assured there and I would be its guardian; then I would not have to listen with loathing to the burrowing of the small fry, but with delight to something that I cannot hear now at all: the murmurous silence of the Castle Keep.

—Franz Kafka, "The Burrow," 1924

Kant's keeping of the peace is the essence of his "Second Supplement" to the three definitive articles for perpetual peace. The philosopher, who is neither a theologian nor a lawyer but a philosopher of moral law, is incapable of forming seditious factions or clubs.[138] Because the philosopher is immune from *stasis*—because the philosopher's *anamnêsis* is precisely an antidote to the recollection of past wrongs[139]—he should be permitted to speak freely within, and should be given a hearing by, the state that in effect hosts him. Since the universal, morally legislative reason to which the philosopher owes his fidelity contradicts the desire of states to establish peace through war, the philosopher's exchanges with the state must remain secret. This secrecy does not violate the first definitive article for perpetual peace: Even though it marks a silent critique of the sovereign peace, it is not kept out of ill will and does not compel the philosopher to perjure himself. It does not then qualify as a mental reservation. On the contrary, because the maxims of international right are incompatible with publicity, the state's secret exchanges with philosophers provide the state with its only chance to tacitly align itself with moral law.[140] The philosopher of moral law is internally excluded within, is even a hostage of, the state that, as a rule, does not obey the moral law. Yet while the philosopher of moral law cannot tell a lie,[141] he is not obliged to speak. When Kant's "Perpetual Peace" passes over the problem of cosmopolitan right "in silence," Kant says that its maxims are easy to infer by analogy to the right of nations.[142] But the maxims of cosmopolitan right directly contradict the territorial claims of the sovereign state.[143] Here, too, Kant's silence keeps the sovereign peace.

The silence is at its most striking in the description of the "day of atonement" Kant offers in a pivotal footnote to "Perpetual Peace." This footnote is, not coincidentally, appended to the same passage where Kant cuts short his account of Saint-Pierre's analogy. If the true peace of a world republic is indeed impossible, Kant argues, we are left with the second-best form of peace, the "pacific federation." [144] In exactly the place where Wolff's account of peace depended entirely on amnesty, Kant writes that the "pacific federation" will include what he calls a "day of atonement."

> At the end of a war, when peace is concluded, it would not be unfitting for a nation to proclaim [*ausgeschrieben*], after the festival of thanksgiving, a day of atonement [*ein Buβtag*], calling upon heaven, in the name of the state, for grace [*Gnade*] on the human race for the great sin of which it continues to be guilty, that of being unwilling to acquiesce in any lawful constitution in relation to other nations but, proud of its independence, preferring instead to use the barbarous means of war (even though what is sought by way, namely the right of each state, is not decided by it). Festivals of thanksgiving during a war for a *victory* won, hymns that (in the style of the Israelites) are sung to the *Lord of Hosts*, stand in no less marked contrast with the moral idea of the father of human beings; for, beyond indifference to the way nations seek their mutual rights (which is regrettable enough), they bring in joy at having annihilated a great many human beings or their happiness. [145]

Kant's note on the day of atonement (or *fête du Grand Pardon*) must be read alongside his argument, in the *Critique of Practical Reason*, that "the Christian principle of *morals* itself is not theological (and so heteronomy)" but is instead the "autonomy of pure practical reason itself[.]" [146] Christianity, in other words, is for Kant the only confession that approximates rational religion, and it is on this basis that Kant issues his critique of the day of atonement. The day of atonement is no longer an amnesty because it is no longer part of a peace treaty aimed at terminating only one *particular* war. Just as the pacific federation aims at a lawful future in which the possibility of war has *in general* disappeared as much as possible, so too does the day of atonement involve an appeal for grace for the human race's *general* failure to learn from its history in spite of that history. Whereas amnesty's modern function is to not apply law in order to preserve the possibility and hope for lawlike relations between states, the day of atonement asks for grace from heaven for a human race that knows the good but, for reasons of pride, prefers not to do it. As distinct from amnesty, the day of atonement assumes the permanence of that for which it asks for grace. It turns heteronomy into a ritual.

Neither amnesty nor grace, the day of atonement nevertheless partakes in both. "Perpetual Peace" poses a question about the conditions under which a lasting peace would be possible. To respond to this question, it departs from the *mere* peace treaty or truce, the *mere* suspension of hostilities, of which amnesty is, for Wolff, the necessary condition. But even though the purpose of the essay "Perpetual Peace" is therefore to rethink the root and branch of the *mere* peace treaties in which amnesty is implied, in order to arrive at the conditions for a true and enduring peace, Kant nevertheless does not mention "amnesty" even once in "Perpetual Peace."

This raises a question related to the readability of Kant's text. A Straussian reader might propose that, for reasons related to the political conditions under which Kant wrote, Kant was obliged to make his most controversial arguments between the lines. The claim of this reading would be that Kant could not have openly articulated his arguments without placing his philosophical utterances, as well as his very self-preservation, at the mercy of Prussian censors: Kant could not have publicly argued, for example, that it is the principle of state sovereignty that keeps the republic from progressing to the cosmopolitan peace that providence invites the republic to see as its future. The purpose of reading Kant in this manner would be to discern the dangerous, unpopular, or untimely philosophical truths articulated only in the silences of Kant's essay, to teach these truths to a few diligent students, and in so doing, to preserve the very possibility of political philosophical inquiry. On this read, Kant's footnotes would become especially significant. The footnotes of "Perpetual Peace" refer to the relation between the sovereign monarch and God, to miracles, and to revealed religion. They are the theological footnote to the text's political body. In between grace and amnesty, between *paradiso* and *purgatario*, the "day of atonement" is also discussed in the eighth of the essay's sixteen footnotes. It occupies the precise middle of Kant's essay. The relation of indiscernibility between amnesty and grace in Kant's footnote on the "day of atonement" would thus also be a point of indiscernibility between, on the one hand, the political philosophical problem silently at issue in Kant's essay (how a peace treaty grounded in amnesty could be grounded instead in moral law) and, on the other hand, the theological frame that appears only, or perhaps especially, at the essay's edges. Situated between politics and theology, the day of atonement would, for that same reason, belong neither to politics nor to theology.

On this read, in other words, "Perpetual Peace" would be a clear example of esoteric writing. But there are at least two problems with this reading. The first and most basic concerns its presupposition about the relation of philosophy and law. The second, which follows from the first, concerns its foreknowledge of the modality of silence for which it searches. On the basis of his reading of Platonic political philosophy, Strauss treats censorship as the exemplary relation of law to philosophy[147] and therefore proceeds as if what remains unspoken between the lines may always be interpreted as a symptom of an antinomy between law and philosophy. Yet because of the way "Perpetual Peace" takes up the problem of amnesty and the unspoken from Wolff, Kant's text poses a special case for this style of reading.[148] Is it not the sovereign ban, rather than censorship, that structures the relation between law and philosophy in this text? Wouldn't potentiality, rather than antinomy, be the modality governing that relation? And wouldn't Kant's silences then point to a problem that is the very opposite of the persecution of the philosophical few by the nonphilosophical many? Not least because Kant openly describes philosophical secrecy in "Perpetual Peace," the Straussian reading that, on the basis of a determinant judgment, apprehends Kant's "Perpetual Peace" as a clear example of esoteric writing will push at an already open door. The reader who, out of loyalty to the principles of esoteric writing, seeks to divide Kant's writing into its esoteric and exoteric dimensions will not be able to understand that *the political ontological modality* of the unspoken in Kant's "Perpetual Peace" derives from a problem more fundamental than law's censorship of philosophical inquiry.

I shall outline that problem in detail in the second part of this chapter, but we may signal it here epigrammatically by saying that *Kant's "Perpetual Peace" observes the amnesty in exactly the same way that the unnamed animal in Kafka's "Burrow" stands guard over its Castle Keep.* Kant does not dwell within the sovereign peace; he stays in the free spaces outside it to better guard over it. *"Perpetual Peace" is written from a limit external to the same sovereign peace it also keeps.* Because a standpoint of this type is the indispensable condition for the esoteric writing that wishes to philosophize about law without also suffering law's censorship of philosophy, the reading that scans Kant's text for esoteric writing without first thematizing amnesty as a problem for reading cannot but remain ignorant of the ban that *links* law and philosophy, and hence too of the oblivion that governs its own interpretation of political philosophical silences. In short, Straussian reading is compelled, by its own immanent principles, to misrecognize the exemplary relation between the said and the unsaid that actually governs Kant's "Perpetual Peace."

The difficulty of reading the murmurous silence of "Perpetual Peace" is not that Kant quietly ensures the preservation of political philosophy against the risk of persecution by law. This is plain not only in the content of the essay's opening passages (its announcement of the "little saving clause" that underwrites the text as a whole) but also in the way the essay works to reconcile the conflict of the faculties (its internal attempt to resolve the strife among the disciplines of law, philosophy, and theology). The challenge of reading Kant's "Perpetual Peace" is rather that *both its manner and its matter imply an unactualized capacity to pose amnesty as a problem for critique*. The "Peace" that appears in Kant's title cannot be limited either to its self-evident grammatical function, its satirical reference to death, or its status as a citation of Saint-Pierre. It indexes only a vanishing point or degree zero of visibility, a point that is at once *the very center of the field of intelligibility upon which Kant speculates* and, at the same time, is *entirely absent from that field*. This point is the very pivot point of Kant's essay: Kant's explicit arguments circle silently around it with geometrically rigorous equidistance. It provides the measure that governs Kant's critique of amnesty and, for this same reason, must be kept from view. The "Peace" of Kant's title is a catachresis: It marks the threshold in Kant's text where Kant observes the sovereign peace without also observing it, while also guarding that peace by saying nothing that would amount to its critique.

From what space, in the name of what principle, does Kant then guard the sovereign peace? Both Kant's politics, which is to say his privately articulated but well-documented sympathy for the revolution that banned the power of pardon outright,[149] as well as his theological writings, which hold that grace should not be reduced to a mere means, point to one and the same conclusion. The purpose of the day of atonement, in Kant's understanding, is to ask for grace for the unforgivable.[150] This is not merely because "knowing the good and preferring not to do it" is the precise opposite of "knowing not what one does" (Luke 23: 34–35). In the closing passages of "Religion Within the Boundaries of Mere Reason," Kant draws on the traditional distinction between nature and grace to define the principles that would later govern his severe limitation on the sovereign right of grace in *The Metaphysics of Morals*. In this text, which was published in Easter of 1793, Kant argues that the act of summoning the effects of grace cannot be incorporated into the maxims of reason if reason is to remain within its legitimate bounds.[151] Whereas reason must restrict its acts of understanding to the natural laws of cause and effect, acts of grace follow no laws of nature at all: Grace is an effect without a comprehensible cause. Though, in this, acts of grace resemble acts of freedom (which, as Kant shows in the *Critique of Pure Reason*, must also break from the laws of nature) and are therefore "limit cases" or *parerga* to reason,[152] the power of grace is ultimately unlike freedom in that it "totally escapes us."[153] To act as if grace is a possibility at one's disposal is to forfeit one's claim to reason altogether: In so doing one thereby incorporates into one's will an unreasonable maxim, a maxim of heteronomy that has no basis in the laws of nature.[154] But it is also to forfeit one's claim to grace and doubly so. Insofar as we begin to incorporate grace into our reasoning, Kant argues, we begin to expect the unpredictable. Instead of striving for grace, we become lazy and idle. We begin to expect from above possibilities we ought to find in ourselves (for example, peace).[155] Wherever grace is not, as Kant counsels, properly limited to the idea that it will "work in us what nature cannot, provided we have made just use of that nature," then incorporating grace into our maxims will cause in us an idleness that precludes our making just use of nature and that thus disqualifies us from grace too. Wherever we summon grace in any but the most strictly immaterial form, in other words, grace shall no longer retain its place in the noumenal divine kingdom. To presume to address God in speech, as do the prisoners of Kant's Schlossgraben, is to presume equality of speech with an omniscient, omnipresent, and omnipotent being.[156] To clothe a request for grace in material or sensuous form is to conceive of God on the model of a mere sovereign monarch—that is to say, as a finite being who would be dependent on the senses to comprehend a request for grace. Even and especially if such a request remains internal and silent, as a mere "act of thought," its form still presumes to address or even persuade God, and it thus remains an act of human pride.[157] Whenever grace is not the end in and for itself of a rebirth into prayerful life, but remains a mere means to the acquisition of virtue, Kant will consider it a form of self-delusion that abandons reason and forfeits faith at one and the same time.

From these passages, in which Enlightenment thought and a certain Protestant work ethic merge into what Adorno might call the sadism of idealist rage, we may infer how Kant might understand the people's call for grace on the day of atonement. This grace would have to include grace for the "intelligible deed" or act of thought by which the human race knowingly integrates maxims into their power of choice that do not accord with the moral law.[158] The use of war would be one such maxim, but it would not be the only or even most extreme example. Because the day of atonement is a public invocation of grace for war's persistence, it would have a specifically sensuous or material form, and it would violate Kant's rule about the distinction between grace and nature. Reducing grace to a mere means, it would diminish its addressee to a natural or immanent being, a mere sovereign.[159] But why are the people forced to beg for grace in the first place? The strong implication of what Kant writes is that the radical evil for which the people ask for grace is not so much war or even pride as *the materialization of pride into an enduring institution*—namely, the necessary evil that is the Leviathan itself. Since it is the state that is jealously unwilling to give up its independence and its war-making powers, it is the state that prevents knowledge of the good from being acted on, and it is the state that is the primary reason for the postponement of progress toward the very perpetual peace the sovereign state claims to desire as its most fundamental law of nature. It is the state, then, that would be a "crime against human nature" as Kant defines it—namely, a crime against the possibility of progress.[160] Because the state's maxims are immoral, it is also the state, in its very principle, that restores the principle of guilt to international law. Thus does Kant's "Perpetual Peace" provide a prolegomena to contemporary anti-statism both left and right. To ask for grace in the name of the state for the human race is, for Kant, also to ask for grace in the name of the human race for the state. When the people call upon heaven, they atone for this thing that will only ever turn heteronomy and anomie into institutions. The state claims to redeem humanity from its state of nature. But it is only a simulacrum of grace, a false messiah: The state forces the people to incorporate not only war but also grace into their maxims of reason. Kant may observe the amnesty, but the substance of his unactualized critique is plain. Even as the day of atonement improves upon amnesty by endowing it with generality, it soils grace by reducing it to amnesty's supplement.

Amnesty as a Problem in Plato's *Laws*

Kant's unactualized critique of amnesty is the antipode of Schmitt's disavowed mourning of amnesty. Even as Kant's explicit statement on amnesty preserves the possibility of the just enemy, his critique of amnesty from the standpoint of grace reintroduces into international law the possibility of the unjust enemy. Yet precisely in their extreme opposition, Kant and Schmitt share a basic problematic. Kant joins in the political theological refrain in a paradoxical manner. Kant separates grace as much as possible from any material phenomena to reserve grace's purity as a form of noumenal rebirth and, thus, *in the name of grace* restricts as much as possible its appearance in the republic. Kant's monarch must embody grace (in order to glow with the halo of sovereignty) without also embodying it (because to give grace sensuous expression is to taint it). Although it seems commonsensical that the principle of Christian charity would encourage the exercise of the right of grace, Kant shows that charity's pure form actually points to a higher *kharis*, the material expression of which is unmitigated punishment. By taking *kharis* seriously, Kant thus arrives at a more extreme conclusion on this point than even Pufendorf.[161] Kant does not disagree with Pufendorf that the primary duty of the supreme sovereign is to the *salus*—the safety, security, health, well-being, and welfare, but also the salvation or immunity—of the public or population.[162] The sovereign may suspend positive law and may remit deserved punishment, but *kharis* and its cognates articulate the standard that governs these exceptions: There is no sovereign exception that is not declared for the sake of some *kharis*. Were a sovereign to pardon a criminal who has injured the public or population, that sovereign would risk violating the holy obligation to keep the public or population safe and sound, to indemnify it from damage or injury, to secure it against internal or external enemies, to preserve and protect its immunity, to ensure its self-preservation and salvation. When Pufendorf argues that, "by the granting of pardon in the proper place and time, the safety of a state is not undermined but is in fact sometimes strengthened," he offers a variation of Seneca's argument that clemency is an excellent way to ensure the safety of the state and the king.[163] But when Kant argues that the monarch cannot even pardon a wrong committed against his own person if that pardon would endanger the security of the people,[164] he articulates the logical conclusion of not only Cicero's principle of *salus* but also the medieval doctrine of the King's Two Bodies. Kant's "most notorious polemic against pardons"[165] is not, despite its mercilessness, a break with the political theological refrain. On the contrary, that mercilessness is the political theological refrain's exemplary, if paradoxical, expression.

What would it mean, then, to break with this refrain? How might we think peace outside of its restricted economy in pardon and amnesty? Because Kant regarded Plato's *respublica noumenon* as the norm for all civil obligation, we may raise these questions with more precision by bringing them to bear on Plato. One purpose of our reading will be to understand the limits of the Platonic archive that governs the relation of the said to the unsaid in Kant's critique of amnesty. This will require a special approach to the text of Platonic philosophy. Loraux has shown how the appropriation of "Athens" as an object of knowledge by various modern disciplines was enabled, from the beginning, by certain ancient writers whose own political participation consisted of inventing and then conferring paradigmatic status upon a decidedly partial account of Athenian life.[166] The amnesty of 403 B.C. is an exemplary case of this dynamic. Loraux argues that amnesty is the "forgetting that founds the political" and suggests that amnesty is a motivated forgetting designed to obliterate, above all, the meaning of the word "democracy."[167] To understand the amnesty of 403 B.C., Loraux writes, we must turn canonical classical texts like Plato's *Laws* back against themselves, submitting the conceptual innovations of these mostly aristocratic writers to the questions and thinking their writing implicitly silences.[168]

What would we learn about Kant's critique of amnesty by bringing Loraux's reading to bear on Plato's *Laws*? In the *Laws*, unlike the *Republic, stasis* emerges explicitly as a problem for thought, where "thought" is understood in a very specific sense. Plato writes in Book VII of the *Republic* that the awakening of thought (*dianoia*) occurs only when thought encounters some paradox, perplexing aporia, or problem that *provokes* it to come into being; only when a "provocative" confounds the senses and leaves the soul at a loss does thought get its start.[169] Gilles Deleuze neatly summarizes the *Republic*'s exemplary provocative: "The sign or point of departure for that which forces thought is the coexistence of contraries, the coexistence of more and less in an unlimited qualitative becoming."[170] In his commentary on the same passages, Badiou emphasizes that the problem of the coexistence of more and less requires special recourse to mathematics.[171] Turned back upon the *Republic*, this paradigm of thought's start throws into relief the difference between the *Republic*'s treatment of *stasis* and the *Laws*'. Whereas the *Republic* approaches *stasis* as the object of a nosological discourse, configuring it as a malady suffered *only accidentally* by the individual soul and, by analogy, the city,[172] the *Laws* presupposes that this same malady will *necessarily* strike whenever there are excessive inequalities in the amount of property, land, and power among citizens who otherwise coexist as equals.[173] According to the paradigm of thought laid out in the *Republic, stasis* only becomes a problem for thought in the *Laws*.

Let us turn, then, to the *Laws*, and in particular to Book I, which, as Loraux notes, frames *stasis* in such a way as to permit us an understanding of how Platonic thought is constituted by what it refuses.[174] What's thought-provoking about Book I is that, at its very outset, the Athenian stranger who is the *Laws*' primary interlocutor mentions amnesty, almost in passing, in the same passages that culminate in the definition of the task of the lawgiver (or *nomothete*) as the task of creating the best *politeia*. The word the Athenian uses is διαλλαγῶν (*diallagôn*), which most translators of the *Laws* have rendered as "reconciliation," which Plato uses elsewhere to describe a peace pact,[175] and which was one of three terms used by Plato's contemporaries to indicate the amnesty of 403 B.C.[176] The Athenian uses the word as part of his refutation of Klinias's bad understanding of the lawgiver's task. Whereas Klinias argues that the lawgiver ought to prescribe laws primarily with a view to success in external warfare and defines good laws as laws that prepare citizens to win external wars, the Athenian's refutation of this argument draws a distinction between external wars and internal wars. Because internal wars are worse and bitterer than external wars, he argues, the lawgiver's primary task is to prescribe laws that preclude internal wars. Because amnesty serves precisely this purpose, it falls squarely within the Athenian's line of questioning.

ATH: Now what about someone who brings harmony to the city? Would he order its way of life with a view more to external war or more to that internal war called *stasis*, which occurs from time to time and which everyone would wish never to come to pass in his city and, if it does, would wish to end as soon as possible?

KL: Clearly, with a view to this latter.

ATH: Now which of two courses would one prefer? That peace [*eirênên*] should be restored by the victory of one party or the other to the faction [*staseôs*], and the destruction of its rival, or rather that friendship and amity should be re-established by a reconciliation [*diallagôn*], and the citizens compelled [*anankên*] to bestow their attention on an external enemy?

KL: Everyone would prefer the latter rather than the former for his own city.

ATH: Then wouldn't the lawgiver also?

KL: How could he not?

ATH: And doesn't everyone set up all his lawful customs for the sake of what is best?

KL: How could he not?

ATH: The best, however, is neither *polemos* nor *stasis*—which are abominable things we must be without—but rather peace [*eirênê*] and at the same time goodwill towards one another. Moreover, it is likely that even that victory of the city over itself belonged not to the best things [*aristôn*] but to the necessary things [*anankaiôn*]. To think otherwise is as if someone had held that a sick body, after it had received a medical purgation [*katharseôs*], were in the best active condition, and never turned his mind to a body which had no need of such remedies at all. Likewise, with regard to the happiness of a city or of a private person, anyone who thought this way would never become a correct statesman, if he looked first and only to external wars, and would never become a lawgiver in the strict sense, if he didn't legislate the things of war for the sake of peace rather than the things of peace for the sake of what pertains to war.[177]

Three sets of oppositions govern the Athenian's discourse in this passage. The first and most basic is the opposition between *mere necessity* and *the best*, the second between *polemos* and *stasis*, and the third between two kinds of peace: *diallagôn* and *eirênê*. The significance of this passage, at least according to Leo Strauss, cannot be underestimated. Because it is only in the *Laws*, Strauss argues, that Plato sets forth the best possible political order (so much so that Strauss will call the *Laws* Plato's "only political work proper,"[178] his "political work *par excellence*,"[179] and his "most political work"[180]), and because the *Laws*' inquiry into the best regime provides the guiding question for all classical political philosophy,[181] the passages we will here consider, which raise the question of the best regime for the first time in the *Laws*, will, on Strauss's read, stand as the inaugural passages of classical political philosophy as such. Yet what is fascinating about these passages is that the Athenian's capacity to pose this all-important question is, precisely as Loraux suggests, constituted by what it refuses: The Athenian's *criticism* of amnesty will also *appropriate its functions* in order *to hypostasize them* in and as *the substance of the political itself.*

Let us consider the passage in greater detail. When the Athenian argues that the peace a city establishes in its victory over itself is merely a lamentable necessity, he presents a veiled criticism of democracy. As Loraux shows, the *"kratos"* that gives "democracy" its root is a victory of precisely this type.[182] The Athenian's criticism of the necessity of *kratos* is, of course, part of political philosophy's more general criticism of merely necessary or compulsory things.[183] Because *kratos* is a need akin to eating, sleeping, laboring, and punishment, it is of the order of the same animal body whose life is governed not by reason but by all manner of contingencies and accidents: Chance is the corollary of mere necessity.[184] This same criticism of the necessary supplies the Athenian with his argument against *diallagôn*. *Diallagôn* may be necessary to avert internal war, but its opposition to *stasis* does not mean that it is the same as peace. In a passage that would be crucial for Schmitt's development of the concept of the enemy, the Athenian claims that *diallagôn* ends *stasis* only by beginning a *polemos*.[185] The fundamental opposition the Athenian establishes here is not then between *diallagôn* and *stasis* but between *stasis*, *diallagôn*, and *polemos*, on the one hand, and *eirênê*, on the other. *Diallagôn*, like the purge that cures a sick body, is a mere necessity. *Eirênê*, a peace beyond both *polemos* and *stasis*, is to be preferred over *diallagôn* just as a perfectly healthy body is to be preferred over a sick body that has been cured. As the best or most excellent peace, it is the thing toward which proper political philosophical inquiry should strive. Yet the very gesture through which the Athenian consecrates *eirênê* depends for its validity on its appropriation of one of the functions of the same amnesty he criticizes. Whereas amnesty instituted a forgetting of *kratos* through a compulsory oath,[186] the Athenian here achieves that same forgetting in the very act by which he poses the question of the best regime. When the Athenian displaces amnesty's compulsory forgetting to raise the inaugural question of classical political philosophy, he also turns one of the amnesty's characteristic powers—forgetting—against itself. Classical political philosophy here calls itself into being both by *partaking in* and *imitating part of* the very amnesty it rejects.

This dynamic becomes clearer in the Athenian's discourse in the well-known passages of Book IV that lay out the concept of the rule of law (715a8–715d9). The Athenian opens these passages by describing the conditions of *stasis* that persist even after divided cities have attempted to reconcile. Under conditions where *stasis* is suppressed *merely* or *only* by amnesty, says the Athenian, one cannot speak of a *politeia* at all. For amnesty does not actually produce the reconciliation at which it aims. It merely preserves in a suspended state of watchful hate the memory of past wrongs that belongs to the two factions it proposes to reconcile. Directly after issuing this criticism, the Athenian will then proceed to speak of law as a "ruler over the rulers," arguing that the presence or absence of rule of law is that which "above all determines whether the city survives or undergoes the opposite."[187] The rule of law is a better—a more *dianoetic*—solution than amnesty to the problem of the divided city. In such a city,

> [t]he ruling offices become matters for battle, and those who are victorious take over the city's affairs to such an extent that they refuse to share any of the rule with those who lost out—with either them or their descendants—and the two sides live keeping watch on one another lest someone ever get into office who might remember [*memnêmenos*] the old wrongs [*kakôn*] and start an insurrection. [The Athenian here invokes the language of the amnesty oath, which was sworn in the first person by every Athenian in 403 B.C.: "I shall not recall past wrongs" (*mê mnêsikakein*).[188]] These we presumably declare now not to be regimes, nor do we declare any laws correct that are not laid down for the sake of what is common to the whole city. Where the laws exist for the sake of some, we declare the inhabitants to be "partisans" [*stasiôtas*] rather than citizens, and declare that when they assert their ordinances to be the just things they have spoken folly.[189]

The Athenian's criticism of amnesty, which is voiced outside Athens to two non-Athenian interlocutors, here, as in Book I, treats amnesty as little more than the counterpart of *stasis* and the prelude to *polemos*. Here too, as before, the Athenian's criticism is predicated on a very specific understanding of both amnesty and *stasis*, and the specificity of his criticism is only partially related to its setting (namely, the ability or inability of his non-Athenian interlocutors to hear an Athenian praise an Athenian law).

It is more fundamentally related to the very writing of Plato's text. The word the Athenian uses to describe amnesty is not *adeia*, which, as Carl Buck wrote in 1920, means "freedom from fear," and which, aside from being "a technical term for 'amnesty, immunity, license,'" also gave rise to a sense of freedom as "being unoccupied" that then extended to "objects which were unoccupied, empty." [190] Nor does the Athenian say *dialusis*, which is a homonym that means both "to reconcile" and "to unbind," which was the word most commonly used to describe reconciliation after *stasis,* such that Loraux, without referring to Badiou's definition of the state, will even sum up amnesty as "an attempt to unbind what dissociates." [191] Plato, Loraux notes, almost never uses this word, and when he does, he acknowledges only one of its two antithetical meanings, as though it meant nothing more than "unbinding" *as a form of* "dissolution." [192] The *Laws* is no exception. The Athenian criticizes *diallagôn* without also criticizing *dialusis* or *adeia*. Why?

Diallagôn carries a quantitative as well as a qualitative sense. Loraux writes that the term belongs to "the sphere of exchange," [193] while Liddell and Scott record that it means not only "to change enmity for friendship, to reconcile one to another" but also "to give and take in exchange." [194] Friendship presupposes equality, and the commercial exchange of monies or other goods supplies a specifically numerical form of equality. [195] By choosing *diallagôn* and not *adeia* or *dialusis* as the point of departure for his discussion of amnesty, Plato clears the way for a more extended argument against any form of amity based on numerical equality. Plato's use of *diallagôn* in the *Laws* is designed to refute the principle that a certain use of arithmetic could be called upon to avert *stasis*. [196]

Plato's argument on this point is supported by an intricate epistemology. Plato held that the numerical order presupposes a mode of connection that is distinct from that of the geometrical order. Geometry, more than arithmetic, offers support for a concept of *koinon* or the common. The singularity of the *stigme* or point that is the basic geometrical unit is that it can extend beyond itself in and through a kind of "prosthesis." [197] Because any given geometrical point is qualitatively and quantitatively similar to every other geometrical point, the geometrical order constituted by these points can support the concept of a basic community or *koinoia* between all points that are points.[198] Not so the arithmetical order. Because every integer or *monad* that constitutes the numerical order is defined by its unique quantitative difference, and hence can only ever be in its own place, there is no single integer that can extend itself over or substitute itself for the other integers that constitute the numerical order.[199] Though the arithmetical order does admit of a community between the integer one and the all-encompassing One,[200] and is in this sense more originary than the geometrical order, its inability to support "prosthetic extension" permits no community between the integers or monads themselves.

Because there is no way for the numerical order to support the concept of a common, the political friendship that is based on numerical equality alone would likewise be based on no common. Because only equals are capable of *stasis*, and because *diallagôn* attempts to resolve *stasis* by instituting a numerical equality modeled on exchange, *diallagôn* would not so much reconcile the divided city as reproduce the necessary condition for the wrath that divided the city in the first place.[201] This is why the *Laws* will rename *stasis* as *diastasis*, which means "evenness" or "equal division."[202] Friendship based on equality requires that one be equal to oneself; but friendship for oneself tends toward the immoderation, the quantitative excess, that is the very hallmark of wrong.[203] When Kant critiques the assumption of equal worth on the basis of its relation to self-love, he repeats Plato's criticism of numerical equality on the basis of its relation to the commercial competition, rivalry, and jealousy that, in turn, lead to *stasis, diallagôn,* and *polemos.*[204] Plato's objection to amnesty, where amnesty is qualified as *diallagôn*, is that it fails to solve the vicious circle that is *stasis*. The comparisons facilitated by numerical equality not only fail to cancel out enmity within the city but also redouble its force outside the city.

Platonic political philosophy proposes to break out of this circle in an ecstatic movement that we should not fail to recognize as the very origin of political theology. Plato turns the weakness of the numerical order, namely, its lack of any prosthesis, into the source of an originary relation of the political to the One. The singularity of Plato's account of number, and the essence of the political theological refrain, consists in this simultaneous *departure from* dianoia and *unmathematical use of arithmetic*: Plato transforms the number one from a mere integer or monad into the concept of an indivisible One of which all is a part.[205] Platonic political philosophy solves the problem of *stasis* by refusing to count past one: It is this refusal that gives the political theological emphasis on immeasurability its non-theological and nonpolitical basis. For Plato, one is the only number that counts. It is the beginning and, more important, the end of the numerical order as such. It is the point at which the numerical order most resembles the perfect geometrical circle the One itself is.[206] It follows that the only *politeia* that really counts is a *politeia* that is one. The best regime is the best because its oneness of property and speech precludes any comparison and hence also any split into two.[207] The indivisibility that would become a hallmark of sovereign power here emerges where Plato turns the arithmetical order against its own tendency toward *stasis*.

It should be clear, then, why the *Laws* frames amnesty as *diallagôn* rather than as *adeia* or *dialusis*: To pose the problem of *stasis* as nothing more than a problem of arithmetic is to clear a space in which the question of the best regime can point self-evidently to political theology for its resolution. By framing amnesty merely as *diallagôn*—which is to say as nothing more than a problem of the insufficiency of the commercial, numerical order—the *Laws* puts itself in a position to demonstrate the superiority of the One to the endless comparison, recounting, and enmity that ostensibly compels *stasis* to turn into *diallagôn* and thence into *polemos*. To set into motion the harmony this recounting ruins, Plato will introduce a philosophical recollection of the ecstatic, incomparable One, the One that cannot be measured because it is the very condition of all measurement.[208] The vicious circle gives way to a virtuous one. In a summary of Plato that closely tracks the argumentation of the *Laws* at 715a8–715d9, Rancière describes what he considers Plato's definitive intervention.

> Philosophy's atomic project, as summed up in Plato, is to replace the arithmetical order, the order of more or less that regulates the exchange of perishable goods and human woes, with the divine order of geometric proportion that regulates the real good, the common good that is virtually each person's advantage without being to anyone's disadvantage. For this, a science, the science of mathematics, will provide the model, the model of an order of numbering whose very rigor derives from the fact that it escapes the common measure. The path of good lies in substituting a mathematics of the incommensurable for the arithmetic of shopkeepers and barterers.[209]

Political philosophy claims to give a more *dianoetic* response to *stasis* than *diallagôn*, in other words, because the philosopher is able to subordinate the merely arithmetical order to the divine order of geometrical proportion. The rule of law that is grounded in this order can thus also claim to give a more *dianoetic* response to *stasis* than *diallagôn*, for it is able to reconcile equality with inequality. Geometry allows the political philosopher to postulate a "proportional, though unequal, distribution" of honors and offices.[210] Political philosophy's subordination of arithmetical equality to geometrical equality permits it to theorize a resolution of *stasis* in which numerical contraries—the democratic many who possess less, the oligarchic few who possess more—can coexist as proportional equals. The nontheological reason that political philosophy points to its resolution in political theology is that only a geometrical equality grounded in an unmathematical use of the One can heal the divided city.

No similar argument can be made on behalf of *diallagôn*. But *diallagôn* is only one among many ways to think about amnesty; Plato's silence on *adeia* and *dialusis* points to another. If, as Loraux suggests, Platonic thought is constituted by what it refuses, and if, in the *Laws*, the Athenian's introduction of the very question of the best regime constitutes itself by imitating and appropriating the amnesty it also rejects and criticizes, then *classical political philosophy will inaugurate its inquiry by internally excluding a certain concept of amnesty*, and will, for this same reason, *tacitly participate in a dispute over the essence of amnesty itself*. Just as Plato himself was, as he writes in his Seventh Letter, implicated in the *stasis* of 403 b.c., so too does Plato's *Laws* partake in a disagreement over amnesty's substance. By virtue of its very form, the Athenian's forgetting of *adeia* and *dialusis* already implies a partisan standpoint on amnesty. The Athenian accepts the idea that amnesty is nothing more than a compulsory forgetting in order to turn just this *one part of amnesty* against *amnesty as a general class*: The Athenian's account of amnesty consigns to oblivion the possibility that amnesty might also be understood not as oblivion but as freedom from fear or an unraveling of a hatred that binds. Plato's *Laws* argues against amnesty, and simultaneously calls political theology into being, not only *by homonym* (by accepting only one meaning of *dialusis* and *stasis*) but also *by metonym* (by criticizing only one part of amnesty). When we today circulate the worn coin that amnesty is synonymous with amnesia, we are more Platonic than we recognize. But there is another way, besides political theology, to institute friendship in the city, and another way, too, to think about the politics of amnesty.

Intellection, or Immanent Critique

This becomes clearer once we consider the *Laws'* account of equity. Because equity in the *Laws* is, like clemency, a name for the necessary incalculability no judgment can avoid, equity belongs to an order of reasons grounded, above all, in the possibility of calculation. Let us consider this order of reasons as it appears in the *Laws*. The best possible city is not the same as the best city; the colony of 5,040 lots is not the same as the communism of elite guardians and warriors. There will still be inequality in the best possible city, and so the possibility of *stasis* will remain. In the passages of Book VI on arithmetical and geometrical equality, we find the *Laws'* third and most explicitly *dianoetic* discussion of *stasis*. In these passages, the Athenian now explicitly cites the maxim he criticized only implicitly in Book I, namely, the idea that "equality produces friendship." The Athenian qualifies this maxim by warning that if equality takes either a purely democratic or a purely monarchic form, it will lead to *stasis*. The best possible regime would thus be the mixed regime, a regime that mixes the two orders of equality. This mix is not a synthesis: Because the geometrical order is more *dianoetic* than the arithmetical, the two axes of equality are not, despite their homonymy, equal. But even though the geometrical order is superior, the Athenian will here acknowledge the necessity of violating it. In a monologue that will shadow Socrates' strange account of number and *stasis* in the *Republic*,[211] the Athenian will say that a violation of this type is necessary only because avoiding *stasis* is necessary. He will thus implicitly return to the distinction between the necessary and the best he introduces in Book I. But between Book I and Book VI, there also will be a slight shift in the way the Athenian criticizes necessity. Whereas in Book I he criticizes the necessity of reconciliation through the exchanges of *diallagôn*, in Book VI he will criticize the necessity of preventing *stasis* through *epieikeia* and *sungnômon*. The former has been translated as "clemency." Pangle translates the latter as "forgiveness."

> For slaves and masters would never become friends, nor would lowly types and serious gentlemen, if they were both held equal when it comes to honors. Both these situations fill regimes with civil strife [*staseôn*]; equal rewards would become unequal if they were distributed to men who are unequal, unless the distribution struck a proper measure. The ancient pronouncement is true, that "equality produces friendship": the saying is both very correct and graceful. But just whatever is the equality that has this effect? Because this is not very clear, we get into a lot of trouble.
>
> For there are two equalities, the same in name, but in many respects almost diametrically opposed in deed. Every city and every lawgiver is competent to assign honors according to the other sort—the equality that consists in measure and weight and number—and by the use of the lot applies it in distributions. But it's not so easy for everyone to discern the truest and best equality. For it is the judgment that belongs to Zeus, and it assists human beings only to a small degree, on each occasion; still, every bit of assistance it does give to cities or private individuals brings all the good things.

By distributing more to what is greater and smaller amounts to what is lesser, it gives due measure to each according to their nature: this includes greater honors always to those who are greater as regards virtue, and what is fitting—in due proportion—to those who are just the opposite as regards virtue and education. Presumably this is just what constitutes for us political justice. It is for this that we should now strive, and it is to this equality that we should now look, Kleinias, to found the city that is now growing [i.e., the Cretan colony the laws of which the interlocutors are now laying down]. The same holds in the case of another city someone might found sometime: it is to this that one should look while giving laws, not to the tyranny of a few, or of one, or some rule by the populace, but always to justice. And this is what has just been described—the natural equality given on each occasion to unequal men.

Nonetheless, necessity [*anankaion*] compels every city to employ even this equality in a modified degree, if it is to avoid partaking of civil strife [*staseôn*] in some of its parts. For equity [*epieikes*] and forgiveness [*sungnômon*[212]], whenever they are applied, are always an infringement or infraction of the perfection and exactness that belong to strict justice. Because of the discontent of the many they are compelled [*anankê*] to make use of the equality of the lot [this is a reference to 690c4–690c8, the same passage to which Rancière refers when he describes Plato's denigration of democracy as the complete absence of qualifications to govern[213]], but when they do, they should pray both to the god and to good luck [*tuchên*] to correct the lot in the direction of what is most just. Thus, of necessity [*anankaiôs*], both equalities ought to be employed, though the type that depends on chance [*tuchês*] as rarely as possible. A city that is going to last is compelled [*anankaion*], for these reasons, to do things this way, my friends.[214]

Before entering into a reading of this passage, the last word of which attests to conditions in which some kind of peace is already in effect, let us briefly outline its place in the history of the idea of clemency. The concept of *epieikeia* is usually traced less to Plato than to Aristotle and thence to its translation into Latin as *aequitas* by Cicero and *clementia* by Seneca, whose letter to Nero is then treated as the first fully self-conscious doctrine of clemency.[215] This history of ideas prepares the way for an argument about the essence of clemency. The basic claim of this argument is that Aristotle's appropriation of equity from Plato remedies Plato's scorn for any law that would swerve from unyielding geometrical principles. Book V of Aristotle's *Nicomachean Ethics* is supposed to soften up the tyranny of Plato's strict justice with a bit of situational "yield,"[216] "flexibility,"[217] "free play," "elasticity,"[218] or in short, "give." This give is then understood to open up the space for discerning judgment to supplement the dead, fixed, and tyrannical letter of the law, which, on its own terms, is presumed incapable of grasping the unpredictable singularity of each given case. Everything is then in place for Paul's distinction of letter and spirit.

Pufendorf is no doubt correct to argue that tempering a punishment out of a sense of equity is not the same as pardoning a criminal,[219] but as Jankélévitch suggests, the difference is more quantitative than qualitative: Like equity, "pardon surfaces in the extralegal, extrajuridical domain of our existence. Like equity, but still more, it is an opening in a closed morality, a type of halo around strict law; is equity not the welcome infringement that we sometimes make on strict justice?"[220]

Understood within the standard history of ideas, then, the "give" in equity and the "gift" in pardon both emerge in the space that inevitably appears between law's written generality and the concrete particularity of the incomparable case.[221] On this read, judgment per se is predicated on *epieikeia*, and insofar as *epieikeia* is translatable by "equity" or "clemency," we may say that there is no legal judgment that does not entail either the application or the nonapplication of clemency. *Epieikeia* is then the very thing that is at stake in any and all judgment because without it judgment consists of nothing more than a punitive application of basic arithmetical calculations. To law's demand for strict accountability, *epieikeia* adds wiggle room: It adds a determinate range of indeterminacy, a set of variables that confer value upon the constants to which it relates. *Epieikeia* saves law from being simple arithmetic by turning it into algebra.

What happens to *sungnômon* in this history of ideas? Even though *epieikeia* and *sungnômon* are still conjoined in Aristotle's *Nicomachean Ethics, epieikeia* will subsequently be translated into "clemency" and *sungnômê* not only into "pardon" and "forgiveness" but also into "indulgence" and "conscience." Martha Nussbaum will translate *sungnômê* awkwardly but much more literally as "judging-with."[222] But Nussbaum will also bind *sungnômê* tightly to eighteenth-century concepts of sympathy and pity.[223] Although *sungnômê* and sympathy are no doubt linked in Aristotle,[224] their translation into modern humanitarianism is questionable, even perilous. Because the Aristotelian account of tragic pity, or *eleos*, would eventually be subsumed within the Christian doctrine of specifically lordly mercy,[225] which then, in turn, would be institutionalized as an imperial prerogative,[226] the history of ideas that translates *sungnômê* into a precursor of modern pity risks understanding it as little more than an underdeveloped version of Christian charity. When *sungnômê* is translated as "pardon" and "forgiveness," it is assimilated into a theological discourse with which it has nothing in common. The "shared judgment" at issue in *sungnômê* is incommensurable with the gratuitous, passionate, miraculous decision of pardon or forgiveness. Though Nussbaum runs this risk in her theory of literary judgment, her translation of *sungnômê* as "judging-with" also provides an antidote. The "syn-" that turns *gnomê* into *sungnômê* is related less to the *pathos* of legal humanitarianism as we imagine it today (the passion of charity, mercy, or pity, the animate laws of the heart) than to the mode of sharing, division, or partaking that is the very essence of political friendship.[227]

When Jankélévitch argues that *sungnômê* is a mode of intellectual love, he in effect situates *sungnômê* as an *eros* without *eros*, a love indistinct from the properly political mode of *philia* (which Freud called "aim-inhibited *eros*"). The critical judgment this political intellectual love implies is, Jankélévitch argues

> not only "with," it is also "in the interior." The one who understands is neither merely opposite, nor merely on the exterior, as is the spectator of a spectacle of a speculative cognition, but is also inside; he penetrates into the depths of the reprehensible act. He is inside and outside at the same time. In a singular paradox, he englobes and is englobed at the same moment. Insofar as he is outside, he knows the misdeed as an object; insofar as he is inside, he participates ontically in the drama of the guilty person. *Inter-legere* ["Read within"]. Intellection is a reading, but this reading reads in the interior and from the interior. The enveloped reader and the enveloping sin penetrate one another in a lived sort of intimacy that blurs the contours of cognitive objectivity. It is, thus, useless to look for the moment at which intellection becomes love, since it is continually loving, and it is no less useless, therefore, to ask oneself if intellection loses all clear-mindedness in turning towards love, or conversely, if love loses all of its loving fervor when its eyes are opened in order to know and to understand.[228]

So incommensurable is *sungnômê* with theology that we may even translate it as *immanent critique*. *Critique* because, as Aristotle writes, the faculty of judgment or *gnômê* is precisely a capacity for *krisis*.[229] And *immanent* because *sungnômê* arrives at its critique *not* by referring to its object from above and beyond, but by reading *in* the interior and *from* the interior. It is no doubt true, as Jankélévitch will proceed to argue, that *sungnômê* provides insufficient grounds for a Kierkegaardian poetics of miraculous sovereign grace. But because, as Schmitt's citation of Kierkegaard in *Political Theology* implies, Kierkegaard's poetics of the instant gives modern political theology its most indivisible kernel, and hence too a way to renew sovereignty's foundation in Plato's ecstatic, immeasurable One, it is Jankélévitch's own dialectic—namely, his argument that the only response to the unforgivable is a sudden, gratuitous, and miraculous act of forgiveness—that obliges us to read Jankélévitch's book by dividing it against its own Kierkegaardian premises.

What's significant about *sungnômê* is not that it is an underdeveloped form of political theological pardon but that political theology needs to romanticize *sungnômê* to consolidate its monopolistic claim to give the best and only metanarrative of political friendship. The most glaring symptom of this romanticization is the assimilation of *sungnômê* into the cliché that "to understand is to forgive." This cliché muffles everything that is critical about immanent critique even as it converts the latter's power to undo, unbind, or unravel into nothing more than a miniature replica of transcendent, sovereign grace. But to read Plato's *Laws* is to recognize this conversion for the profound metalepsis that it is. Because the concept of *sungnômê*, *read on its own terms*, is as unrelated to the miracle as it is to the decision, it may double as a point of departure, at once autonomous and antinomic, for an immanent critique of the very political theology that cannot abide by immanent critique. Political theology insists upon translating *sungnômê* into pardon because *sungnômê* marks a hollow within the architecture of sovereignty where the wrong on which it is founded becomes legible for critique.

For so far is it from being the case that *sungnômê* is commensurable with divine geometrical principles that the Athenian even calls it a violation and an infringement of those principles. As we reread the *Laws* at 756e9–758a4, let us begin by noting that *sungnômon* and *epieikeia* here fall into the same category as did *diallagôn* at the *Laws'* outset. Like *diallagôn*, *sungnômon* and *epieikeia* are a mere necessity. Like *diallagôn*, their mere necessity derives only from the necessity of avoiding *stasis*. Unlike *diallagôn*, however, they are no longer an attempt to cure an already sick body. In this, they are more like the preventive medicine of cathartic colonization Plato describes at 736c5–737b10. *Sungnômon* and *epieikeia* belong to the best possible *politeia*, which, unfortunately, Plato writes, is not the same as the best *politeia*: It must run the risk of including a democratic faction within itself. Blackstone may have considered pardons incommensurable with democracy, but the *Laws* speaks of *sungnômon* and *epieikeia* as dangerously democratic principles, principles forced upon the best possible *politeia* by the appearance, within it, of a democratic faction. Mathematics and the unbinding movement of *stasis*, not theology or *polemos*, here give Plato the reason the best possible form of written law cannot assume an unswerving form.

This is why, as Saunders notes, the *Laws* will make every attempt to render *epieikeia* redundant.[230] Prior to Plato, Saunders argues, the concept of *epieikeia* emerged in relation to the risk that legal punishment would resemble and thus result in retaliation and that *stasis* would therefore emerge within the very rule of law designed to avert it.[231] After arguing that the *Laws'* passages on *epieikeia* are unique for the way they integrate *epieikeia* into constitution making, Saunders then notes that *sungnômon* in particular implies a concession of political power to what he calls the "common man."

> It is therefore "reasonable" to grant him [the "common man"] some share, i.e. to abate the *extreme* practice which is geometrical equality—though of course not as much as democratic theory would demand. That might be the point of *sungnômên*: one "indulges" a limited claim, perhaps on a greater scale than one should. The chief thought, however, is that conceding such power in face of democratic pressure represents a *loss* to those who ought ideally to enjoy total political control.[232]

Saunders's argument is supported by no less a theorist of sovereignty than Jean Bodin. In Book II of his 1583 *République*, Bodin observes that Plato's *Laws* gives the people, and not the sovereign magistrate, "the power of life and death, of passing condemnations, and of granting pardons, all of which are clear indications of a democratic state."[233] Plato's *Laws*, Bodin argues, is thus even more democratic than Athens itself, in which "the Athenian people, alone and to the exclusion of the magistrates, had the power of granting pardons, as was shown in the case of Demosthenes, Alcibiades, and several others."[234]

But what neither Bodin nor Saunders make sufficiently clear is the direct relation, in the internal order of problems that structures Plato's *Laws*, between amnesty, on the one hand, and *sungnômon* and *epieikeia*, on the other. Whereas *diallagôn* restores the polity from enmity and *stasis* to conditions of amity and peace by instituting an arithmetical equality, *sungnômon* and *epieikeia* prevent the possibility of enmity and *stasis* by introducing a slight twist into arithmetical equality itself. *Sungnômon* and *epieikeia* therefore serve the same necessity as *diallagôn* but achieve it more *dianoetically* than *diallagôn*. Each introduces into legal accountability the necessity of maintaining political order in and through its violation. This violation does not take the form of a sovereign exception. It takes the form of a *small* miscount that is designed, in effect, to avert the *big* miscount that is *stasis*.[235] *Sungnômon* and *epieikeia* here follow the logic of the *pharmakon*: They offer a cure for *stasis* that partakes in the illness that is *stasis* itself. Whereas *diallagôn* prevents full health by turning the illness against itself, but in the process preserves the illness in the cure, *sungnômon* and *epieikeia* preserve health by preventing the illness through an inoculating dose of the poison itself. *Sungnômon* and *epieikeia* are here both *the substitute for* and *the precise converse of diallagôn*.

This has implications for the way we understand pardon in its modern form. If Kant is correct that the right of pardon is the most majestic of the monarch's sovereign powers,[236] and if the modern theory of pardon is, like other European discourses on decision making, comprised of a Christian thematic that has been grafted onto a Platonic paradigm,[237] then precisely these most undemocratic thinkers' most undemocratic texts will also point to a way out of the same political theological refrain they set into motion. Nussbaum's translation of *sungnômê* as "judging-with" provides a way not only to reverse Schmitt's claim that "all significant concepts of the modern theory of the state are secularized theological concepts"[238] but also to displace Schmitt's Heideggerian claim that *polemos* is the essence of the political. By returning to the account of *sungnômê* in Plato's *Laws*, we find that the most theological concept of the modern theory of the state derives genealogically from an irreducibly democratic understanding of *stasis*.

From the standpoint of genealogy rather than the history of ideas, the problem to which *sungnômon* and *epieikeia* respond in the *Laws* thus has nothing to do with pity or sympathy. Like amnesty, these two powers emerge as part of a political calculation, the necessity of which derives primarily from the necessity of averting *stasis*. This order of reasons remains in effect even in Seneca. Though Roman law will ignore amnesty almost entirely, Seneca still conceives of clemency in relation to the civil war amnesty was designed to quell. To offer clemency to no one, Seneca writes, would be just as dangerous as using clothing to distinguish slaves from citizens: Just as distinct modes of dress would permit slaves to count the number of citizens and hence to recognize that slaves form a majority, so too would a lack of clemency demonstrate publicly that the wicked are preponderant.[239] But by that same token, "to pardon [*ignoscere*, closer to "overlook" or "ignore"] everyone is as cruel as to pardon none."[240] Because clemency is admirable only to the degree it is rare, clemency cannot take the form of a general pardon [*ignoscere*].[241] Clemency's qualitative difference from amnesty is here reducible to a difference of degree. Whereas amnesties punish the fewest number possible, clemency remits punishment from the fewest number possible.[242] Clemency, like amnesty, is primarily a problem of political economy.

Ignorance of the Law

By reading Plato's *Laws* against itself, we find a paradigm for the remission of deserved punishment that casts Seneca's *clementia* in a different light. Seneca's *clementia* is, like Plato's *epieikeia*, less a timeless virtue of the beautiful soul or an animate law of the heart than a specifically aristocratic or imperial reiteration of amnesty's calculated attempt to avert *stasis*. The geometry of the unswerving fits only the best city; in the best possible city, accident and necessity reign. The inclusion of *sungnômon* and *epieikeia* in the best possible city is the result of a strict calculation about the limits of strict calculation in that city.[243] The laws appropriate to that *politeia* cannot take the form of unbending lines without also bending one of the city's constitutive factions badly out of shape. This is a chance no lawgiver can take: *Stasis* must be averted even at the cost of leaving equality up to chance.

We also find another way to think about a problem of translation that emerges in Seneca: the rendering of *ignoscere* as "pardon."[244] The problem of ignorance is central to what is perhaps the most interesting example of *sungnômon* in the *Laws*. This example appears in Book XI, where the Athenian considers the problem of the citizen who dies without leaving any children to inherit his share of the colony's 5,040 lots. The number in the arithmetical order that admits of an unusually high number of proportional divisions is 5,040: It is "divisible by every integer from one to twelve with the exception of eleven."[245] It is thus a number that "can very readily put right": It is unusually able to divide up the arithmetical order according to geometrical principles of community. The best possible number of lots for a city is 5,040.

A man who dies intestate poses a problem for the city so arranged. The unoccupied lot he leaves behind could disrupt the city's need to keep the 5,040 lots constant.[246] If the colony's number of lots is not to drop to 5,039—a number that is not divisible without remainder—each citizen must therefore leave a will designating a single son to inherit his lot (whether his natural son, the husband of his daughter, or if he leaves behind an unwed daughter, an appointed son).[247] But because there is a chance that, despite the colony's numerous laws ordering sex difference and organizing sexual reproduction, a citizen might die childless, the interlocutors are forced to discuss the best possible way for law to respond to this contingency.

The Athenian's solution is to command that "a female and male from the family [of the deceased man] shall mate, as we may express it, and be placed in the deserted homestead, the allotment being legally assigned to them."[248] This law does not command incest; it carefully qualifies its order by adding that this mating should take place as consanguinity and religion demand.[249] But it does command the aristocratic practice of endogamous union, which is to say union between uncles and nieces, nephews and aunts, and so on.[250] To determine how exactly this union will take place, the Athenian specifies that "the order of succession shall be: sister, brother's daughter, father's sister, father's brother's daughter, father's sister's daughter."[251] Multiplied by the six corresponding possibilities in the male order of succession (brother, brother's son, sister's son, father's brother, father's brother's son, father's sister's son), the Athenian's command implies hundreds of permutations. Endogamous union would then certainly provide an aristocratic solution to the problem of the intestate citizen, since it would remove the absence or void that threatens to interrupt the patrimonial transmission of the colony's 5,040 lots. But it would also create a new problem.

The Athenian realizes that his law may seem burdensome to those to whom it is applied. He therefore adds a special "preamble" [epode] to the command. The concept of a "preamble," which is considered unique to the *Laws*, is consistent with the *Laws*' more general account of the mixed regime: The preamble offers a gentle and persuasive spoken introduction to a law that is itself unyielding, tyrannical, and written.[252] Preambles were to act like doctors who do not merely treat their patients but explain to them the causes of their ills: Preambles educate the citizens about the laws that command them.[253] Unlike any of the other preambles in the *Laws*, the Athenian's preamble to the law on intestate citizens consists of a proposal for *sungnômên* that is almost shared between lawgiver and citizen.[254] This proposal is not, as we might perhaps expect, related to the proximity of the lawgiver's command to incest. The lawgiver does not appeal for shared *sungnômên* because he has violated a taboo. He appeals for *sungnômên*, and is prepared to extend it to those he commands, because his command to marry endogamously is predicated on a kind of ignorance.

That ignorance derives from a double bind in which the lawgiver is placed by law's very structure. Since the lawgiver cannot *not* subordinate the arithmetical to the geometrical order, he is bound to issue laws that maintain the 5,040 lots. Yet the command through which the lawgiver fills the empty lot left by the intestate man multiplies the possibilities of compliance to a point where even and especially the lawgiver can no longer calculate the compliance he himself commands. The lawgiver cannot know which permutation of endogamous union would be the best possible permutation. The very structure of the best possible city thus forces the lawgiver to issue law in ignorance. The question at hand is not whether the lawgiver can *avoid* or *correct* this ignorance (he cannot, because it pertains to an error that is constitutive of law). It is whether or not the lawgiver is *ignorant of his ignorance*—that is to say, whether the lawgiver has given law in a philosophical manner. When Blackstone argues that pardon is impossible in a democracy, his reason is that its very exercise would force judges to violate the law of noncontradiction: In the absence of a monarch whose exercise of equity would obey the laws of the heart alone, the democratic magistrate whose pardons would unmake decisions would often be the same person who made those decisions in the first place. This self-contradiction would introduce an arbitrariness into law that would confound law's very form.[255] Whereas Blackstone takes no chances with ignorance, and hence rules out any possibility for a purely democratic pardon, the lawgiver in the *Laws* who is compelled to make use of the democratic power of *sungnômên* takes a different approach: He proposes joint *sungnômên* precisely to show that he is not ignorant of his ignorance.

> Let's not overlook the oppressiveness of such laws, the harshness sometimes involved in their ordering the next of kin of the deceased to marry his kinswoman, and their *apparent* failure to consider *the tens of thousands of impediments* that come into being among human beings and make one unwilling to obey such commands [emphasis mine: By enumerating what the lawgiver "apparently" fails to take into account, the Athenian is acknowledging the limit at which the arithmetical order necessarily implies a virtually innumerable set of contingencies, which is why Saunders here translates, "numberless impediments"[256]], and indeed make them ready to suffer anything whatsoever rather than obey, when diseases or maimings of the bodies or the mind arise in some of those they are commanded to marry or be married to [*gamein ê gameisthai*]. It might seem to some people that the lawgiver gives no thought to these things, but that impression would be incorrect. So let there be something spoken on behalf of the lawgiver and on behalf of the man to whom the law is given, almost as a shared [*koinon*] prelude, requesting those who are given the orders to judge-with the lawgiver [*sungnômên men tôi nomothetêi*], because in his supervision of the common things he would never be able at the same time to manage the private calamities of each man, and on the other hand requesting judging-with from those to whom the legislation is given [*sungnômên d' au kai tois nomothetoumenois*], because it's likely that sometimes they are unable to carry out fully the orders of the lawgiver, which he issued in ignorance.[257]

The lawgiver's proposal for joint *sungnômên* here is as unrelated to the act of forgiving the transgression of a primordial taboo (incest)[258] as it is to a decision based on purely personal or arbitrary discretion.[259] The lawgiver's prelude, which the Athenian raises to the status of the almost common, responds instead to the possibility of a miscount internal to law. The lawgiver's command to enter into endogenous union requires an appeal for joint *sungnômên* because it compels the lawgiver to count what cannot be counted. But the lawgiver's inability to count exposes one of the polity's most sensitive nerves. The most generic definition of *stasis* is war within the family; the Athenian insists that the first laws passed in the *Laws* should pertain to matrimonial practices.[260] And when Aristotle criticizes Plato for maintaining a constant number of lots rather than a constant population rate, Aristotle writes that the risk of the lots falling out of joint is precisely *stasis*.[261] The stakes are therefore high, indeed the very concept of the political is at stake,[262] and yet the lawgiver who is here compelled to take account of what cannot be counted is also, precisely, a lawgiver who reveals himself to be without the only knowledge that qualifies him to be a lawgiver.[263] So identical is counting with lawgiving that, when summarizing the *Laws*, Jean-François Pradeau will even render the two equivalent, stating, simply, that "to legislate is to count."[264] Where the lawgiver shows himself to be unable to count, so too then does he show himself to be incapable of legislating.

The case of the intestate man is not then merely one among many contingent situations in which the numerical order drops out of joint with the principles of geometry. It reveals the way in which the very possibility of an unoccupied lot, a void or vacuum—even if it is not introduced by the part that has no part, even if it is instead only the empty lot that remains after a part of the city has departed— can throw law's count into question.[265] By both appealing for and extending *sungnômên* for the uncountable obstacles that lie in the way of the law on endogamous unions, the lawgiver in effect makes manifest the absent foundation of his own lawgiving. The appeal for joint *sungnômên* in the *Laws* marks a point where a legal order that is founded on the possibility of a *dianoetic* count is forced to admit that it cannot count only on the philosophical lawgiver to govern the best possible city. If there is such a thing as a specifically democratic power of pardon, we might find its paradigm in this "co-mercy," this relation to law's miscount that derives its governing principle not from the indivisible one but, on the contrary, from a *dianoetic* politicization of the divisive, numerical, commercial equality that both Kant and Plato reject. If philosophy is knowledge of ignorance, then the philosophy of law requires knowledge of the ignorance of law. What Book XI of the *Laws* shows is that joint *sungnômon* is the site where this ignorance emerges as a problem for thought. The resolution of this problem has nothing to do with a sovereign decision or the protection of the *salus publica*. It is nothing more than a limit where the philosophy of law is obliged to offer an immanent critique of the miscount that founds law itself.

Law Degree Zero

> What is found at the historical beginning of things is not the inviolable iden-
> tity of their origin; it is the dissension of other things. It is disparity.
>
> —Michel Foucault, 1971

Taken to its limit, this immanent critique points to the origins of the pardon power
in a political ontological problematic that is without relation to the political theological refrain. We may discern this problematic by reading the *Laws* against itself a
last time. Faced with the contingency of an intestate citizen, the philosophical lawgiver's obligation to maintain the 5,040 lots requires him to admit a certain quo-
tient of anarchy into lawgiving to avert anarchy as such. We have already seen how
political philosophy not only imitates but also attempts to render redundant the
democratic principles it refuses.[266] What democratic principles, if any, may we infer from joint *sungnômon*?

Because it implies the potential absence of the *arche*—the starting point and
commanding principle—that grounds lawgiving itself, joint *sungnômon* first of
all implies a *general* equality between lawgiver and subject of law. This equality is
not reducible to the implicitly aristocratic concept of democratic equality the *Laws*
elsewhere articulates: It does not collapse democratic equality into commercial, arithmetical equality in order to then criticize and reject arithmetical and democratic
equality alike. On the contrary, the "co-mercy" we find in Book XI of the *Laws* no
longer belongs either to the geometrical order (since, as Plato writes, *sungnômon*
is precisely a violation of strict geometrical principles) or to the arithmetical order
(since it involves a set of permutations that, in effect, cannot be counted). It points
to another order altogether.[267]

Saunders notes that one provision of the complicated oath Athenian lawgivers
were required to swear before entering office pertained directly to *gnômê*: "on matters on which laws do not exist," the lawgivers swore, "I shall reach a decision by
a judgment (*gnômê*) which is most just."[268] If *gnômê* already indicates a power of
legal judgment that emerges only at that limit of law where law cannot apply, then
joint *sungnômên* will imply a power of legal judgment that must be both multiplied
and divided if it is to be judgment at all. *Sungnômên* multiplies and divides legal
judgment first by adding to *gnômê* the prefix "sun-" (indicating a judgment that
is "together" or "with") and then by requiring *sungnômên* of both lawgiver and
subject. It implies that law can encounter a miscount, even and especially in Plato's
best possible city, that *can only* be put back in joint by the multiplication of shared

or divided judgment. A constitutively shared or divided judgment—not an indivisible decision—is here the only possible way to repair the disjuncture the empty lot opens up between the arithmetical and geometrical orders.

Although this judgment is part of an attempt to avert *stasis*, we should note that it has nothing to do with the merely numerical amnesty criticized by Plato. Whereas *diallagôn* produces a political relation that can support nothing in common, the lawgiver's appeal for joint *sungnômên* repairs the political relation with reference to an empty site—an unoccupied or empty lot, a departed life, a shared loss—that not only *can* but also *can only* be held in common. Instead of using numerical integers to establish equality or instituting peace through an unmathematical use of the one, the lawgiver's joint *sungnômon* implies *an unmathematical use of the void*. Whereas the common that emerges from the One gives the lawgiver a paradigm for an indivisible political community, the prosthetic extension of the void indexes another common altogether. It marks an unoccupiable emptiness for which Plato's philosophy of number cannot account and which the philosophical lawgiver must ignore if he is to begin counting at all. Joint *sungnômon* is not a prohibition of unbinding; it is an unbinding of prohibition. Law's move here is not to use an indivisible One to stop the endless divisions of arithmetic. It is *to divide the power of division against itself*. In this, its imitation of *stasis*, joint *sungnômon* points to its origins in a political ontological problematic that is incommensurable with the indivisible political community that appropriates it to its own end. Joint *sungnômon*, a power *to unbind law without also unbinding law*, receives its distinctive ontological composition from the immanent potential of *stasis* to not be.

As remote as this formulation may seem, it actually cuts to the quick of the political theological refrain we have been tracing. In Kant's footnote on the day of atonement in "Perpetual Peace," amnesty is displaced by grace at the exact threshold where politics becomes indiscernible from theology. But from the immanent critique of Plato's *Laws*, we find that amnesty is the condition of possibility for the political theological in the first place. Prior to any opposition between *stasis* and *polemos*, between the state of nature and the city of grace—prior even to the messianic "division of the division" Agamben finds in Paul's letter to the Ephesians[269]—there is void that not only supplies the political with its characteristic antagonism but also gives the theological its paradigm for peace.[270] To trace the refusal of this void in Plato's *Laws* is to realize that political theology, with its attendant poetics of immeasurable indivisibility, is not the only or most desirable way to inquire into the peace at stake in the relation of pardon and amnesty. "There is no question which we might simply ask," writes Theodor Adorno, "without knowing of the past things that are preserved in the question and spur it."[271] Political theology claims to safeguard law's power to keep the peace, but it is not capable of turning around to face the force that blows it forward into war.

Notes

I thank Andrew Dole, Andrew Parker, James Montana, Jill Stauffer, the participants of "Forgiveness, Mercy, and Clemency," and an anonymous reviewer for comments on earlier drafts of this essay.

1. Carl Schmitt, *The* Nomos *of the Earth in the International Law of the* Jus Publicum Europaeum, trans. G. L. Ulmen (New York: Telos Press, 2003), 151, see also 121 and ff.; Carl Schmitt, "The Theory of the Partisan: A Commentary/Remark on the Concept of the Political," trans. A. C. Goodson, *CR: The New Centennial Review* 4: 3 (Winter 2004), 6, 7, 24, 64.

2. Carl Schmitt, *The Concept of the Political*, trans. G. Schwab (Chicago: U of Chicago P, 1996), 28–29; Schmitt, *The* Nomos *of the Earth*, 51–52, 187, 266.

3. Schmitt, *The* Nomos *of the Earth*, 168–171, 320–322; Schmitt, "Theory of the Partisan," 21–25, 37.

4. Schmitt, *The* Nomos *of the Earth*, 58, 120–121, 141, 143; Schmitt, "Theory of the Partisan," 36, 61.

5. Schmitt, *The* Nomos *of the Earth*, 142, 148; Schmitt, "Theory of the Partisan," 6.

6. Schmitt, *Concept of the Political*, 36, 56; Schmitt, "Theory of the Partisan," 36.

7. Schmitt, *The* Nomos *of the Earth*, 123, 299–304, 321. See also Carl Schmitt, *War/Non-War? A Dilemma*, trans. S. Draghici (Corvallis, OR: Plutarch Press, 2004), 41, 44, 58–59.

8. Schmitt, *The* Nomos *of the Earth*, 147, 321.

9. Ibid., 246.

10. Ibid., 121, 140–143, 157.

11. Schmitt, *Concept of the Political*, 26, 35, 39, 45.

12. See, for example, the special issues on Schmitt in *Cardozo Law Review* 21: 5–6 (2000), *CR: The New Centennial Review* 4: 3 (2004), and *The South Atlantic Quarterly* 103: 2 (2005).

13. See, variously, Hugo Grotius, *De Jure Belli ac Pacis Libri Tres*, vol. 2, trans. F. Kelsey (Washington, DC: Carnegie Institution of Washington, 1916), 644–645; Thomas Hobbes, *Leviathan,* ed. R. Tuck (Cambridge: Cambridge U P, 1996), 121–129; Samuel Pufendorf, *De Jure Naturae et Gentium Libri Octo,* ed. J. Scott, trans. C. H. Oldfather and W. A. Old-father (Oxford: Clarendon Press, 1934), 1011–1013, 1015, 1017; Jean-Jacques Rousseau, *The Social Contract; and, The First and Second Discourses*, ed. S. Dunn (New Haven, CT: Yale U P, 2002), 176–178; Cesare Beccaria, *On Crimes and Punishments,* ed. R. Bellamy, trans. R. Davies (Cambridge: Cambridge U P, 1995): 66; Friedrich Nietzsche, *On the Genealogy of Morals/Ecce Homo*, ed. and trans. W. Kaufmann (New York: Vintage Books, 1989), 71–72;

Michel Foucault, *Discipline and Punish: The Birth of the Prison*, trans. A. Sheridan (New York: Vintage Books, 1979), 48; Michel Foucault, *The History of Sexuality, Volume I: An Introduction*, trans. R. Hurley (New York: Vintage Books, 1990), 135, 137–138.

14. Hobbes, *Leviathan*, 106. Hobbes adds that the peace granted in pardon is not peace at all. Because those to whom pardon is granted in the state of nature persevere in their hostility, pardon does not put an end to the state of war. It should be granted anyway, Hobbes argues, because to *not* grant it is to signify an aversion to peace, which is contrary to the Fundamentall Law of Nature.

15. See *The Federalist* (No. 74), "The Command of the Military and Naval Forces, and the Pardoning Power of the Executive," in *The Federalist, A Commentary on The Constitution of the United States*, ed. H. C. Lodge (New York: G. P. Putnam's Sons, 1888), 462–465. See also Daniel Kobil, "The Quality of Mercy Strained: Wresting the Pardoning Power from the King," *Texas Law Review* 69 (1991), 584, 588.

16. See, for example, *Black's Law Dictionary*, which defines amnesty as "a declaration of the person or persons who have newly acquired or recovered the sovereign power in a nation, by which they pardon all persons who composed, supported, or obeyed the government which has been overthrown"; *Words and Phrases*, which states that "[a]n amnesty is an act of oblivion or forgetfulness. It is an act of sovereign mercy and grace, flowing from the appropriate organ of government. 'Amnesty' is defined to be the act of the sovereign power granting oblivion or a general pardon for a past offense"; *The Oxford English Dictionary*, which identifies the specific power of an "Act" or "Bill of Oblivion" as the power of *amnestia* or oblivion, and clarifies that power by emphasizing that it is an act or bill that "grants a *general pardon* for political offenses."

17. Schmitt, *Concept of the Political*, 33, 79; Schmitt, "Theory of the Partisan," 36, 41, 60, 64–65. See also Hobbes, *Leviathan*, 88–89; John Locke, *Two Treatises of Government and A Letter Concerning Toleration*, ed. I. Shapiro (New Haven, CT: Yale U P, 2003), 107.

18. Schmitt, "Theory of the Partisan," 42.

19. Nicole Loraux, *The Divided City: On Memory and Forgetting in Ancient Athens*, trans. C. Pache (New York: Zone Books, 2002), 113, see also 95–97.

20. Ibid., 155–169.

21. Vladimir Jankélévitch, *Forgiveness*, trans. A. Kelley (Chicago: U of Chicago P, 2005), 5.

22. Ibid., 154, cf. 5, 36, 69–70, 88, 101–104, 117–118, 150–151.

23. Hobbes, *Leviathan*, 92.

24. Schmitt, *The Nomos of the Earth*, 169; Randall Lesaffer, "Peace Treaties from Lodi to Westphalia," in *Peace Treaties and International Law in European History: From The Late Middle Ages to World War One*, ed. R. Lesaffer (Cambridge: Cambridge U P, 2004), 39.

25. Lesaffer, "Peace Treaties from Lodi to Westphalia," 39. Compare Schmitt, *The Nomos of the Earth*, 147–148.

26. Schmitt, *The Nomos of the Earth*, 170.

27. See, on this point, Jankélévitch, *Forgiveness*, 144.

28. Schmitt, *The* Nomos *of The Earth*, 160.

29. Grotius, *De Jure Belli ac Pacis*, 826–827, see also 645, 804–807.

30. Schmitt, *The* Nomos *of the Earth*, 160.

31. See, on this point, Heinhard Steiger, "Peace Treaties from Paris to Versailles," in *Peace Treaties and International Law in European History*, 84.

32. Just as "a supreme sovereign is able to abrogate a complete positive law under just cause," Pufendorf writes, "so he can remove its effect in a certain person or case, although it remains in force in every other respect." Pufendorf, *De Jure Naturae*, 1191. Compare, on this point, Magnus Fiskesjö, *The Thanksgiving Turkey Pardon, the Death of Teddy's Bear, and the Sovereign Exception of Guantánamo Bay* (Chicago: Prickly Paradigm Press, 2003), 1–3, 52–57.

33. Carl Schmitt, *Political Theology: Four Chapters on the Concept of Sovereignty*, trans. G. Schwab (Cambridge, MA: MIT Press, 1988), 38.

34. Carl Schmitt, *On the Three Types of Juristic Thought*, trans. J. Bendersky (Westport, CT: Praeger, 2004), 61.

35. Schmitt, *The* Nomos *of the Earth*, 261.

36. Ibid., 262. Compare Hans Kelsen, *Peace Through Law* (Chapel Hill: U of North Carolina P, 1944), 90; Hans Kelsen, *Principles of International Law* (New York: Rinehart: 1952), 38–39; Christian Tomuschat, "The 1871 Peace Treaty and the 1919 Versailles Treaty," in *Peace Treaties and International Law*, 391–392; Randall Lesaffer, "Conclusion," in *Peace Treaties and International Law*, 399–403.

37. Carl Schmitt, "The Plight of European Jurisprudence," *Telos* 83 (Spring 1990), 54, 57.

38. Schmitt, *The* Nomos *of the Earth*, 75.

39. Ibid., 148.

40. Ibid., 75.

41. Ibid., 159.

42. Hobbes, *Leviathan*, 88. See also Locke, *Two Treatises*, 108.

43. Schmitt, *The* Nomos *of the Earth*, 83, 137, 349–350.

44. Martin Heidegger, *Introduction to Metaphysics*, trans. G. Fried and R. Polt (New Haven, CT.: Yale U P, 2000), 162; Martin Heidegger, *Hölderlin's Hymn 'The Ister,'* trans. W. McNeill and J. Davis (Bloomington: Indiana U P, 1996), 79–91, 94.

45. Jankélévitch, *Forgiveness*, 46, see also 98.

46. Quoted in Giorgio Agamben, "Bartleby, or On Contingency," in *Potentialities: Collected Essays in Philosophy*, trans. D. Heller-Roazen (Stanford, CA: Stanford U P, 1999), 262.

47. "To wish that which has been done to be undone," Kant warns, is to succumb to a kind of desire for superhuman perfection and fantastical bliss that is immorally nourished by novels and similar mystical representations. See Immanuel Kant, *Critique of the Power of Judgment*, trans. P. Guyer and E. Matthews (Cambridge: Cambridge U P, 2000), 32, compare 65, 155.

48. Martin Heidegger, *What Is Called Thinking?* trans. J. Glenn Gray (New York: Harper & Row, 1968), 92–105.

49. Ibid., 64–73, 83, 88. At no point does Heidegger mention President Konrad Adenauer's amnesty of 1949, which supplied Heidegger's lectures with their concrete social and legal conditions of possibility, if not also the sociogenesis of their very substance. On Adenauer's amnesties, see Norbert Frei, *Adenauer's Germany and the Nazi Past: The Politics of Amnesty and Integration*, trans. Joel Golb (New York: Columbia U P, 2002).

50. Agamben, "Bartleby, or On Contingency," 262.

51. Giorgio Agamben, *Homo Sacer: Sovereign Power and Bare Life*, trans. D. Heller-Roazen (Stanford, CA: Stanford U P, 1998), 46.

52. Perhaps this explains Agamben's interest in amnesty as a technique for bringing the sovereign exception to a close. See, on this point, Giorgio Agamben, "Du bon usage de la mémoire et de l'oubli," trans. Y. Moulier-Boutang, in Antonio Negri, *Exil* (Paris: Mille et une Nuits, 1998), 57–60.

53. G. W. F. Hegel, *The Philosophy of Right*, trans. T. M. Knox (Oxford: Oxford U P, 1952), 186.

54. Christian Wolff, *Jus Gentium Methodo Scientifica Pertractatum*, vol. 2, trans. J. Drake (Oxford: Clarendon Press, 1934), 502.

55. Emmerich de Vattel, *Le Droit des Gens, ou Principes de la Loi Naturelle, appliqués à la Conduite et aux Affaires des Nations et des Souverains*, vol. 2, ed. J. B. Scott (Washington, DC: Carnegie Institution of Washington, 1916), 267.

56. Ibid., 164.

57. Adam Sitze, "At the Mercy Of," in *The Limits of Law*, ed. A. Sarat, L. Douglas, and M. M. Umphrey (Stanford, CA: Stanford U P, 2005), 263–267.

58. By "indiscernible" I mean the sense in which differences of *quantity* (one versus many), *space* (extension to entire territories versus application to single individuals), and *time* (future prosecutability versus past guilt), among other differences, are not sufficient grounds for concluding that amnesty and pardon are two clear and distinct powers. This is not to ignore the very apparent differences between the two powers, only to suggest that the difference between amnesty and pardon is not a *qualitative* difference. To inquire into the indiscernibility of amnesty and pardon is then to study the sense in which the potential either–or between these two powers amounts to *a division internal to the same basic power*. One implication of this indiscernibility is that we can no longer approach the jurisprudence of mercy as if it emerged out of, and belonged to, a separate order of reasons than the jurisprudence of emergency (to which amnesty belongs). On relations of indiscernibility, see Gilles Deleuze, *The Fold: Leibniz and the Baroque*, trans. T. Conley (Minneapolis: U of Minnesota P, 1993), 65.

59. Schmitt, "Plight of European Jurisprudence," 48; Schmitt, "Theory of the Partisan," 23.

60. Barbara Cassin is right to claim that "*stasis* is clearly one of those Freudian Greek words." "Politics of Memory: On Treatments of Hate," *The Public (Javnost)* 8 (2001), 10.

Loraux explains that in tragic and comic poetry, ancient history, and some ancient philosophy, *stasis* is "synonymous with *kinêsis*, movement, or, more specifically, agitation." She then notes that "[f]or philosophers interested in characterizing Being, there is another *stasis* as the name of the being at rest and of the standing position in its motionlessness" (*Divided City*, 104). The result is that *stasis* means both rest and unrest. Since *stasis* is therefore a "homonym" in Rancière's sense of the word—since its very meaning is a point of disagreement—I will take seriously Loraux's objections to its translation by "civil war," leaving it untranslated wherever possible *Divided City*, 107. See also, on this point, Derrida's commentary on Schmitt's political theological conception of *stasis*. Jacques Derrida, *Politics of Friendship*, trans. G. Collins (New York: Verso, 1997), 108–109. Derrida does not pursue Schmitt's enthusiastic designation of *stasis* as a "theologico-political goldmine."

61. Compare Heidegger, *Introduction to Metaphysics*, 65, 149.

62. Wolff, *Jus Gentium*, 502.

63. Loraux, *Divided City*, 197–213.

64. Schmitt, *The* Nomos *of the Earth*, 141.

65. Conceived as fratricide, *stasis* already contains the principle of its own resolution: Fratricidal *stasis* leads naturally to reconciliation on the basis of kinship and purely fraternal equality. It lives and dies on the principle of "*suggeneia*," which is to say, as Derrida puts it, "friendship founded on *homogeneity*, on *homophilia*, on a solid and firm affinity stemming from birth [*gen*], from native community." Derrida, *Politics*, 92, emphasis in original; see also 90, 93; Loraux, *Divided City*, 205. As I shall discuss in what follows, it is this paradigm of reconciliation that the amnesty of 403 B.C. calls into question.

66. See, on this point, Loraux, *Divided City*, 246; cf. Derrida, *Politics*, 90.

67. See Loraux, *Divided City*, 25; Aristotle, *Athenian Constitution*, 38.4; Andrew Wolpert, *Remembering Defeat: Civil War and Civic Memory in Ancient Athens* (Baltimore: Johns Hopkins U P, 2002), 4, 75.

68. Nicole Loraux, *The Invention of Athens: The Funeral Oration in the Classical City*, trans. A. Sheridan (Cambridge, MA: Harvard U P, 1986), 201.

69. Edmund Husserl, "The Origin of Geometry," in Jacques Derrida, *Edmund Husserl's Origin of Geometry: An Introduction*, trans. J. P. Leavey Jr. (Lincoln: U of Nebraska P, 1989), 108, compare 34–51.

70. Schmitt, *The* Nomos *of the Earth*, 52–55.

71. Loraux, *Divided City*, 10.

72. On the significance of Kant's account of peace today, see *Philosophy in a Time of Terror: Dialogues with Jürgen Habermas and Jacques Derrida*, ed. Giovanna Borradori (Chicago: U of Chicago P, 2003), 38–39, 130. On the fundamental character of Kant's account of grace, see Jacques Derrida, "To Forgive: The Unforgivable and the Imprescriptable," in *Questioning God*, ed. J. D. Caputo, M. Dooley, and M. J. Scanlon, trans. E. Rottenberg (Indianapolis: Indiana U P, 2001), 33–34.

73. Schmitt, *The* Nomos *of the Earth*, 168–171.

74. See Giorgio Agamben, *State of Exception*, trans. K. Attell (Chicago: U of Chicago P, 2005), 85; cf. Giorgio Agamben, *The Time That Remains: A Commentary on the Letter to the Romans*, trans. P. Dailey (Stanford, CA: Stanford U P, 2005), 119–124. See also Émile Benveniste, *Le Vocabulaire des Institutions Indo-Européennes, Tome 1: Économie, Parenté, Société* (Paris: Les Éditions de Minuit, 1969), 201; Ernst Kantorowicz, "*Deus per Naturam, Deus per Gratiam*: A Note on Medieval Political Theology," in *Selected Studies* (Locust Valley, NY: J. J. Augustin, 1965), 121–137.

75. William Shakespeare, *The Merchant of Venice*, act 4, sc. 1.

76. See, on this point, Sigmund Freud, *Totem and Taboo*, trans. J. Strachey (New York: W. W. Norton, 1950), 190–191. See also, generally, Immanuel Kant, "Religion Within the Boundaries of Mere Reason," in *Religion and Rational Theology*, trans. and ed. A. W. Wood and G. di Giovanni (Cambridge: Cambridge U P, 1996), 208–209, 213–214; cf. Derrida, *Politics*, 202–203, 232–233, 260–261, 284–285; Nicole Loraux, *Divided City*, 206–208; Hannah Arendt, *Love and Saint Augustine*, ed. J. V. Scott and J. C. Stark (Chicago: U of Chicago P, 1996), 99–106.

77. On deconstruction and democracy, see Derrida, *Politics*, 101–106. On the commensurability of dictatorship and a certain concept of democracy, see Carl Schmitt, *The Crisis of Parliamentary Democracy*, trans. E. Kennedy (Cambridge, MA: MIT Press, 1985), 8–17, 22–32.

78. Immanuel Kant, "The Conflict of the Faculties," in *Religion and Rational Theology*, 306.

79. See Jacques Rancière, "Ten Theses on Politics," *Theory & Event* 5: 3 (2001), ¶17, cf. ¶9–10. http://muse.jhu.edu/journals/theory_and_event/v005/5.3ranciere.html (last checked June 2005) see also Jacques Rancière, "Who Is the Subject of the Rights of Man?" *South Atlantic Quarterly* 103: 2/3 (Spring–Summer 2004), 305. In the same paragraph of *Origins of Totalitarianism* where Arendt discusses the "right to have rights," she turns to Book IV of Plato's *Laws* (716c–d) to clarify how political theology obscured the same political ontological problem that Giorgio Agamben, in his reading of the subsequent paragraph, would come to call "the ban." See Arendt, *Origins of Totalitarianism*, 299. Alain Badiou, meanwhile, argues that it is in Book X of Plato's *Laws* that Plato "gives up on the ethics of philosophy and exposes the whole of his thinking to disaster." *Manifesto for Philosophy*, trans. Norman Madarasz (Albany: SUNY Press, 1999), 134. For his part, Leo Strauss argues that the "only philosophic part" of the *Laws* is Book Ten, "in which the existence of the gods is demonstrated, i.e. in which the problem of the gods is directly faced." See Leo Strauss, *The Argument and the Action of Plato's Laws* (Chicago: U of Chicago P, 1975), 129; see also Leo Strauss, *Philosophy and Law: Contributions to the Understanding of Maimonides and His Predecessors*, trans. E. Adler (Albany, NY: SUNY Press, 1995), 76.

80. Schmitt quotes Plato on the relation of *polemos* to *stasis* to clarify why the political must be defined as a decision on the friend–enemy distinction. Schmitt, *The Concept of the Political*, 28–29. Derrida critiques Schmitt for, in effect, failing to conceive of *stasis* on its

own terms, showing how Schmitt transports the conceptual apparatus of *polemos* onto the state, treating *stasis* as a mere matter for the army or the military. *Politics*, 83, 108 n 13, 121, 132, 139. The implication of Derrida's argument seems to be it is possible to read Schmitt against himself on the point of *stasis*, that the latter can even be treated as a site for the theorization of a democracy to come.

81. Plato, *Epistle VII*, 324c–324d4.

82. See, on this point, Jacques Derrida, *Rogues: Two Essays on Reason*, trans. P-A. Brault and M. Naas (Stanford, CA: Stanford U P, 2005), 31–32.

83. Francisco Lisi argues that the influence of the *Laws*, which he calls "the first attempt to give a rational organization to the juridical system of a State," was "much wider than that of the *Republic*." While "[t]he Aristotelian treatises and Cicero's work were the origin of most of the indirect influence the *Laws* exerted during the Middle Ages in Western Europe," Lisi suggests, "the *Laws* seems to have been read with care in the Byzantine Empire," adding that "[t]hrough Pletho's *Laws* the dialogue has probably had an influence on Thomas More's *Utopia*." Lisi does not mention the influence of the *Laws* upon Islamic philosophy. Among the elements of contemporary legal thought Lisi traces to the *Laws* are the principle of the rule of law ("law is the ruler over the rulers" [715d7]) and the notion of the mixed constitution. See Francisco Lisi, "Contemporary Readings of Plato's *Laws*," in *Plato's Laws and Its Historical Significance, Selected Papers of the 1st International Congress on Ancient Thought, Salamanca, 1998*, ed. F. L. Lisi (Sankt Augustin: Academia Verlag, 2001), 11, 15–16. See also Hannah Arendt, "What Is Authority?" in *Between Past and Future: Six Exercises in Political Thought* (New York: Viking Press, 1961), 106; Agamben, *Homo Sacer*, 33–35.

84. Jacques Rancière, *Disagreement: Politics and Philosophy*, trans. J. Rose (Minneapolis: U of Minnesota P, 1999), 10.

85. See, on this point, Jankélévitch, *Forgiveness*, 101.

86. Schmitt, *The* Nomos *of the Earth*, 128.

87. See, on this point, Heidegger, *What Is Called Thinking?* 83, 150–151.

88. Immanuel Kant, *The Metaphysics of Morals*, trans. M. Gregor (Cambridge: Cambridge U P, 1996), 118.

89. Compare, on this point, Robert Tuck, *The Rights of War and Peace: Political Thought and the International Order from Grotius to Kant* (Oxford: Oxford U P, 1999), 13, 108, 189, 193–194; Schmitt, *The* Nomos *of the Earth*, 160–161.

90. Immanuel Kant, "Metaphysics of Morals," in *Practical Philosophy*, trans. and ed. M. Gregor (Cambridge: Cambridge U P, 1996), 486. Cf. Immanuel Kant, "Toward Perpetual Peace," in *Practical Philosophy*, 326–327; Grotius, *De Jure Belli ac Pacis*, 808–809; Wolff, *Jus Gentium*, 500–501; De Vattel, *Le Droit des Gens*, 264.

91. Kant, "Metaphysics of Morals," 482.

92. Ibid., 484; cf. "Perpetual Peace," 320, 326–327.

93. Kant, "Metaphysics of Morals," 484.

94. Ibid., 485; cf. "Perpetual Peace," 320.

95. Vattel, *Le Droit des Gens*, 265.

96. Kant, "Metaphysics of Morals," 470.

97. Ibid., 486; cf. Pufendorf, *De Jure Naturae*, 1325.

98. Kant, "Metaphysics of Morals," 486.

99. Wolff, *Jus Gentium*, 502.

100. Grotius, *De Jure Belli ac Pacis*, 811.

101. Wolff, *Jus Gentium*, 502. See also Vattel, *Le Droit des Gens*, 266.

102. Wolff, *Jus Gentium*, 503.

103. Wolff will write that "the effect of amnesty is that acts wrongfully done are to be considered *as though* they had not been done" and speak of property occupied "*as if* by right," deeds done "*as if* without wrong," and peace treaties that are "to be considered *as* law." See Wolff, *Jus Gentium*, 501.

104. Vattel will thus write, "if a town has been razed or dismantled during the war, such damage, being done in the exercise of the rights of war, is set as naught by the act of amnesty. When a sovereign has ravaged a country he is not bound, upon restoring it at the conclusion of peace, to give it back in its former condition; he gives it back in the condition in which it happens to be." *Le Droit des Gens*, Chapter III, Book IV.

105. Steiger, "Peace Treaties from Paris to Versailles," 84–85.

106. Kant, "Metaphysics of Morals," 485; cf. "Perpetual Peace," 320.

107. Kant, "Metaphysics of Morals," 487.

108. Kant, "Perpetual Peace," 322.

109. Ibid., 317.

110. Cf. Ibid., 322, 328.

111. Ibid., 317.

112. Ibid.

113. Ibid., 347. Since Kant argues that maxims that require publicity as part of their intrinsic purpose are commensurable both with morality and with politics (350), we may infer that while the archive is, in principle, certainly *capable* of being made public, it does not *require* publicity to achieve its purpose. It is thus an open question whether, on Kant's terms, a closed archive is compatible with right and politics. For a discussion of the "programmed time of latency" that governs state retention of archival secrets, see Cassin, "Politics of Memory," 17.

114. Kant, "Perpetual Peace," 317–318.

115. On the relation of dignity, timelessness, and sovereignty, see Ernst Kantorowicz, "Mysteries of State: An Absolutist Concept and Its Late Mediaeval Origins," in *Selected Studies*, 394.

116. Kant, "Perpetual Peace," 347.

117. Kant, "Religion Within the Boundaries of Mere Reason," 79–80. By "human race," I refer to the anthropological category Kant designates with the phrase "*das menschliche Geschlecht.*" This is a category that entails subdivisions for savages, barbarians, and nomads, as well as subdivisions of sex, such that Kant's references to "men" are never neutral.

118. Kant, "Religion," 83.

119. Ibid. Cf. Immanuel Kant, "Foundations for the Metaphysics of Morals," in *Practical Philosophy*, 45–46, 52 ff.

120. Kant, "Religion," 75.

121. Ibid.

122. Kant, "Perpetual Peace," 317, 322, 328–329; Kant, "Metaphysics of Morals," 484.

123. Kant, "Religion," 75. Kant's 1793 account of the vices of culture reappears in his 1797 definition of the right to wage preventive war. Quite apart from any *act* of war on the part of a greater power, Kant will argue, the bare fact of increased magnitude *alone* provides a legitimate basis for the lesser power to attack. The assumption of equal worth, which Kant calls the "right to a balance of power," will therefore ground the justification of preventive war. See Kant, "Metaphysics of Morals," 484 (emphasis in the original).

124. Kant, "Religion," 75, 78.

125. Immanuel Kant, "Idea for a Universal History with a Cosmopolitan Purpose," in *Political Writings*, ed. H. Reiss, trans. H. B. Nisbet (Cambridge: Cambridge U P, 1991), 44–46.

126. Kant, "Perpetual Peace," 336–337, but cf. 319. On commerce in Kant, see Pheng Cheah, "The Necessary Stranger: Law's Hospitality in the Age of Transnational Migrancy," in *Law and the Stranger*, ed. A. Sarat, L. Douglas, and M. M. Umphrey (Stanford, CA: Stanford U P, forthcoming).

127. Compare, on this point, Thomas Keenan, *Fables of Responsibility: Aberrations and Predicaments in Ethics and Politics* (Stanford, CA: Stanford U P, 1997), 99–133.

128. Tuck, *Rights of War and Peace*, 141.

129. See, on this point, Michel Foucault, *Hermeneutics of the Subject, Lectures at the Collège de France, 1981–1982*, ed. F. Gros, trans. G. Burchell (New York: Palgrave Macmillan Press, 2005), 54.

130. Kant, "Perpetual Peace," 336, cf. 318.

131. Ibid., 328 (emphasis in the original).

132. Kant, "Conflict of the Faculties," 248–249, 257–261; Kant "What Is Enlightenment?" *Practical Philosophy*, 22, but compare 17.

133. Kant, "Metaphysics of Morals," 461 (emphasis in the original).

134. Cf. Jacques Derrida, *Archive Fever: A Freudian Impression*, trans. E. Prenowitz (Chicago: U of Chicago P, 1996), 1–4; Rancière, *Disagreement*, 13; Loraux, *Divided City*, 69, 260.

135. See, on this point, Achille Mbembe, "The Power of the Archive and Its Limits," in *Refiguring the Archive*, ed. C. Hamilton et al. (London: Kluwer Academic Publishers, 2003), 23.

136. Kant, "Metaphysics of Morals," 490, cf. 480. See also Kant, "Perpetual Peace," 339. None of this means that the *arkhê* of state power is antinomic with the transcendental formula of public right. To the contrary, the state's maxim is perfectly compatible with it being

made public, and Kant will argue regularly, in the name of the philosopher class, against the censorship of such inquiry, particularly in the event that an entire people should wish to voice its "grievances" against the state. Kant, "Perpetual Peace," 337–338; see also "Conflict of the Faculties," 305. What would *not* be commensurable with the *arkhê* of the state, however, would be the archive Kant imagines in "Perpetual Peace."

137. Kant, "Metaphysics of Morals," 488; see also, on this point, "Perpetual Peace," 350–351.

138. Kant, "Perpetual Peace," 338.

139. Whereas *anamnêsis* ("recollection") has a double object (a content that is recalled as well as a subject who is reminded), the memory (*mnêsi-*) of wrongs (*kakein*) that amnesty banned has only a single object: its target. *Mnêsikakein* implies that one can "wield memory like a weapon, that one attacks or punishes someone, in short, that one seeks revenge." The *álaston* that produces it thus has only a superficial resemblance to *alêtheia* (truth). See Loraux, *Divided City*, 149, 161.

140. Kant, "Perpetual Peace," 350.

141. See, on this point, Immanuel Kant, "Proclamation of an Imminent Conclusion of a Treaty of Perpetual Peace in Philosophy," in *Theoretical Philosophy After 1781*, ed. H. Allison and P. Heath, trans. G. Hatfield et al. (Cambridge: Cambridge U P, 2002), 459–460.

142. Kant, "Perpetual Peace," 337.

143. Ibid.

144. Particularly since Kant defines his "pacific federation" primarily by differentiating it from the peace treaty of which amnesty is a part. See Kant, "Perpetual Peace," 327.

145. Ibid., 328 (emphasis in the original, translation modified).

146. Kant, "Critique of Practical Reason," 243.

147. Leo Strauss, "Persecution and the Art of Writing," in *Persecution and the Art of Writing* (Chicago: U of Chicago P, 1988), 25–26.

148. Ibid., 33, n 12.

149. See Lebigre, "Pardon, Grâce, Amnistie," 88; cf. Kathleen Dean Moore, *Pardons: Justice, Mercy, and the Public Interest* (Oxford: Oxford U P, 1989), 24.

150. See, on this point, Jean Bodin, *On Sovereignty: Four Chapters from* The Six Books of the Commonwealth, trans. J. Franklin (Cambridge: Cambridge U P, 1992), 77.

151. Kant, "Religion," 96–97.

152. Ibid., 96.

153. Ibid., 207.

154. Ibid.

155. Ibid., 208.

156. Ibid., 210.

157. Ibid., 210–212.

158. Ibid., 79–81.

159. Ibid., 214–215.

160. Kant, "What Is Enlightenment?" 20. Kant would almost have to consider the day of atonement a specifically hopeless gesture, a gesture made by the "moralizing politicians" who "by glossing over political principles contrary to right on the pretext that human nature is not *capable* of what is good in accord with that idea, as reason prescribes it, *make* improvement *impossible* and perpetuate, as far as they can, violations of right." "Perpetual Peace," 341 (emphasis in the original). If hope for progress only becomes possible by adopting pure principles into one's power of choice ("Religion," 92), then the day of atonement would redouble despair: Not only does it ask for grace for the way the human race has pridefully incorporated war as a maxim, but on top of that, it included grace as part of this same maxim.

161. Pufendorf, *De Jure Naturae*, 1190.

162. Ibid., 1118–1119.

163. Ibid., 1187. Cf. Seneca, *On Clemency*, 1.19.4–7, 1.24.1–2.

164. Kant, "Metaphysics of Morals," 477–478. Compare Hobbes, *Leviathan*, 237–238; Locke, *Two Treatises*, 104, 110.

165. Moore, *Pardons*, 28. On what might be called the mercilessness implied in the Kantian philosophy of law, see Jacques Derrida, *Of Hospitality*, trans. R. Bowlby (Stanford, CA: Stanford U P, 2000), 69–70; but cf. "To Forgive," 34.

166. See Loraux, *Invention of Athens*, 172, 176, 183, 202–204, 218, 220; Loraux, *The Divided City*, 15, 19, 21, 49, 51, 55–56, 61.

167. Loraux, *Divided City*, 7, 42–43, see also 10, 19–20, 22, 40, 96, 122, 153, 155, 240, esp. 254–258.

168. Ibid., 52, 59, 79.

169. Plato, *Republic*, 522b9–525e4, esp. 524a6–7, 524e1–525a.

170. Gilles Deleuze, *Difference and Repetition*, trans. P. Patton (New York: Columbia U P, 1994), 138–139, 141. For his part, Heidegger emphasizes that *dianoia* is not the same as thought per se but is the mode of thought that corresponds to the *koinon* or "common," where what thought thinks when it thinks the common are things that *share their difference* or *differ over what they share*. Heidegger also suggests that *dianoia* is a specifically litigious mode of thought, involving a cross-examination of what is heard and seen, which is to say of the *koinon aisthêsis* or "common sense." See, on these points, Martin Heidegger, *Towards the Definition of Philosophy*, trans. T. Sadler (New York: Continuum, 2002), 131, 141–142. *Dianoia*, we might say, opens a litigious relation not only to what Rancière would call the "division of the sensible" but also to the "common" and is therefore what Rancière might call political thought itself. See Rancière, *Disagreement*, ix, 5, 26–27, 57–58, 66.

171. Alain Badiou, *Theoretical Writings*, ed. and trans. R. Brassier and A. Toscano (New York: Continuum, 2004), 12–13, 21, 28–32.

172. See Loraux, *Divided City*, 78–84; Derrida, *Politics*, 92; cf. Cassin, "Politics of Memory," 11.

173. *Laws*, 728e8–729a3, 744d4–745b1; cf. Derrida, *Politics*, 134, n 7. Consider the inaugural discussion of *stasis* in the *Republic*, which occurs as part Socrates' refutation of

Thrasymachus (351c6–352a3). The question at hand does not concern *stasis* in any *diano-etic* sense but inquires instead into whether justice is the advantage of the superior man (338c5–6). The discussion turns to *stasis* only by way of analogy: The purpose of Socrates' hypothetical questions regarding *stasis* is to show that, like the divided city, the unjust man is less capable of action than the just man. At no point do these hypothetical questions regarding the nature of *stasis* come close to grievance regarding a past *stasis*. On the contrary, as Rancière has observed, what drops out entirely during Socrates' exchange with Thrasymachus is the problem of "wrong." *Disagreement*, 4.

174. Loraux, *Divided City*, 120–121.

175. See Plato, *Epistle VIII*, 356c.

176. See Loraux, *Mothers in Mourning*, 90–91; *Divided City*, 96, 240; Charles Hignett, *History of the Athenian Constitution* (Oxford: Clarendon Press, 1952), 294 n1. See also Isocrates, "Special Plea Against Callimachus," in *Isocrates I*, trans. D. Mirhady and Y. Lee Too (Austin: U of Texas P, 2000), 104. See, more generally, Herodotus, *The Histories*, 1.22.1; Appian, *The Civil Wars*, ed. Horace White, 1.14.121; Aristophanes, *Peace*, 1049.

177. Plato, *Laws*, 628a8–628e. I have here relied on the most recent translation of the *Laws*, namely, *The Laws of Plato*, trans. T. Pangle (Chicago: U of Chicago P, 1980). Where doubt or ambiguity has emerged, I have consulted *Laws*, Vols. I and II, trans. R. G. Bury, The Loeb Classical Library, Volumes X and XI, ed. Capps et al. (New York: G. P. Putnam's Sons, 1926); "Laws," trans. A. E. Taylor, in *The Collected Dialogues of Plato, Including the Letters*, ed. E. Hamilton and H. Cairns (New York: Pantheon Books, 1961), 1225–1513; and *The Laws*, trans. T. J. Saunders (New York: Penguin, 1970).

178. Leo Strauss, "Plato," in *History of Political Philosophy*, 3rd ed., ed. L. Strauss and J. Cropsey (Chicago: U of Chicago P, 1987), 78, cf. 67–68, 72.

179. Leo Strauss, "What Is Political Philosophy?" in *What Is Political Philosophy? And Other Studies* (Chicago: U of Chicago P, 1988), 29.

180. Strauss, *Argument and the Action*, 1.

181. Strauss, "What Is Political Philosophy?" 34.

182. Loraux, *Divided City*, 251, 257.

183. See Rancière, "Ten Theses," ¶2.

184. See Plato, *Laws*, 709a2–709d4. Cf. Rancière, "Ten Theses," ¶10; Derrida, *Politics*, 30.

185. See, on this point, Jean-François Pradeau, *Plato and the City: A New Introduction to Plato's Political Thought*, trans. J. Lloyd (Exeter: U of Exeter P, 2002), 27.

186. Loraux, *Divided City*, 29, 129, 149, 171.

187. Plato, *Laws*, 715d3–4.

188. Loraux, *Divided City*, 29, 149, 171. Wolpert notes that this phrase was also used in each of the three amnesties preceding the amnesty of 403 B.C. *Remembering Defeat*, 77.

189. Plato, *Laws*, 715a8–715b7.

190. Carl Buck, "'Empty' from 'Free,'" *Classical Philology* 15: 2 (1920), 198.

191. Loraux, *Divided City*, 95.

192. Ibid., 96, 121.

193. Ibid., 96.

194. See H. G. Liddell and R. Scott, *Greek-English Lexicon* (Oxford: Oxford U P, 1987), 190. See also, on this point, Emmanuel Levinas, *Otherwise Than Being, or, Beyond Essence*, trans. A. Lingis (Pittsburgh, PA: Duquesne U P, 1981), 4–5.

195. See Derrida, *Politics*, 19–22, 101. This would not be the last time that a peace would be sealed with gestures of the marketplace. See, on this point, Giorgio Agamben, *The Idea of Prose*, trans. M. Sullivan and S. Whitsitt (Albany: SUNY Press, 1995), 81.

196. Jean-Pierre Vernant quotes Pythagorean philosopher Archytas to this effect: "rational computation [*logismos*] puts an end to the condition of *stasis* and introduces *homonoia* [concord or harmony]; for there is truly no more *pleonexia* [greed], and *isotês* is achieved; and it is equality that permits business to be carried on in matters of contractual exchange. Thanks to all this, the poor receive from the mighty and the rich give to those in need, all groups having the *pistis* [trust] that by these means they will have *isotês*, equality." *Origins of Greek Thought*, 96; see also Vernant, *Myth and Society*, 30–31. It is worth noting, in this connection, that Aristophanes' *Frogs* included a parabasis that urged the victorious democrats to restore citizenship to the oligarchs from whom it had been stripped as punishment for their involvement in the overthrow of 411 B.C. The relevant passages of the *Frogs* (687–690) justify the restoration of equality to those implicated in the oligarchic overthrow by placing all blame for it on its leader, Phyrnichus. By restoring citizenship to all oligarchs involved in the events of 404 B.C. except The Thirty, who were put to death, the amnesty of 403 B.C. implicitly repeated the measures Aristophanes recommended: It limited harsh justice to the smallest number possible. But it also went further: It silenced the litigious subject, where Aristophanes' comedy proposed only equality.

197. See, on this point, Martin Heidegger, *Plato's Sophist*, trans. R. Rojcewicz and André Schuwer (Indianapolis: U of Indiana P, 1997), 77, 83.

198. Ibid., 80.

199. Ibid., 82.

200. Jacob Klein, *Greek Mathematical Thought and the Origin of Algebra*, trans. Eva Brann (Mineola, NY: Dover Books, 1992), 90.

201. As Vernant puts it, "all *eris* presupposes a relationship of equality." *Origins of Greek Thought*, 47. Wolpert notes that "[f]ar from preventing antagonisms from erupting, the amnesty was itself a source of contention. It did not end hostilities; rather, it redirected, rechanneled, and reconfigured them." *Remembering Defeat*, 57.

202. Plato, *Laws*, 744d7; cf. Loraux, *Divided City*, 118; Derrida, *Politics*, 134, n. 7.

203. Plato, *Laws*, 731e4–731e6. See, on this point, Vernant, *Myth and Tragedy*, 137.

204. Rancière, *Disagreement*, 15.

205. Klein, *Greek Mathematical Thought*, 92, 98; cf. Heidegger, *Plato's Sophist*, 81.

206. Plato, *Letter VII*, 342c4.

207. Plato, *Laws*, 739b8–e; cf. *Republic*, 462b–c; see also Rancière, *Disagreement*, 64.

208. See, on this point, Klein, *Greek Mathematical Thought*, 87–99, esp. 92.

209. Rancière, *Disagreement*, 15.

210. Plato, *Laws*, 744c3–4.

211. Plato, *Republic*, 546a–547c3.

212. *Sungnômon* is in the independent nominative case, indicating a thing or quality capable of standing alone. As a noun, it appears only in the *Laws*, not in any of Plato's other works, and it appears three more times, at 770c, 906c, and 921a.

213. Rancière, "Ten Theses," ¶10.

214. Plato, *Laws*, 756e9–758a4.

215. On Seneca's translation of *epieikeia* into Latin by *clementia*, see Martha Nussbaum, "Equity and Mercy," *Philosophy and Public Affairs* 22 (Spring 1993), 85, n. 3, 102. On Seneca's account of *clementia* as the starting point for the history of the idea of mercy, see John Tasioulas, "Mercy," in *Proceedings of the Aristotelian Society* 103 (January 2003), 101.

216. See John Pattantyus, "Aristotle's Doctrine of Equity," *The Modern Schoolman* 51 (March 1974), 213.

217. Nussbaum, "Equity and Mercy," 86, 87, 93, 96.

218. Hans-Georg Gadamer, *Truth and Method*, 2nd ed., trans. J. Weinsheimer and D. G. Marshall (New York: Continuum, 2003), 518–519.

219. Pufendorf, *De Jure Naturae*, 1191.

220. Jankélévitch, *Forgiveness*, 9.

221. See Cornelius Castoriadis, *On Plato's* Statesman, ed. and trans. D. A. Curtis (Stanford, CA: Stanford U P, 2002): 140, 142, 159; cf. Nussbaum, "Equity and Mercy," 86; Gadamer, *Truth and Method*, 318.

222. Nussbaum, "Equity and Mercy," 86.

223. Ibid., 94, 97, 110, 125.

224. Jankélévitch, *Forgiveness*, 88–89.

225. See Kenneth Burke, "On Catharsis, or Resolution," *The Kenyon Review* 21: 3 (Summer 1959), 344; cf. Kenneth Burke, "Catharsis—Second View," *Centennial Review of Arts and Science* 5 (Spring 1961), 115.

226. See Lebigre, "Pardon, Grâce, Amnistie," 86–87; Peter Brown, "Vers la Naissance du Puratoire: Amnistie et pénitence dans le christianisme occidental de l'Antiquité tardive au Haut Moyen Age," *Annales: Histoire, Sciences Sociales* 6 (November–December 1997), 1250–1251.

227. See, on this point, Giorgio Agamben, "Friendship," *Contretemps* 5 (December 2004), 6–7.

228. Jankélévitch, *Forgiveness*, 89.

229. In the *Nicomachean Ethics*, Aristotle will define *epieikeia* as the very thing of judgment and *sungnômên* as the mode through which equitable judgment is exercised. "What is called judgment [*gnômê*], in virtue of which men are said to be conscientious [*sungnômonas*] is the faculty of distinguishing correctly what is equitable [*epieikous esti krisis*

orthê]. This is indicated by our saying that the equitable man is above all conscientious [*sungnômonikon*], and that it is equitable to have conscience [*sungnômên*] in certain cases. Conscience is judgment that distinguishes [*kritikê*] what is equitable and does so correctly; and correct judgment is that which judges what is true [*alêthous*]" (1143a 19–24, translation modified).

230. Saunders, "*Epieikeia*," 81, 88.

231. Ibid., 77, cf. 70–71.

232. Ibid. 83.

233. Bodin, *On Sovereignty*, 103.

234. Ibid., 73.

235. On the relation between *stasis* and the "miscount" in Rancière's sense, see Agamben, *Time That Remains*, 58.

236. Kant, *Metaphysics of Morals*, 109.

237. See Jacques Derrida, *The Gift of Death*, trans. D. Wills (Chicago: U of Chicago P, 1995), 23–29. John Dillon notes that the *Laws'* 756e9–758a4 have been among the more significant passages for Neoplatonism. See "The Neoplatonic Reception of Plato's *Laws*," in *Plato's* Laws *and Its Historical Significance*, 249.

238. See Schmitt, *Political Theology*, 36; see also Schmitt, *Concept of the Political*, 42.

239. Seneca, *On Clemency*, 1.24.1.

240. Ibid., 1.2.2.

241. Ibid., 1.5.4; 1.2.1.

242. See, on this point, Lebigre, "Pardon, Grâce, Amnistie," 87.

243. This same logic reappears in Portia's command to Shylock to be merciful. Shylock must show mercy to Antonio not out of charity but because his demand for a strictly calculated penalty is impossible on strictly calculative terms: Shylock cannot cut out a pound of Antonio's flesh without also shedding an ounce of Christian blood. The merciless mercy that governs the unequal relation between these two merchants is grounded in a political theological reiteration of *diallagôn*: Like the other bonds at issue in Shakespeare's comedy, the bond of hatred between Shylock and Antonio is governed by the laws of commerce.

244. Sitze, "At the Mercy Of," 267–273.

245. Ibid., 771c2–4; cf. 737e1-738b.

246. Ibid., 740e2.

247. Ibid., 740b6.

248. Cf. Capps et al.: "Whosoever dies intestate, being without any issue, male or female, in all other matters shall be governed by the previous law [namely, the law governing *epiklêros*]; and a man and woman from the family shall in each such instance go into the deserted house as joint assignees, and their claim to the lot shall be made valid." Taylor: "If a man decease intestate leaving no issue, male or female, in all other respects the law above stated shall apply to the case, but a female and male from the family shall mate, as we may express it, and be placed in the deserted homestead, the patrimony being legally assigned to

them." Pangle: "In the case of a man without any male or female children at all who should die without having made a will, what pertains to such a man in other respects should be governed by the aforementioned law, but a female as well as a male from the family shall proceed as mates to the deserted house each time, and the allotment shall become legitimately theirs."

249. Plato, *Laws*, 925d2–3.

250. See Jean-Pierre Vernant, *Myth and Society in Ancient Greece*, trans. J. Lloyd (New York: Zone Books, 1990), 70–71; cf. David Schaps, "Women in Greek Inheritance Law," *Classical Quarterly* 25: 1 (May 1975), 56. It is worth noting that, despite translators' frequent use of the Latinate *marriage* to indicate the union between a man and a woman, there is no support for this translation in the original Greek. See Vernant, *Myth and Society*, 59–60.

251. Plato, *Laws*, 925d2–3.

252. Ibid., 722e7–8, 859a4–6.

253. Ibid., 857c5–857e7. There is disagreement among commentators on the *Laws* regarding the status of the preambles. Some find the preambles to be propagandistic, others understand them to be educative or persuasive, and still others find them even dialogic. See Andrea Nightingale, "Writing/Reading a Sacred Text: A Literary Interpretation of Plato's *Laws*," *Classical Philology* 88: 4 (October 1993), 290–293; R. F. Stalley, "Persuasion in Plato's *Laws*," *History of Political Thought* 15: 2 (Summer 1994), 157–159; Arendt, "What Is Authority?" 108.

254. This is not the only preamble in the *Laws* that involves a lawgiver requesting *sungnômon*. In the case of the *epiklêros* (the daughter who, like Portia, inherits the property of her dead father but who cannot partake in the city because she is not a man), the lawgiver asks for her *sungnômon* before assigning her a mate but does not also extend *sungnômon* to her. See Plato, *Laws*, 924c8–d5.

255. William Blackstone, *Commentaries on the Laws of England*, vol. 4 (Chicago: U of Chicago P, 1979), 390–391.

256. Saunders, "*Epieikeia*," 85.

257. Plato, *Laws*, 925d8–926a5.

258. Foucault describes how the problematization of incest in what he calls "classical Greek culture" had less to do with a foundational taboo than with the question of the "right time" [*kairos*]: Parents were not to have sexual intercourse with their children primarily because they were no longer at the peak of their health and would necessarily beget badly. Because Socrates' precept against incest remains merely one among many precepts, it is neither a paradigm for entrance into human culture nor an exemplar for the form of law as such. See Michel Foucault, *The Use of Pleasure*, volume 2 of *The History of Sexuality*, trans. R. Hurley (New York: Vintage Books, 1985), 59.

259. See Saunders, "*Epieikeia*," 85.

260. Plato, *Laws*, 721a1–a10.

261. Aristotle, *Politics*, 1265a38–1265b13, 1266b9–14.

262. See, on this point, Plato, *Laws*, 715a8–715b7.

263. See Ibid., 738b1–5, 746e4-747a7.

264. Pradeau, *Plato and the City*, 159. Pradeau goes on to say that legislating involves "ways of setting down single and multiple elements in order together."

265. See, on this point, Rancière, "Ten Theses," ¶21.

266. Rancière, *Disagreement*, 65.

267. Ibid., 19.

268. Saunders, "*Epieikeia*," 86.

269. Agamben, *Time That Remains*, 50–54.

270. Compare, on this point, Loraux, *Divided City*, 55; Jacques Derrida, "Faith and Knowledge: The Two Sources of 'Religion' at the Limits of Reason Alone," in *Religion*, ed. J. Derrida and G. Vattimo (Stanford, CA: Stanford U P), 18–19.

271. Theodor Adorno, *Negative Dialectics*, trans. E. B. Ashton (New York: Continuum, 1983), 54.

Index